The Rhetoric of Failure

SUNY Series,
The Margins of Literature

Mihai I. Spariosu, Editor

Ewa Płonowska Ziarek

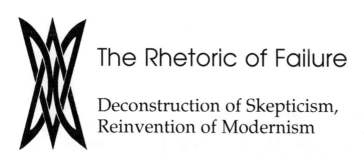

The Rhetoric of Failure

Deconstruction of Skepticism, Reinvention of Modernism

STATE UNIVERSITY OF NEW YORK PRESS

Production by Ruth Fisher
Marketing by Theresa Abad Swierzowski

Published by
State University of New York Press, Albany

© 1996 State University of New York

For information, address State University of New York Press, State University Plaza, Albany, N.Y., 12246

Library of Congress Cataloging-in-Publication Data

Ziarek, Ewa Płonowska, 1961–
    The rhetoric of failure : deconstruction of skepticism, reinvention of modernism / Ewa Płonowska Ziarek.
        p. cm. — (SUNY series, the margins of literature)
    Includes bibliographical references and index.
    ISBN 0-7914-2711-0 (alk. paper).—ISBN 0-7914-2712-9 (pbk. : alk. paper)
    1. Deconstruction. 2. Postmodernism. 3. Ethics, Modern—20th century. 4. Aesthetics, Modern—20th century. 5. Skepticism.
    I. Title. II. Series: SUNY series, margins of literature.
B809.6.Z53   1996
149—dc20   95-1439
                                                                     CIP

10 9 8 7 6 5 4 3 2 1

To my mother,
Halina Płonowska

Contents

Acknowledgments

With great pleasure I would like to acknowledge many friends and colleagues who read and commented on my work in its various stages. I am especially indebted to Carol Jacobs, Henry Sussman, Raymond Federman, Rodolphe Gasché, and Neil Schmitz, who guided this project from its inception. Their teaching and research have been a source of continuous inspiration for my work. I would also like to thank my colleagues at Notre Dame: Gerald Bruns, Joseph Buttigieg, Fred Dallmayr, Stephen Fredman, Teresa Krier, James Robinson, and Stephen Watson for their illuminating suggestions. I would like to express special thanks to Kathy Psomiades and Hilary Radner for their perceptive readings, friendship, and warm support. I am grateful to Derek Attridge, Rebecca Comay, Drucilla Cornell, Simon Critchley, Daniel Herwitz, Kelly Oliver, Marjorie Perloff, Herman Rappaport, Jill Robbins, and especially, Alexander Gelley, for their insightful comments on various sections of this book. Ziba Rashidian's suggestions and careful reading have made this a better book.

I am especially grateful to Krzysztof Ziarek for his endless encouragement and intellectual companionship. Special thanks go to my son *Łukasz*, for his enthusiasm about this book and his patience. And finally, I would like to thank Rita and Richard Lipsitz for their extraordinary hospitality and generous help during difficult times.

Sections of this work appeared before in print. Chapter 4 is reprinted from *Unruly Examples: On the Rhetoric of Exemplarity*, edited by Alexander Gelley, with the permission of the publishers, Stanford University Press. © 1995 by the Board of Trustees of the Leland Stanford Junior University. I thank the editors of Stanford Press for their permission to reprint. Part of the chapter on Derrida will appear in *Selected Studies in Phenomenology and Existential Philosophy*, Vol. 21, eds. John D. Caputo and Lenore Langsdorf, forthcoming from SUNY Press. Finally, I extend my thanks to the Institute for Scholarship in Liberal Arts in the College of Arts and Letters at the University of Notre Dame for a research grant on Gombrowicz.

Grateful acknowledgement is make to the following publishers who have generously given permission to use quotations and illustration from the following works:

Illustration for cover design from *The Trial: Definitive Edition* by Franz Kafka, translated by Willa and Edwin Muir, copyright 1935, (c) 1956 by Alfred A. Knopf, Inc. Copyright renewed 1964, 1984 by Alfred A. Knopf. Reprinted by permission of Schocken Books, published by Pantheon Books, a division of Random House, Inc.

From Samuel Beckett, *How It Is*, copyright 1963 by Grove Press, by permission of the publisher.

From Stanley Cavell, *The Claim of Reason*, copyright 1975 by Oxford University Press, by permission of the publisher.

From Jacques Derrida, *Margins of Philosophy*, translated by Alan Bass, copyright 1982 by The University of Chicago Press, by permission of the publisher.

From Witold Gombrowicz, *Cosmos and Pornografia*, translated by Alastair Hamilton, copyright 1985 by Grove Press, by permission of the publisher.

From Witold Gombrowicz, *A Kind of Testament*, translated by Alastair Hamilton, copyright 1973 by Temple University Press, by permission of the publisher.

1

Introduction: Deconstruction of Skepticism, Reinvention of Modernism

Try again. Fail again. Better again. Or better worse.
Fail worse again. Still worse again.

Samuel Beckett, *Worstward Ho*

All these parables really set out to say merely that the incomprehensible is incomprehensible, and we know that already.

Franz Kafka, *On Parables/ Von Den Gleichnissen*

If the preoriginal reason of difference, non-indifference, responsibility, a fine risk, conserves its signification, the couple *skepticism and refutation of skepticism* has to make its appearance.

Emmanuel Levinas, *Otherwise than Being or Beyond Essence /Autrement qu'être ou au-delà de l'essence*

But to distance oneself thus from the habitual structure of reference, to challenge and complicate our common assumptions about it, does not amount to saying that there is *nothing* beyond language.

Jacques Derrida, "Deconstruction and the Other"

1

I.

Deconstructive interpretation has always been a rather difficult and risky enterprise, perhaps delivering too much and not promising enough. Without proposing a complete break from the received paradigms or assuring the critical overcoming of the past, this mode of inquiry implies both continuity and rupture, repetition and difference, affiliation and disconnection. Neither faithful preservation nor complete destruction, deconstructive intervention operates instead as a reinscription and a transformation of the established patterns of thinking. In this book, I examine two crucial moments in poststructuralist theory—its affiliation with modernism and its revision of skepticism— where this mode of intervention characteristic of deconstruction has been most frequently ignored or misread. As a result, deconstruction of skepticism has been notoriously mistaken for the skepticism of deconstruction, and a certain reinvention of modernism confused with the impasse of aestheticism.

The effects of this misreading are rather familiar and widespread. In the numerous debates concerning the impact of deconstruction, charges of skepticism and aestheticism are levied almost interchangeably to repudiate the paralyzing consequences of language severed from the task of representation and reduced to pure textuality. When deconstruction is perceived as the most extreme manifestation of postmodernity, the very appearance of the term "skepticism" implies a strong and reductive value judgment about the impasse, deadlock, or exhaustion of postmodern thinking.[1] Just as frequently, Derrida's work is seen as a continuation of modern aestheticism with its rejection of representation for the sake of formal experimentation.[2] Needless to say, this wholesale repudiation of deconstruction closes and distorts the debate from the very start. In this book, I argue that the reductive claims about the "skepticism" or "aestheticism" of poststructuralist theory make us overlook the deeper consequences of the *deconstruction* of skepticism carried out in both the philosophical and the literary discourses of modernity. Because the issue of skepticism is so frequently associated with the most superficial dismissals of deconstruction, poststructuralism's own engagement with skepticism remains an untheorized and often ignored problem. A similar observation can be made about the affiliation of deconstruction with modernism.

I bring together these two areas of inquiry—deconstruction of skepticism and the aesthetic turn of poststructuralist theory—not merely because they are the most frequently misread issues but because they are in fact interrelated and complementary projects. Deconstruction of skepticism and the poststructuralist affiliation with modernist aesthetics represent two different moments of the critique of reason—two different scenes where the transparency of truth and the generality of linguistic structures is brought into question. In both cases, the interruption of the totality of knowledge reveals the excess of signification incompatible with the coherence of discourse. Questioning the sweeping comprehensiveness of the negative thesis about the impossibility of knowledge in general, the deconstruction of skepticism severs the bond between the particular and the universal, that is, between the failure of the specific claim to knowledge and the totalizing conclusion about the impossibility of knowledge as such. This incompatibility between the particular and the general is reread as a positive interruption of the totality of knowledge—an interruption which makes an affirmation of radical alterity possible. Bringing into a sharper focus the uniqueness of style and the excess of rhetoric, the affiliation between deconstructive theory and modern aesthetics discloses another location where the transition between the generality of linguistic structures and their particular manifestation is irremediably broken. The main difficulty here lies in the interpretation of rhetoric, so that its local instability is not generalized too quickly, as it is sometimes assumed, in terms of the negative epistemology of figurative language or in terms of the endless recesses of linguistic self-reflection. I argue that the aesthetic turn of deconstruction allows us to reread the instability of rhetoric as the figuration of an unpredictable event, whose occurrence cannot be derived from the generality of linguistic structures. The possibility of such an unexpected event sustains the signification of the other and the non-identical in language. What deconstructive intervention performs in the case of both skepticism and modern aesthetics is, therefore, a shift from the negative epistemological consequences of linguistic instabilities to the emphatic affirmation of the other of reason and the other of the subject.

This project began with the intention of rethinking the relationship between deconstruction and modern aesthetics. As Derek Attridge eloquently argues, the significance of modern literature for Derrida's project can hardly be overestimated: "as a peculiar institution which sheds light on institutionality, as a site of resistance to the philosophical tradition of conceptual thought, as a series of singular (but repeatable) acts that demand singular (but responsible) responses...literature is clearly of major importance in Derrida's work."[3] And yet, despite numerous studies devoted to Derrida's readings of key modernist figures (Artaud, Mallarmé, Joyce, Kafka), and despite the proliferating deconstructive analyses of modern texts, this crucial relationship is far from being sufficiently articulated because it is all too often associated with the celebration of textual experimentation, self-reflective language, or the aesthetic subversion of meaning.[4] What needs to be explicitly addressed here are the two interrelated difficulties generated by the complex positioning of modernist aesthetics within deconstructive theory. On the one hand, we are confronted with the more general problem of the connection between literature and philosophy (the relation, which strangely bifurcates deconstruction into philosophical and literary criticism); on the other hand, we are faced with the specific crisis characteristic of modernism, namely, with the difficult relation between aesthetics and social practice. In the context of philosophy, the affinity between poststructuralist criticism and modernist aesthetics is interpreted either as a rhetorical subversion of philosophical categories or as a suspect evasion (either on the part of Derrida himself or on the part of his followers) of philosophical argumentation.[5] In the specific context of modernism, however, this quarrel between philosophy and literature, performed both in Derrida's work and in deconstructive criticism, is supplanted by a different debate concerning the ethico-political stakes of deconstruction. Because of the problematic social positioning of modern aesthetics, the effects of the rhetorical subversion of meaning can be misread as the infinite play of self-reflective language, separated from the tasks of representation and social obligations. Here the detractors of deconstruction, like Habermas, Schulte-Sasse, or Huyssen, argue that Derrida's investment in modernism, evident in the suspension of representation and reference, repeats the characteristically modernist gesture of withdrawal from social praxis and thereby leads to the exhaustion, atrophy, or failure of the deconstructive project.[6] In response, poststructuralist critics, like Derek Attridge or J. Hillis Miller, make a case for "a strong ethico-political summons implicit in the constant attention in . . . [Derrida's literary] essays to the uniqueness of the other, the function of alterity in any movement or consciousness of the self."[7] What emerges from this debate is the question of how "the attention to the uniqueness of the other" can change the place of aesthetics in social praxis.

At stake in these discussions is not only a complex negotiation of Derrida's relationship to literature and literary theory but also a rethinking of modernism. In this context it is a sort of paradox that the critics who, like Schulte-Sasse and Huyssen, most emphatically insist on the homology between deconstruction and modern aesthetics in fact tend to produce the most narrow understanding of both. This sense of constraining closure is perhaps not so surprising, since the argument that "poststructuralism is primarily a discourse of and about modernism" all too often posits both modernism and poststructuralism as the exhausted paradigms to be overcome by a new critical discourse of postmodernism.[8] Interpreted as a belated, and therefore already obsolete, theoretical elaboration of the modernist project, Derrida's philosophy is construed as a continuation of modern aestheticism with its emphasis on the autonomy of art, self-referential language, and formal experimentation. Like modernist experimentation, the interventions of deconstruction seem to be confined to formal and aesthetic concerns, that is, to writing, language, and textuality. Arguing that poststructuralist problematization of representational language leads to an increasing separation from social and ethical concerns, Huyssen and Schulte-Sasse dismiss deconstruction on the grounds that it merely offers a theory of "a modernism all too confident in its rejection of representation and reality, in its denial of the subject, of history, and the subject of history"—that is, as a theory of modernism *"at the stage of its exhaustion."*[9] As the rhetoric of exhaustion, atrophy, or impasse suggests, such a narrow understanding of Derrida's investment in modernist aesthetics in fact closes the debate rather than opens up new interpretative possibilities or critical reassessments.

In order to diagnose the philosophical and linguistic presuppositions informing this misreading of both deconstruction and modernism, I became engaged in another, this time philosophical, scene of contestation over Derrida's work, that is, in the attempt to define deconstruction as a kind of skepticism. Skepticism, usually understood as a negative or critical attitude questioning the possibility of knowledge and truth, is not so much a specific philosophical position as it is a challenge to the legitimation of knowledge: "skepticism has not functioned in philosophy as merely one more position alongside idealism, materialism, and realism. Instead, it has been like an anonymous letter received by a dogmatic philosopher who does hold a position. The letter raises fundamental problems for the recipient by questioning whether he had adequate grounds for his assertions and assumptions."[10] It is somewhat ironic that the dissemination of Derrida's texts in the last thirty years is more and more frequently seen as a surreptitious circulation of such a deadly letter—a letter which, however, raises more problems for its sender than its recipients. In the aftermath of French poststructuralism, the problem of skepticism is persistently raised in both philosophical and literary studies in order to dramatize the "paralyzing" consequences of the postmodern critiques of reason: "postmodernism . . . [is] a continuation of the metaphysical skeptical tradition, reaching its dead end in deconstruction."[11]

As the most extreme philosophical conceptualization of the impasse of thinking, the charge of skepticism not only responds to a similar linguistic problem discussed in the context of modern aesthetics but also interprets this problem in an analogous manner. Here, too, the debated issues are the apparent rejection of representation and the subject for the sake of "pure" textuality. The arguments about the skepticism of deconstruction invariably claim that Derrida's critique of representation and reference destroys the correspondence between language and the world and in effect leads to a paralyzing notion of linguistic immanence. Severed from any relationship to the external world, language becomes self-referential, leaving the subject trapped in the "prison-house" of textuality. Although the debates about the skepticism of deconstruction situate Derrida firmly in the context of the postmodern critiques of reason, this different contextualization (within philosophical postmodernity rather than literary modernism) does not introduce any critical breakthrough in the reception of Derrida's work. On the contrary, it reproduces the same rhetoric of exhaustion, atrophy, or paralysis—paralysis which this time is extended to the postmodern scene in general. The fact that these very different critiques of deconstruction—perceived as a continuation of either philosophical skepticism or modernist aestheticism—share the same presuppositions about Derrida's problematization of representation and reference points to the necessity of bringing these two areas of inquiry together.

Engaging both of these critiques, my book is composed of two parts. The first part discusses the reinterpretations of skepticism in the thought of Stanley Cavell, Ludwig Wittgenstein, Jacques Derrida, and Emmanuel Levinas; the second part traces the affinity between poststructuralist discourse and modern aesthetics through detailed readings of literary texts by Franz Kafka, Samuel Beckett, and Witold Gombrowicz. It is the central argument of my book that the signification of alterity and its relation to the limits of rationality figures as a crucial concern in both the poststructuralist rereading of skepticism and its affiliation with modernist aesthetics. This focus on the critical revision of skepticism and modernism allows for a significant intervention not only into a reception of deconstruction but also into the broader debate on postmodernism. The implications of my argument make it possible to move past the endless discussions of the impasse of postmodernity, the exhaustion of subjectivity, or the collapse of reason, and to articulate instead an alternative interpretation of postmodern discourse—an interpretation that would account for the crucial role of alterity in language, community, and aesthetics.

By deconstructing the subject-centered understanding of language, the critical rereading of skepticism in the philosophical texts I discuss discloses those social and ethical aspects of signification that exceed the limits of rationality. Consequently, the reconceptualization of skepticism in poststructuralist discourse is not just motivated by a failure of knowledge and representation; rather, it is intertwined with a critique of subject-centered reason and with subsequent conceptualization of language beyond the "exhausted" paradigm of the subject. More specifically, this reinterpretation implies that the significance of skepticism is not confined to the familiar negative thesis regarding the impossibility of knowledge or truth. As Cavell, Levinas, and Derrida suggest in different ways, there is an entirely different aspect of skepticism—let us call it provisionally "an affirmative" signification of skepticism— which both skepticism's self-understanding and its philosophical refutation fail to register. Preceding the distinction between the negative and the positive, this peculiar mode of affirmation discloses what remains excluded from positive knowing. If skepticism's self-interpretation negates the possibility of knowledge about the world and others, the reappraisals of skepticism at work in Cavell, Levinas, and Derrida take it to be an interruption of the totality of knowledge—an interruption that confronts us with a disquieting encumbrance of alterity. Consequently, Cavell, Levinas and Derrida neither advance new skeptical arguments "cast in linguistic metaphors" nor refute the classical claims of skepticism. They focus instead on changing the significance of skepticism and its place in the philosophical tradition. No longer concerned with the subject as the center of meaning, such a critical reassessment of skepticism allows the discussion of language to be resituated in the context of alterity and the discursive community. In other words, the interpretation of the failure of the subject-centered conception of language is not an end in itself (although it has been frequently misread as a dead end) but a preliminary, and risky, step in articulating those aspects of signification that are incommensurate with the coherence of rational discourse: in Levinas and Derrida, the emphasis falls on the articulation of a non-thematizable alterity; in Cavell, on the precedence of community and intersubjective agreements underlying linguistic praxis. Consequently, the reappraisal of skepticism provides an answer to the widespread objection that the poststructuralist critique of representation merely exhausts the paradigm of the subject underlying Western conceptions of reason and language without, however, overcoming this paradigm in any significant way.[12]

The deconstruction of skepticism not only raises the issue of the other of reason and the other of the subject but also points to different, and seemingly conflicting, articulations of alterity within the post-structuralist project: from the textual emphasis on the excess of the materiality of language questioning the self-evidence of truth to the socio-ethical considerations of the claims of the other person and linguistic community. What allows for a certain rapprochement between these two articulations of the other of reason is precisely a turn to modern aesthetics where the intense confrontation between the claims of alterity and the claims of rationality is perhaps more readable than in philosophical discourse. In my readings of the literary texts of modernism, I am especially interested in those aspects of literary form, figurative language, and rhetoric that stage the conflict between alterity and rationality in ways inaccessible to philosophical argumentation. What I ask here is why modern aesthetics is, to use Cavell's phrase, so "haunting"—that is, what kind of disturbing demands does it make upon reason, the subject, and philosophy itself.[13] In order to recognize these demands, however, we need to rethink the effects of rhetoric in the social typography of language. Irreducible to the mere manifestation of linguistic undecidability, or to the failure of representation, rhetoric in this context reveals the signification of alterity as an irreparable discord in the grammar of language games. Although frequently interpreted as a recoil into the self-referential language of aestheticism, the limits of representation dramatized through the excess of rhetoric in fact contest any unproblematic assertions of the autonomy of the work of art, not the least because such claims are inseparable from the corollary claims of truth in the separate domain of reason.[14] My readings of modernist texts not only disclose and criticize the often unacknowledged complicity between skepticism and aestheticism (insofar as both terms suggest the idea of language severed from the task of representation and reduced to formalism) but also propose a different articulation of modern aesthetics—aesthetics no longer limited to textual experimentation devoid of any social or ethical significance. In contrast to interpretations of modernism based on the autonomy of art, I argue that these texts focus instead on those aspects of literary language and aesthetic form which enact an intense conflict between the signification of alterity and the unifying function of discursive community.

In what way does this rereading of modernism change our understanding of the relation between the philosophical critiques of rationality and modern aesthetics? For the philosophers we are considering, the act of overstepping the bounds of philosophy—moving beyond or outside the reason and the subject—leads to a renewed interest in literary language. This focus on the literary features of language—on the uniqueness of style or the excess of rhetoric— opens another path of intervention into the transparency of truth and generality of knowledge. Consequently, Derrida's interpretations of modern texts and Cavell's readings of romanticism are not peripheral but, rather, integral to their philosophical projects. Yet, what is at stake in this intersection between philosophy and literature is obviously not a rejection of philosophical rigor in favor of the pursuit of literary criticism. Nor is it the case that interest in modern aesthetics is motivated by a desire to evade the contradictions characteristic of the totalizing critique of reason.[15] On the contrary, the rereading of skepticism in the context of both philosophy and literature poses a new, crucial question as to whether the signification of alterity can be contained within the logic of non-contradiction, that is, the logic that assimilates divergent meanings into a coherent system. If the concern for "the other of reason" and "the other of language" leads to a renewed interest in aesthetics (especially modern aesthetics), it is because the rhetorical aspects of language open the possibilities of signification beyond the logic of identity.

As the title of my book implies, the signification of alterity requires a rethinking of the relation between logic and rhetoric—a rethinking that goes beyond the usual opposition of the grammatical stability of meaning and rhetorical undecidability.[16] This reinterpretation of the significance of rhetoric emerges not only from the interpretation of literary texts but also from the philosophical revision of skepticism. The philosophical revisions of skepticism suggested by Cavell, Levinas, and Derrida rely on the shift from the logic of non-contradiction to the rhetoric of temporality. Interested neither in the contradictions hidden in the skeptical argument nor in the philosophical refutation of skepticism that discovers these contradictions, these writers focus instead on the rhetorical model of signification enacted by the skeptical thesis. Consequently, the emphasis falls not on what is said in the skeptical argument but, to paraphrase Emmanuel Levinas, on the *way* of saying, on the temporal mode of signification. As Stanley Cavell's comment— "I have wished to understand philosophy not as a set of problems but as a set of texts"—suggests, at stake here is not the philosophical problem of skepticism but the problematic relationship between the rhetoric and the logic of the skeptical argument. If the focus on logic reveals a contradiction inherent in the skeptical argument (which, by negating the possibility of truth, undercuts its own meaning), the attention to rhetoric manifests a temporal disjunction between two different significations: between the negation of truth and the affirmation of alterity. One of the main effects of rhetoric here is therefore a disjunction between the epistemological and the ethical significance of skepticism.

Can we speak of a similar disjunction between the epistemological and the ethical effects of rhetoric in literature? What are the implications of this disjunction for the social significance of modern aesthetics? In my readings of Kafka, Beckett, and Gombrowicz I argue that the rhetorical instability of language not only suspends the epistemological functions of representation and truth but also reveals the ethical signification of alterity as an unpredictable event. Irreducible to the aporia of language reflecting only itself, rhetoric understood as an event creates a sense of incommensurability in the collective conditions of enunciation. Consequently, it is only by confining the effects of rhetoric to negative epistemological consequences that we arrive at an interpretation of modernism as self-reflective art deprived of any social significance.

By reading together philosophical and literary texts, I am thus interested in how this intersection enables crucial reformulations of both the philosophical and the aesthetic critiques of modernity. As I argue, the philosophical deconstruction of skepticism is already contingent on the change in emphasis from the logical (epistemological) to the rhetorical (literary) aspects of language and therefore situates aesthetics at the very center of the philosophical project. However, the signification of alterity and community disclosed by the philosophical revision of skepticism also allows us to intervene in the discussions of modern aesthetics, where the limits of representation have been interpreted either in terms of the dissociation of art from the realm of social praxis and ethical obligations or in terms of mere formal experimentation.[17] In other words, this focus on the intersection between aesthetics and philosophy—on the way aesthetics challenges philosophy and philosophy inhabits aesthetics—alters not only the stakes of deconstruction but also the significance of modernism.

One of the main implications of my book is that the very persistence of themes like exhaustion, impasse, uncertainty, skepticism, or failure in the debate on postmodernism indicates a certain inability to link the philosophical or aesthetic critique of representation with the signification of otherness. Even more so, this fixation on the exhaustion of postmodernism betrays an obstinate refusal to acknowledge the claims of alterity as such. Jürgen Habermas's well-known critique of the impasse of postmodernity—one of the most eloquent and rigorous responses, to be sure—provides an excellent illustration of this refusal. According to Habermas, the poststructuralist critique of reason merely "exhausts the paradigm of the philosophy of consciousness," but the symptoms of this exhaustion are not alleviated by any alternative ways of thinking.[18] Habermas's argument articulates at once what he perceives to be the most significant advance of the postmodern critique of modernity and its severest limitation. In *The Philosophical Discourse of Modernity*, Habermas claims that the distinctive feature of modernity, a feature that has dominated philosophy since Kant, lies in subject-centered rationality. Although the primacy of the subject and reason has been consistently called into question—from Nietzsche to Heidegger, from Foucault to Derrida—these philosophical critiques of modernity limit themselves to "the abstract negation of the self-referential subject," and therefore do not advance any alternative paradigms of thought or language. In this context, Derrida's philosophy presents for Habermas one of the most striking illustrations of the impasse that plagues the postmodern scene generally. Consequently, for Habermas, Derrida's critique of logocentric language remains incomplete and inadequate because it does not exceed the model of decentered subject in any positive way.

Although based primarily on philosophical discourse, Habermas's misunderstanding of postmodernity stems in a large degree from a very reductive understanding of the significance of modern aesthetics in the "postmodern" critiques of rationality.[19] Like many other critics commenting on the intersection between modernism and poststructuralism, Habermas likewise suggests that deconstruction, influenced by the practice of the avant-garde, can be read as a certain reenactment of aesthetic modernity. Yet for Habermas, this engagement between modern aesthetics and the philosophical critique of reason is in itself a symptom of exhaustion rather than a meaningful solution to the "crisis" of modernity. For Habermas, any theory that steps outside the horizon of reason, that "borrows" criteria from "the basic experiences of aesthetic modernity" (in this case, from the experiences of decentered subjectivity liberated from rational constraints and ethical/practical norms) is suspect because it evades or postpones the problem of its own legitimation.[20] Thus, the recourse to modern aesthetics, Habermas claims, becomes almost synonymous with an inability or unwillingness to account for the aporia that results when the totalizing critique of reason undercuts its own foundation. Without this turn to aesthetics, without this violation of the distinction between philosophy and literature, postmodern discourses would be forced to appear as what they really are: either self-contradictory critiques of reason or expressions of skepticism. What this narrow focus on "the illicitly borrowed aesthetic criteria" allows Habermas to disregard is the signification of alterity in poststructuralist discourse. Such a rigid separation between philosophy and aesthetics is compounded in Habermas's critique with a narrow understanding of "aesthetic criteria" as either subjective irrationalism or formal experimentation. He argues therefore that the solution to the impasses of postmodernism can come only from reason itself, albeit from a different paradigm of reason based on "mutual understanding between subjects capable of speech and action."[21] Thus, any contestation of Habermas's interpretation of postmodernism has to resume the question about the relation between aesthetics and the signification of the other.

The reason Habermas (and other critics who, like Jay Cantor, Michael Fischer, Eugene Goodheart, Hazard Adams, M. H. Abrams, Andreas Huyssen, and even sometimes Stanley Cavell, see in deconstruction an "unacknowledged" expression of skepticism or aestheticism)[22] disregards the alternative modes of signification emerging in the wake of the deconstruction of the subject is because these alternatives exceed both the bounds of subjectivity and the bounds of rationality. Whether the "excess" of rationality is interpreted as a linguistic form of skepticism or as "illicitly borrowed" aesthetic criteria, in both cases this excess or otherness is identified with the impasse of thinking. Thus, what both of these interpretations of postmodernity—either as modern aestheticism or as epistemological skepticism—have in common is that they are incapable of responding to the question of otherness. As Derrida argues, this inability to address the other of reason is especially striking in the case of skepticism, which expresses the limit of philosophy but still presents itself *as* philosophy. Although the focus on "borrowed aesthetic criteria" seems to recognize the other of reason in a more explicit way, the significance of this alterity is equally disregarded when modern aesthetics is reduced to an aestheticized irrationalism or formal experimentation. At stake in a critical rereading of the engagement between deconstruction and skepticism, and between deconstruction and modern aesthetics, is not only the expression of a limit (in particular, the limit of the subject, reason and representation) but also the signification of otherness.[23]

As my book illustrates, the issues of skepticism and modern aesthetics not only disclose two interrelated sites of the intense interrogation of Derrida's project but also reveal a strange discursive disorder where the very criteria according to which Derrida's work is contested break down or become insufficient. In the course of the heated discussions on deconstruction and skepticism, or deconstruction and modernism, the oppositions between representational and self-referential language, epistemological uncertainty and ethical obligation, internal and external critiques of reason, subject and the other, and finally, between logic and rhetoric, philosophy and literature become slippery and unmanageable. In fact, the tiring repetition of the charge of skepticism functions in these debates as an obsessive yet unsuccessful attempt to master this discursive disorder. Because of its strong rhetorical force, the term skepticism promises to fix the terms of the discussion from the very start, to close the polemics in a decisive way. Yet, instead of drawing the firm boundaries of discourse, the repetition of skepticism reproduces the disorder it claims to master, and thereby testifies to the disturbing effects of what Derrida calls "the other and the other of language."

II.

The first chapter of this study, "Stanley Cavell and the Economy of Skepticism," examines the work of Stanley Cavell with a particular focus on his engagement with the language philosophy of the later Wittgenstein. Although Cavell is not usually associated with poststructuralism or postmodernism (or, when he is, he is usually cast in the role of a critic of deconstruction),[24] his discussion of how the problem of skepticism occurs in the philosophy of Wittgenstein clarifies and dispels many presuppositions behind the critiques of poststructuralism.[25] Placing the emphasis on the revision of skepticism rather than on its refutation, Cavell shifts the discussion of language from the paradigm of the subject to the context of the linguistic community, while at the same time emphasizing the fragility of such a community: "mutual understanding, and hence language, depends upon nothing more and nothing less than shared forms of life, call it our mutual attunement or agreement in our criteria."[26] My reading focuses on the conflict in Cavell's revision of skepticism between the notion of discursive community and the significance of alterity. By departing from the paradigm of the subject, Cavell claims that the "truth" of skepticism reveals not only the precedence of the being together of the speakers in a discursive community (what Cavell calls *attunement*) but also the alterity of the other person—or what Cavell terms *acknowledgment*. I argue, however, that these two aspects of language are incommensurate and that Cavell eventually attempts to resolve this discrepancy by subordinating alterity to a vision of communal unity. Although Cavell appeals to aesthetics, especially to the aesthetic judgement, to harmonize the claims of community with the claims of alterity, the very difficulties he encounters in his interpretation of modernism and metaphor point to the impossibility of such an undertaking.

The second chapter, "Deconstruction and the Rhetoric of Failure," pursues the question of the alternatives issuing from the impasse of a subject-centered understanding of language in the context of Derrida's philosophy, which appears to be either completely removed from the problematic of skepticism, or as perhaps the most striking manifestation of its danger.[27] I not only diagnose why Derrida's work so consistently provokes associations with skepticism but also present the affinity between deconstruction and skepticism from a different perspective than the one usually pursued by Derrida's critics. Toward this end, I contrast two very different ways of broaching the problem of skepticism within deconstruction. Operating within post-Kantian epistemology, the first interpretation sees in deconstruction a linguistic version of the classical skeptical argument. In order to make sense of Derrida's claim that the deconstruction of the subject is primarily a search for the "other," I turn to the alternative view of skepticism proposed in Levinas's response to Derrida. The perspective opened by Levinas's reappraisal of skepticism—his emphasis on the incommensurability of the epistemological negation of truth and the ethical affirmation of otherness—clarifies the difference between a classical skeptical attack on the certainty of knowledge and Derrida's emphasis on the undecidability and indeterminacy of meaning produced in the exchange with the other. I argue that by elaborating the scope of responsibility tied to the signification of alterity, Derrida not only deconstructs the notion of linguistic immanence but also extends this critique to the nostalgic visions of social immanence, underlying the theories of discursive community. Rethinking the place of skepticism in Derrida's philosophy of language can open, therefore, an alternative both to the aporia into which the critique of subject-centered rationality falls and to the paradigm of rationality based on intersubjectivity.

Turning to the literary discourse of modernity, the second part of my book examines the way in which the paradigms of the subject and representation have been called into question by conceptions of literary language in the prose of three major modernist writers: Franz Kafka, Samuel Beckett, and Witold Gombrowicz. Focusing primarily on the specific literary practices identified with modernism, I attempt, at the same time, to trace the effects of the aesthetic turn in the post-structuralist critiques of metaphysics. Can deconstruction be read, as is so frequently assumed, as a certain "theory of modernism"? No matter what its content, this interpretation of deconstruction usually implies a profound sense of embarrassment—an embarrassment generated by the fact that the supposed "novelty" of Derrida is already a belated repetition of both the critical impulses and the impasses of modern art. Yet perhaps this embarrassment covers over a different sort of frustration—namely, a frustration with Derrida's refusal of the very desire for "a theory of modernism." By confronting us with the limits of "theory," that is, with the limits of the philosophical reflection on modern art's significance, the uneasy affiliation of modernism and deconstruction calls, instead, for an altogether different "invention" of modern aesthetics—the scope of which I discuss at greater length in the context of my reading of Beckett.

It is perhaps worth recalling at this point that most of the "theories" of modernism converge on the work of the negative—on the privation of truth, the refusal of representation, and the disintegration of form—performed by modern aesthetics. Not surprisingly, the theoretical elaborations of art's negativity sooner or later attempt to account for either the problem of the skepticism or the aesthetic autonomy of the work of art. What these two very different interpretations of the negative have nonetheless in common is their emphasis on the loss of the world or on art's separation from social praxis—a separation that leads eventually to the impasse and failure of the modernist project. As the most extreme manifestation of the so-called "crisis of language," skepticism in particular has generated some of the familiar antinomies shaping both the theories of modernism and the reception of modern writers like Kafka and Beckett.[28] On the one hand, skepticism is regarded as an expression of pessimism or "despair" about the limitations of language and its incapacity to reach the most essential dimensions of self; on the other hand, it is interpreted as the manifestation of a critical attitude toward the ossification of public language. In yet another contradictory formulation, skepticism is interpreted either as a sign of resistance to the increasing instrumentalization of modernity or merely as a logical culmination of the self-referential character of the work of art.[29]

This last opposition between skepticism and aestheticism, informs, for instance, Peter Bürger's diagnosis of the impasse of modernism. In his critical foreword to Peter Bürger's *Theory of the Avant-Garde*, Jochen Schulte-Sasse argues that "what the debate about modernism generally refers to as the writer's skepticism toward language and meaning since the mid-nineteenth century, Bürger considers to be an increasing consciousness on the part of the artist of writing techniques."[30] Yet, although the earlier discussions of modernism formulate art's negativity in epistemological terms, and Peter Bürger points to the historical underpinning of the aesthetic interpretation of the negative, both of these theories share similar assumptions about the effects produced by modern art. Either failing to convey the truth of the real (skepticism) or purposively negating the real in order to disclose new possibilities of signification, which, nonetheless, remain confined to the realm of art (aestheticism), modern art becomes self-referential. For Bürger, the self-referentiality of language reflects the atrophy of aestheticism, evident in more and more extreme declarations of the autonomous status of modern art. Schulte-Sasse concurs with this evaluation of modern aesthetics: "Bürger sees this development as logical and necessary, yet as negative, since it leads toward a state in which art works are characterized by semantic atrophy."[31] The complicity between "linguistic" skepticism and the formal self-consciousness of aestheticism separates modern art from the world of social obligations and results in the impasse of aesthetics as such.

Yet what we need to ask at this point is whether the provocations and impasses of modern aesthetics can be confined to the work of the negative and its various theoretical elaborations. Can we interpret the so-called crisis of modernism otherwise than as the unfortunate predicament of self-reflexive art? As my readings of Kafka, Beckett, and Gombrowicz suggest, the precarious "position" of modern art escapes the very opposition between the separation or integration into social praxis. Avoiding the pitfalls of the self-referential language of aestheticism, and contesting the separation of art from both knowledge and social praxis, Kafka, Beckett, and Gombrowicz are equally suspicious of the alternatives that present themselves under the guise of linguistic community. Consequently, I argue that in order to challenge the "narrow divide" between aesthetic autonomy and social signification of literature, and the corollary opposition between the autotelic and referential aspects of literary language, the discussion of modernism and modern aesthetics has to take yet another turn and account for an "invention" of the task of aesthetics beyond the work of the negative.

Coming to terms with the modern writers discussed in the second part of the book—Kafka, Beckett, and Gombrowicz—presents a peculiar difficulty defined with great precision by Walter Benjamin: "To do justice to the figure of Kafka in its purity and its peculiar beauty one must never lose sight of one thing: it is the purity and beauty of a failure. The circumstances of this failure are manifold. One is tempted to say: once he was certain of eventual failure, everything worked out for him *en route* as in a dream."[32] Underscoring the work of the negative and at the same time exposing its limits, Benjamin's insight inevitably evokes Beckett's famous description of modern aesthetics in terms of a "fidelity to failure"—"to be an artist is to fail, as no other dare fail"[33]— or Gombrowicz's equally paradoxical emphasis on the "fiasco" of modern art. However, the pervasive rhetoric of failure in such formulations of modernism does not merely call attention to the negative epistemological consequences of figurative language or to an unhappy predicament of discourse reflecting only itself, but also performs a certain reinvention of the very notion of "modernism." We can read Benjamin's "beauty of failure" as a striking figure for this invention— a figure which marks a disjunction between the epistemological and the ethical significance of art, between the privation of truth and the unrelenting acknowledgment of alterity.

To return to the main issue implied by the title of my book, I am not only concerned here with the failure of representation, or with the suspension of truth, produced by the instability of rhetoric, but also with a redefinition of rhetoric called for by such staged moments of "failure." Following de Man's famous claim that "rhetoric radically suspends logic and opens up vertiginous possibilities of referential aberration," the majority of the deconstructive criticism in the seventies and eighties has emphasized the negative epistemological consequences of the discrepancy between grammar and figure, logic and rhetoric.[34] Although this project has been of major importance in literary criticism, it is perhaps time to elaborate more explicitly a different kind of discrepancy, namely, the difference between the epistemological and the ethical implications of rhetorical instability.

By shifting the emphasis from the epistemological to the ethical effects of rhetoric, my interpretation of modern aesthetics suggests a certain affinity between what are sometimes perceived as two divergent articulations of "the other of reason": between the more textual emphasis on the instability of rhetoric and the more socio-ethical emphasis on the claims of alterity in linguistic community. Irreducible to the negation of truth or to the aporia of self-reflective language, the surplus of rhetoric in modern literary texts not only suspends the functions of analogy and representation but also, as Derrida reminds us, stages the possibility of an event and the performative address to the Other. This incompatibility between representation and event, between the constative and the performative force of language, is what enables the signification of alterity in language. By suspending the capacity of grammar to calculate or anticipate the unexpected in advance, the undecidability of rhetoric in these texts dramatizes the often unresolved conflict between the signification of alterity and the notion of discursive community, between the shock of otherness and the absorption of this shock within communicative rationality. By displacing incommensurability from the subjective to the collective conditions of enunciation, the unsettling effects of figurative language reveal the discord that the emergence of alterity generates in intersubjective praxis.

My readings of the selected literary texts by Kafka, Beckett, and Gombrowicz locate the disjunction between the epistemological and ethical significance of rhetoric at the very core of their various attempts to "reinvent" the task of the aesthetics beyond the work of the negative. In the third chapter, "'The Beauty of Failure': Benjamin and Kafka on the Task of Transmission and Translation," I focus on Benjamin's attempt to rethink the negativity of Kafka's parables as a peculiar obligation of transmission. As Benjamin argues, what is crucial for understanding Kafka's modernity is not the loss of truth—Kafka is certainly not the first writer to face such a predicament—but the obligation this loss imposes. In Benjamin's words, Kafka's parables perform *the sacrifice of truth* "for the sake of clinging to its transmissibility."[35] In order to develop the implications of this remarkable insight into the temporality of transmission, I discuss Kafka's parables in the context of Benjamin's own theories of translation and mechanical reproduction. Opening a rift between epistemology and ethics, the temporal deferral of meaning in Kafka's parables destroys not only the concept of truth but also, and more importantly, the immanence of a community "speaking with the same lip." By exposing a "fatal" alterity within the common social body, Kafka's texts risk the paralysis of linguistic circulation in order to disarticulate the vision of the unified social space. By returning the social body to "an urn already crumbled to dust,"[36] Kafka's parables intensify the haunting impact of modern aesthetics on the very concept of social praxis: these texts not only destroy the possibility of grounding the exemplary meaning of the text in the common ways of speaking but implicate the very desire for that kind of grounding in violence.

In the forth chapter, "The Paratactic Prose of Samuel Beckett," I read Beckett's "art of failure" in the context of the obligation imposed by the very act of "invention." Neither a subjective initiative nor just a performative effect of anonymous linguistic play, invention for Beckett is intertwined with "the obligation to express" at the very moment when such expression is no longer possible. Figured as a paradoxical task that is simultaneously assumed and given up, Beckett's act of invention opens a passage to the other through the most uncompromising assault on grammar, representation, and the speaking subject. As Beckett's strange reference to "obligation" implies, such an undoing of the order of discourse is not, however, a simple destructive or negative act; rather, it allows for the coming of the unanticipated, for the manifestation of alterity as an unpredictable event.

The sense of urgency associated with the task of Beckett's aesthetics is especially intense in *How It Is*, one of the most difficult, and certainly, one of the most haunting works in Beckett's career, where the disintegration of form stages a violent clash between the signification of alterity and its obliteration by communicative rationality. By juxtaposing the loss of meaning in face of the other, dramatized by the fragmented syntax, with the monstrous vision of discursive community, the text obsessively "calculates" the costs of reclaiming the endangered rationality of language. This persistent desire for a rational being and for a being in common submits the ethical and linguistic difference to the gruesome regulation of "justice"—which in the case of *How It Is* is presented ironically as the "fatal monotony" of pure numbers.

Unlike Kafka or Beckett, whose work has been at the center of the polemics over the significance of modernism, Witold Gombrowicz (1904–1969), a Polish emigre writer, is probably the only figure in the book who requires an introduction to the Anglo-American audience. Gombrowicz is still little known in the United States, even among those American literary critics who study European modernism. And yet, ever since the International Publishers' Prize in 1967, his nomination for the Nobel Prize in 1968, and the numerous translations of his work into over thirty languages, Gombrowicz has emerged, particularly in Europe, as a major eastern-European avant-garde writer and theoretician of modernity. I hope that this discussion of Gombrowicz's work within the broader context of literary and philosophical modernity, the understanding of which, unfortunately, is still too narrowly confined to Western culture, will bring his texts to the serious attention of American academic audiences and at the same time produce a more encompassing view of modernism itself. The recent English translation of Gombrowicz's *Diaries* (Northwestern, 1989, advertised as a major literary event of the year) and of *Trans-Atlantyk* (Yale, 1994) make this discussion especially timely.

What Gombrowicz contributes to the discussion of modernity is his complex understanding of form—one of the central preoccupations in his writings from the early novel *Ferdydurke* to his later texts like *Pornografia* and *Cosmos*—which ties together his philosophical, aesthetic, and social concerns. In order to divorce aesthetics from the passive reproduction of the social forms of life, Gombrowicz's texts incessantly uncover the aporetic structure of the aesthetic form. By under-scoring the aporias of form, modern aesthetics, according to Gombrowicz, does not collapse into mere formalism but testifies instead to the antinomy inherent in social "forms of life": "Here's another antinomy: he alone will know what Form is who never moves a step away from the full intensity of the whirl-wind of life."[37] For Gombrowicz, the aporias of aesthetics dramatize the effects of incongruity in the intersubjective language games and thus reformulate the usual understanding of both "intersubjectivity" and linguistic praxis. Neither simply reproducing nor repudiating the shared forms of life, modern aesthetics registers the breakdown of the intersubjective criteria in a "direct" encounter with the other. A sober testimony to the unsurpassable incommensurability of language games, the decomposition of form in Gombrowicz's texts aims to uncover the social and the subjective levels of "underdevelopment," the refuse and remnants of culture—or what he calls the modes of being "below the level of all values." By bringing the values of modernity—that is, the constraints of rational discourse, codified morality, and aesthetic wholeness—to a crisis, aesthetics registers the disquieting effects of an unpredictable event in the social topography of language.

By elaborating the critical reappraisals of skepticism in the conceptions of both literary and philosophical language, this book challenges the assumption that the philosophical and literary critiques of modernity inevitably lead to the impasses either of self-referential language (aestheticism) or of traditional skepticism, and therefore end up in the crippling versions of linguistic immanence. As an interruption of rational coherence, language, according to Levinas, "is already skepticism." Yet, as Levinas adds, "skepticism in fact makes a difference." In this book, I elaborate the difference which such a rethinking of skepticism makes in our understanding of aesthetic and philosophical modernity.

NOTES

1. For this kind of assessment, see for instance Eugene Goodheart, *The Skeptic Disposition in Contemporary Criticism* (Princeton: Princeton UP, 1984); Christopher Butler, "Deconstruction and Skepticism," in *Interpretation, Deconstruction and Ideology* (Oxford: Oxford UP, 1984), 60–65; Michael Fischer, *Stanley Cavell and Literary Skepticism* (Chicago: U of Chicago P, 1989), 1–9, 30–35. For a critique of this reception, see A. J. Cascardi, "Skepticism and

Deconstruction," in *Philosophy and Literature* 8 (1984): 1–14; and Christopher Norris, *Derrida* (Cambridge: Harvard UP, 1987), 142–161.

2. For a decisive intervention into the reception of deconstruction as a persistence of aestheticism, see Jonathan Loesberg, *Aestheticism and Deconstruction: Pater, Derrida, and De Man* (Princeton: Princeton UP, 1991), 3–10, 74–121.

3. Derek Attridge, "Introduction: Derrida and the Questioning of Literature," in *Acts of Literature* ed. Derek Attridge (New York: Routledge, 1992), 25.

4. For a useful synopsis of the parallels between deconstruction and modernism, see Astradur Eysteinsson, *The Concept of Modernism* (Ithaca: Cornell UP, 1990). For a decisive challenge to the reductive understanding of Derrida's interest in literature, see Derek Attridge, "Introduction: Derrida and the Questioning of Literature" and Jacques Derrida, "This Strange Institution Called Literature": An Interview, trans. Geoffrey Bennington and Rachel Bowlby, both in *Acts of Literature*, 1–29; 33–75. See also, Wlad Godzich, "Domestication of Derrida," in *The Yale Critics: Deconstruction in America* ed. Jonathan Arac, Wlad Godzich, and Wallace Martin (Minneapolis: U of Minnesota P, 1983), 20–40.

5. For a critique of the assimilation of Derrida's philosophy to a literary theory, see, for instance, Rodolphe Gasché, *The Tain of the Mirror: Derrida and the Philosophy of Reflection* (Cambridge: Harvard UP, 1986), 1–5, 255–270; Irene E. Harvey, *Derrida and the Economy of Différance* (Bloomington: Indiana UP, 1986), ix–xii; and Christopher Norris, *Derrida*, 27. For an illuminating discussion of the split between philosophical and literary deconstruction and the corresponding split between Derrida's reading of the philosophical texts and his reading of literary texts, see Derek Attridge, "Derrida and the Questioning of Literature," 10–14.

6. Jürgen Habermas, *The Philosophical Discourse of Modernity: Twelve Lectures*, trans. Frederick G. Lawrence (Cambridge: MIT P, 1987), 185–210; Andreas Huyssen, *After the Great Divide: Modernism, Mass Culture, Postmodernism* (Bloomington: Indiana UP, 1986), 206–216; Jochen Schulte-Sasse, "Foreword: Theory of Modernism versus Theory of the Avant-Garde," in Peter Bürger, *Theory of the Avant-Garde*, trans. Michael Shaw (Minneapolis: U of Minnesota P, 1984), xix–xxix. For an opposite reading of Derrida's philosophy as a dismantling of this version of modernism, see Stephen W. Melville, *Philosophy Beside Itself: On Deconstruction and Modernism* (Minneapolis: U of Minnesota P, 1986), 3–33.

7. Derek Attridge, "Derrida and the Questioning of Literature," *Acts of Literature*, 26. For a related argument that deconstruction performs "a necessary ethical moment" in the act of reading, see also J. Hillis Miller, *The Ethics of Reading* (New York: Columbia UP, 1987), 1–9. For a difference between J. Hillis Miller's "ethics of rhetorical reading" and Levinas's ethics of response to the other person, see Simon Critchley, *The Ethics of Deconstruction: Derrida and Levinas* (Oxford: Blackwell, 1992), 44–48.

8. Andreas Huyssen, *After the Great Divide*, 207.

9. Andreas Huyssen, *After the Great Divide*, 209.

10. Richard H. Popkin, "Skepticism," in *The Encyclopedia of Philosophy* ed. Paul Edwards, Vol. 7 (New York: MacMillan, 1967), 459. For other helpful discussions of the role of skepticism in the history of philosophy see, for instance, *The Skeptical Tradition* ed. Myles Burnyeat (Berkeley: U of California P, 1983); Richard H. Popkin, *The History of Skepticism from Erasmus to Spinoza* (Berkeley: U of California P, 1979); Nicholas Rescher, *Skepticism: A Critical Reappraisal* (Totowa: Rowman and Littlefield, 1980); P.F. Strawson, *Skepticism and Naturalism: Some Varieties* (New York: Columbia UP, 1985); Barry Stroud *The Significance of Philosophical Skepticism* (Oxford: Claredon, 1984).

11. This particular quotation has appeared in the recent SUNY Press advertisement of Don Byrd's new book, *The Poetics of The Common Knowledge*.

12. See, for instance, Habermas, *The Philosophical Discourse of Modernity*, 161–184.

13. Cavell's "haunting aesthetics" anticipates in many ways Derrida's discussion of the spectrality of experience in his recent text, *Specters of Marx: The State of the Debt, The Work of Mourning, and the New International*, trans. Peggy Kamuf (New York: Routledge, 1994).

14. Among many other critics who posit art as a possible locus of the critique of reason, J. M. Bernstein argues perhaps most eloquently that the autonomy of art, a product of the separation of the spheres constitutive of modernity, sustains the claims of truth: "the very idea of aesthetics is based upon a series of exclusions which themselves assume a conception of truth in terms of its isolation from normative and 'aesthetic values.'" *The Fate of Art: Aesthetic Alienation from Kant to Derrida and Adorno* (University Park: Pennsylvania State UP, 1992), 3–4.

15. For such a claim, see for instance, Habermas, "Excursus on Leveling the Genre Distinction between Philosophy and Literature," *The Philosophical Discourse of Modernity*, 184–210.

16. The question of rhetoric and rhetorical criticism is more readily associated with Paul de Man, especially with his two influential essays "Semiology and Rhetoric," in *Allegories of Reading: Figural Language in Rousseau, Nietzsche, Rilke, and Proust* (New Haven: Yale UP, 1979), 3–19 and "The Rhetoric of Temporality," in *Blindness and Insight: Essays in the Rhetoric of Contemporary Criticism*, 2nd ed., rev. (Minneapolis: U of Minnesota P, 1983), 173–209. For an excellent discussion of de Man's rhetorical reading, see, for instance, the collection of essays, *Reading de Man Reading* eds. Lindsay Waters and Wlad Godzich (Minneapolis: U of Minnesota P, 1989). Although de Man's rethinking of rhetoric in relation to grammar is inextricably bound up with the question of temporality in language, the issue of rhetoric in the texts of Derrida and Levinas links temporality more explicitly with the signification of the other. As Jacques Derrida writes about deconstruction, "this writing is liable to the other, opened to and by the other, to the work of the other; it is writing working at not letting itself be enclosed or dominated by this economy of the same in its totality." "Psyche: Inventions of the Other," *Reading de Man Reading*, 61.

17. Robert B. Pippin, for instance, claims that the question of the self-grounding of modernity threatens to "create an unsolvable skepticism problem." He further argues that the "aesthetic crisis in modernism itself [is] very similar to the epistemological problems of philosophic modernity." *Modernism as a Philosophical Problem: On the Dissatisfactions of European High Culture* (Cambridge: Basil Blackwell, 1991), 28, 45. For a discussion of parallel conceptions of the crisis of meaning in modernist literature and poststructuralist theory, see for instance Astradur Eysteinsson, *The Concept of Modernism*, 46–49.

18. Jürgen Habermas, *The Philosophical Discourse of Modernity*, 296.

19. For an intelligent critique of Habermas's reading of postmodernity, see George A. Trey, "The Philosophical Discourse of Modernity: Habermas's Postmodern Adventure," *Diacritics* 19 (1989): 67–79. For a detailed discussion of the place of aesthetics in Habermas's philosophy, see for instance, Martin Jay, "Habermas and Modernism," 1–14 and Richard Rorty, "Habermas and Lyotard on Postmodernity," 32–44, *Praxis International* 4 (1984). For Habermas's response, see "Questions and Counterquestions," *Praxis International* 4 (1984): 229–249.

20. Habermas, *The Philosophical Discourse of Modernity*, 96.

21. Habermas, *The Philosophical Discourse of Modernity*, 295.

22. M. H. Abrams, "Constructing and Deconstructing," in *Romanticism and Contemporary Criticism* ed. Morris Eaves and Michael Fischer (Ithaca: Cornell UP, 1986), 130; Hazard Adams, *Philosophy of the Literary Symbolic* (Tallahassee: Florida State UP, 1983), 199; Charles Altieri, *Act and Quality* (Amherst: U of Massachusetts P, 1981), 26–28; Christopher Butler, "Deconstruction and Skepticism," *Interpretation, Deconstruction and Ideology*, 60–65; Jay Cantor, "On Stanley Cavell," *Raritan* 1 (1981): 50–51; Michael Fischer, *Stanley Cavell and Literary Skepticism;* and Eugene Goodheart, *The Skeptic Disposition in Contemporary Criticism*.

23. For an excellent reading of the way the function of the limit in Derrida's philosophy is "foundational to his more obvious interest in the relationship to the Other," see Drucilla Cornell, *The Philosophy of the Limit* (New York: Routledge, 1992), 1–3, 62–90.

24. For the most recent example of such argument, see for instance Michael Fischer, *Stanley Cavell and Literary Skepticism*, 1–35.

25. As a notable exception, one can cite Stephen Melville's claim that "Derrida and Cavell stand together at a major crossing in modern philosophy" since both of them radically complicate "philosophy's search for its own pure and proper ground." *Philosophy Besides Itself*, 23.

26. Stanley Cavell, *The Claim of Reason: Wittgenstein, Skepticism, Morality, and Tragedy* (Oxford: Oxford UP, 1979), 168.

27. For examples of reading deconstruction in terms of skepticism, see note 14.

28. For a discussion of the specificity of the "crisis" of language in modern literature, see for example Richard Sheppard, "The Crisis of Language," in *Modernism 1890–1930* ed. Malcolm Bradbury and James McFarlane (London: Penguin, 1976), 323–336. See also Irwing Howe, *Decline of The New* (New York:

Horizon P, 1970), 15–27 and Astradur Eysteinsson, *The Concept of Modernism,* 35–49. For a generalized definition of modernity as a "culture of crisis" see Matei Calinescu, *Five Faces of Modernity: Modernism, Avant-Garde, Decadence, Kitsch, Postmodernism* (Durham: Duke UP, 1987), 123–125.

29. Adorno's interpretation of negativity in modern aesthetics calls into question the very opposition between political engagement and formalist autonomy of the work of art. See, for instance, Theodor W. Adorno, "Commitment," trans. Francis McDonagh, in *The Essential Frankfurt School Reader,* ed. Andrew Arato and Eike Gerhardt (New York: Urizen, 1978), 300–318. See also his "Notes on Kafka," in *Prisms,* trans. Samuel and Shierry Weber (Cambridge: MIT P, 1981), 243–271.

30. Jochen Schulte-Sasse, "Theory of Modernism versus Theory of the Avant-Garde," xiii.

31. Jochen Schulte-Sasse, "Theory of Modernism versus Theory of the Avant-Garde," xiii.

32. Walter Benjamin, "Some Reflections on Kafka," in *Illuminations,* trans. Harry Zohn, ed. Hannah Arendt (New York: Schocken, 1968), 144–145.

33. Samuel Beckett, "Three Dialogues," in *Disjecta: Miscellaneous Writings and a Dramatic Fragment* ed. Ruby Cohn (New York: Grove P, 1984) 145.

34. Paul de Man, "Semiology and Rhetoric," *Allegories of Reading,* 10. See also note 6.

35. Walter Benjamin, "Some Reflections on Kafka," *Illuminations,* 144.

36. Franz Kafka, "The Great Wall of China," trans. Willa and Edwin Muir, in *Franz Kafka: The Complete Stories,* ed. Nahum N. Glatzer (New York: Schocken, 1976), 245.

37. Witold Gombrowicz, *A Kind of Testament* ed. Dominique de Roux, trans. Alastair Hamilton (Philadelphia: Temple UP, 1973), 72–73. Originally published in French, *Entretiens de Dominique de Roux avec Gombrowicz,* Editions Pierre Belfond, 1968.

2

Stanley Cavell and
The Economy of Skepticism

. . .what I have called the truth of skepticism, or what I might call
the moral of skepticism, namely, that human creature's basis in the
world as a whole, its relation to the world as such, is not that of
knowing, anyway not what we think of as knowing.

Stanley Cavell, *The Claim of Reason*

Deconstruction is a classical skeptical argument, recast using
linguistic metaphors. What in the skeptic's argument is called *the
world,* is here called *referents* or *signified* . . .

Jay Cantor, "On Stanley Cavell"

Despite his frequent references to Kant, Freud, and Heidegger,
Stanley Cavell does not seem to be engaged in the debate over
the consequences of the continental critiques of modernity, at
least not in any direct way. On the contrary, Cavell's work—
with its focus on the confrontation between traditional epistemology and ordinary language philosophy—appears to have a
more immediate impact on Anglo-American academic philosophy. This is perhaps not surprising, given that one of Cavell's
central concerns is the problem of skepticism. Cavell theorizes
how the significance of skepticism—articulated in the history
of epistemology as a challenge questioning the possibility of
knowledge and truth—changes in the context of the philosophy of language where the main issues are no longer under-

standing and cognition but reference, meaning, and communication.[1] By making the issue of skepticism central for understanding the implications of Wittgenstein's later philosophy, Cavell's own interpretation of skepticism is, however, anything but familiar. According to Cavell, both its philosophical refutation and skepticism's self-understanding in fact obfuscate the deeper significance of skepticism, miss its "truth." Instead of advancing or refuting the claims of skepticism, Cavell changes, therefore, the very parameters of skepticism's confrontation with philosophy.[2] Irreducible to a negation of knowledge, the truth of skepticism, Cavell argues, interrupts the bounds of philosophy and opens up a possibility of rearticulating our understanding of language in the context of discursive community—or, what Cavell calls, after Wittgenstein, the shared "forms of life" [*Lebensform*].

The connection Cavell draws between skepticism and language has frequently been cited in support of arguments that refute deconstruction as a "linguistic" version of skepticism,[3] but this seems to be the least productive, and ultimately, a misleading way to employ Cavell's work in the context of the philosophical discussions of modernity. A more fruitful way to engage Cavell's work is to articulate how his critical revision of skepticism could illuminate the alternative understanding of language informing the counter-discourse of modernity. In fact, the main problems issuing from Cavell's discussion of skepticism—the position of the speaking subject in the discursive community, the function and the limitation of intersubjective linguistic criteria, the relation between the self and the other, the function of rhetoric and aesthetics in ordinary speech—speak directly to the central concerns emerging in the wake of the poststructuralist challenge to modernity. What the poststructuralist critique of modernity demonstrates, according to Habermas, is that the subject-centered paradigm of reason, dominating the philosophical discourse of modernity from Kant onward, has been exhausted. In the aftermath of this critique, the philosophical counter-discourse of modernity is confronted with the task of providing alternative conceptualizations of language and knowledge. For Habermas, such an alternative path lies in replacing the subject-object paradigm of knowledge with "the paradigm of mutual understanding between subjects capable of speech and action."[4] This is the path, Habermas argues, that the philosophical counter-discourse of modernity, from Nietzsche and Heidegger to Foucault and Derrida, has confronted yet not pursued.

Although never speaking directly about the impasses or possible correctives to the discourse of modernity, Cavell's critical revision of skepticism not only confronts but also complicates this alternative notion of language based on intersubjective understanding. One of the central insights of Cavell's reinterpretation of skepticism is that the stability of meaning in ordinary language cannot be confused with conceptual necessity because it rests on a common linguistic practice— on the agreements in judgements reached among the speakers rather than on the rules of reason. Consequently, what the "truth" of skepticism reveals for Cavell is the being together of the speakers in a discursive community (what Cavell calls *attunement*), their participation in the common forms of life. Cavell's conceptualization of language moves, therefore, from the paradigm of the speaking subject (or what Wittgenstein calls "private language") to the paradigm of intersubjectivity. And yet, at the point when Cavell seems to provide an alternative to the paradigm of the speaking subject, this alternative itself becomes increasingly problematic.

First of all, Cavell emphasizes the fact that the appeal to discursive community does not provide a new foundation of knowledge. It does not provide the means for a refutation of skepticism, but merely a therapy, an antidote to its threat. By elaborating the affinities between Freud and Wittgenstein, Cavell suggests, therefore, that the epistemological quest for the legitimation of knowledge becomes supplanted by a project of therapy, by what might be called a psychoanalysis of philosophy. Second, the being in common of the speakers in a linguistic community (*attunement*) is itself put into question by the competing emphasis in Cavell's work on the alterity of the other person—or what Cavell articulates as *acknowledgment*. Although Cavell presents *attunement* and *acknowledgment* as merely two complementary sides of the intersubjective linguistic exchange, I argue that these two aspects of language are incompatible, and that Cavell eventually attempts to resolve this discrepancy by subordinating the alterity of the other person into a vision of communal unity. Even though Cavell does not thematize this issue directly, the unsettling tension between *attunement* and *acknowledgment* shows that intersubjectivity does not provide in itself a workable alternative to the paradigm of the subject, but that this alternative in turn problematizes the relation between otherness and community. When articulated within the larger context of the philosophical critique of modernity, this conflict between *acknowledgment* and *attunement* in Cavell's work not only clarifies what sort of alternatives emerge in the wake of the deconstruction of the subject but also demonstrates their incompatibility with one another.

In order to articulate the consequences of this critical revision of skepticism, I focus primarily on Cavell's reading of Wittgenstein's *Philosophical Investigations*.[5] My argument proceeds in three parts. The first part elaborates how the problem of skepticism occurs in the later philosophy of Wittgenstein and what its implications are for a theory of language. The second part claims that both the insights and the impasses generated by thinking about language in terms of skepticism lead Cavell to a radical reappraisal of the traditional picture of skepticism itself. I focus my discussion on one of the most significant consequences of this revision, namely, the problem of the discursive community that functions as a constitutive framework of knowledge. The third part of my argument inquires into the consequences of thinking about community in the context of a recovery from skepticism, and demonstrates what the unity of the discursive community (articulated as "our" attunement) cannot assimilate—alterity and figurative language. I end with Cavell's analysis of metaphor and modernism, which, I argue, provides a counterpoint to his notion of community as a mode of being in common.

Cavell Reading Wittgenstein: Linguistic Games and the Threat of Skepticism

What is striking about Cavell's reading of *Philosophical Investigations* is his insistence that coming to terms with the complexity of Wittgenstein's understanding of language requires keeping the possibility of skepticism open (or taking its threat seriously). By juxtaposing the epistemological problem of skepticism and the linguistic theory of the later Wittgenstein, Cavell links the skeptical attitude (which conveys a dissatisfaction with the limitations of knowledge) directly to a certain distrust of language. Cavell's insistence on taking the possibility of skepticism seriously might be surprising because *Philosophical Investigations* has frequently been interpreted in just the opposite way: Wittgenstein is supposed to have answered skepticism by providing linguistic criteria regulating the correct use of concepts and by showing the ungrammaticality, that is, incoherence, of the skeptical argument. From the outset, Cavell takes issue with these views (in particular with Malcolm and Albritton)[6] and argues that linguistic criteria settle very little, perhaps too little to be "serious contenders in the battle to turn aside skepticism."[7] The point is not, Cavell argues, to read Wittgenstein as a refutation of skepticism but to explore how the perspective of ordinary language changes the significance of skepticism.

It is not by accident, of course, that Cavell raises the issue of skepticism and its relation to language/text primarily in the context of Wittgenstein's *Philosophical Investigations*—a landmark study in the philosophy of language departing from the classical structure of linguistic reference and meaning.[8] It is as if from the outset Cavell anticipates and questions the main premise of numerous debates arising in the wake of poststructuralism—namely, a prevailing suspicion that, by interrogating reference and by questioning the stability of meaning, linguistic theory cuts us off from access to the world and thereby risks the possibility of skepticism. That is why it is worth repeating the main points of Wittgenstein's critique of the traditional realist conception of language—or what Henry Staten calls the primal scene in philosophy[9]—before discussing Cavell's interpretation of how that critique invites both a suspicion of skepticism and a revision of its significance.

Opening with a famous example from Augustine's *Confessions*, *Investigations* interrogates the classical idea of meaning articulated in terms of correspondence between words and objects: "In this picture of language we find the roots of the following idea: Every word has a meaning. This meaning is correlated with the word. It is the object for which the word stands."[10] Although naming—and its correlative, ostensive definition—certainly has a place in language (as Wittgenstein says, naming is a language game of its own), this is too narrow and misleading a picture of language, which we come up with when we in fact ignore how language works in everyday praxis:

> Naming appears as a *queer* connexion of a word with an object.—And you really get such a queer connexion when the philosopher tries to bring out *the* relation between name and thing by staring at an object in front of him and repeating a name and even the word "this" innumerable times. For philosophical problems arise when language *goes on holiday*. And *here* we may indeed fancy naming to be some remarkable act of mind, as it were a baptism of an object [*PI*, #38].

In this frequently quoted passage, Wittgenstein argues against the assimilation of the model of meaning to the model of perception. What is at stake in this assimilation is the centrality of the solitary subject who grasps the correlation between words and objects by staring at things, pointing to them, and then pronouncing their names. Such a desire to articulate the relation between language and reality as a certain kind of private "seeing" intends to secure an intimate and intrinsic connection between the word and the object through the mental act of the speaker. The scene of naming becomes a contemplation of the presence of the object in the mind of the solitary subject. According to this picture of language, the origin of meaning lies in "some remarkable act of mind," as if seeing and speaking were two sides of the same activity.

This complicity between reference, meaning, and perception indicates that language is thought within the parameters of epistemology, which likewise takes perception to be one of the main (and most frequently doubted) sources of the knowledge of objects. If *seeing the object* posits the essential continuity between linguistic meaning and knowledge based on subject-centered rationality, then traditional skeptical questions ("do you see all of it?" "do you really see it—you might be dreaming?" "do you see it as it is in itself?") seem to cut across both knowledge and language. For that reason, it is easy to misread Wittgenstein's critique of the name/object model of meaning as an epistemological argument that either confirms or refutes skepticism. Let us compare, for a moment, the above fragment from *Philosophical Investigations* with what Stanley Cavell describes as a typical structure of the skeptical argument:

Request for Basis: How, for example, do I know there's a table here?

Basis: Because I see it. Or: by means of the senses.

Ground for Doubt: a) But what do I really see? Mightn't I be, suppose I were, dreaming, hallucinating?
b) But that's not enough. Mightn't it be a decoy?
c) But I don't see all of it . . .

Conclusion: So I don't know.

Moral: I never can know. The senses are not enough to ground our knowledge of the world [*CR*, 144].

Although both linguistic and epistemological analyses refer to "staring at an object" as a source of meaning and knowledge, and both find this foundation insufficient, it does not follow that we end up in both cases with the same skeptical conclusion. What is at stake in Wittgenstein's critique is not a doubt whether perception can provide the link between the object and its name for the speaking subject but a question whether the origin of meaning can be located within subjectivity. Wittgenstein implies that such skeptical conclusions arise out of misreading the nature of the linguistic difficulty, "for philosophical problems arise when language *goes on holiday*." Irreducible to the subject-object relation, Wittgenstein's analysis, on the contrary, points to the aspects of signification exceeding subjectivity.

The first point of Wittgenstein's critique is to replace the misleading picture of reference as "staring at an object," by shifting the analysis from the solitary perception of the object to the intersubjective sphere of communication. Consequently, the discussion of meaning moves from the analysis of the mental act of the speaker to the consideration of social language games and their grammar—that is, from the subjective to the intersubjective and intra-linguistic constitution of meaning. What Wittgenstein argues here is that the relation between words and objects is mediated by social praxis: "Only someone who already knows how to do something with it can significantly ask a name" [*PI*, #31]. And we know "how" to do something with a word when we know its grammar, the rules of the game in which the word occurs. Grammatical rules constitute an intersubjective framework that both precedes and enables seeing and naming objects. Only when, for instance, someone already has some understanding of the game of chess, can she grasp the meaning of a figure called "king." The second point of Wittgenstein's critique of reference is that it obfuscates the fact that speaking is a form of social and cultural practice rather than the unmediated contemplation of an object by a solitary subject. In other words, subjectivity, mental acts, and perception are not prior to but issue from shared forms of life. This is the main issue behind Wittgenstein's critique of so-called private language.[11] Hence Wittgenstein's famous claim that meaning is not established by the word's correspondence with the object but by the word's uses in specific situations. Such an understanding of meaning in terms of use conflicts with the model of reference based on perception, because even words that function as names (and obviously not all words do) do not derive their meaning from a stable relationship with the things in the world but "characterize many different kinds of use of a word, related to one another in many different ways" [*PI*, #38]. Consequently, the apparent unity of meaning based on "seeing the object"—that is, on the unity of the mental act—is put into question by words' diverse social uses.[12]

Cavell argues here that to read Wittgenstein's philosophy in terms of a confirmation or a repudiation of traditional skepticism is to return to the model of reference rooted in perception and to meaning grounded in the mental process—that is, to abridge both the intersubjective and the grammatical character of signification. Focused on the gaps between the world and language, existence and identity, subject and object, an interpretation of Wittgenstein's philosophy in terms of skep-

ticism is misleading for several reasons. First, this reading still perpetuates the correspondence model of meaning and truth; second, it does
not take into account the intersubjective character of signification and
restores instead the centrality of the subject; and finally, it assumes an
unproblematic notion of identity. An alternative approach to
Wittgenstein's philosophy (which, I believe, Cavell elaborates in *The
Claim of Reason*) radicalizes the significance of skepticism in order to
articulate a model of signification that is incompatible with the philosophical paradigm of the subject.

    Before proposing this redefinition of skepticism, Cavell inquires
first into how the suspicion about the gap between identity and existence originates. Let us recall that for Wittgenstein the meaning of an
expression is determined by linguistic practice, and what governs such
a practice are the conventional agreements among speakers. Yet, since
(Wittgensteinian) criteria merely regulate the application of words in
specific contexts, the argument can be advanced that they do not tell
us of a thing's existence but merely determine its identity: "Criteria are
'criteria for something's being so', not in the sense that they tell us of
a thing's existence, but of something like its identity, not of its *being* so,
but of its being *so*" [*CR*, 45]. This disappointment with the limitations
of criteria in turn sounds like a version of the classical skeptical conclusion that we do not really know the existence of things. Yet, the
apparent gap between identity and existence is something
Wittgenstein's definition of the nature of grammatical investigation
both anticipates and responds to:

> We feel as if we had to *penetrate* phenomena: our investigation,
> however, is directed not towards phenomena, but, as one might
> say, towards the *'possibilities'* of phenomena. We remind our-
> selves, that is to say, of the *kind of statement* that we make about
> phenomena . . . . Our investigation is therefore a grammatical one
> [*PI*, #90].

If we think that criteria should help us "penetrate phenomena," or discover their hidden essence, then the grammatical explanations of the
word's usage might seem superficial, somehow out of touch with reality. In that case, criteria would appear to problematize "the relation
between knowing what a thing is . . . and knowing that it is" [*CR*, 49]
(for instance, calling something pain will not tell us whether pain itself
is real or simulated), and therefore would confirm the possibility of
skepticism rather than refute it. Cavell argues, however, that this sense
of failure arises only if we assume that there is a radical difference
between language and world, words and facts, and that language

functions merely as an "access" to the world and facts [CR, 68]. Rather than attempting to bridge the gap between language and the world with familiar constructs like God or universals, Wittgensteinian analysis inquires into the ways in which the intersubjective linguistic practices constitute both the picture of the world and the subject's place in that world. Thus, grammatical investigations not only establish the identities of phenomena but also disclose, in the Kantian sense, the very 'possibilities' of those phenomena.[13] To posit a gap between identity and existence is to misunderstand the role of language—in particular, to confuse the intersubjective constitution of the framework of the world with the subjective representation of that world.[14]

This unquestioned centrality of the subject is particularly striking in the case of skepticism regarding the reality of other minds, where the gap between the world and language is articulated as a discontinuity between the self and the other, which in turn discloses gaps between language and mind, soul and body, the inside and the outside. For Cavell, skepticism of other minds expresses a dissatisfaction that language does not give access to the other's self-knowledge. How can outer criteria—say the grammar of the word "pain"—reach the inner process or the private sensation—the pain itself—in the other person? Especially in the last section of *The Claim of Reason*, Cavell draws shocking parables of violence inherent in this desire to possess the other's self-knowledge and opens interesting ways of revising skepticism of other minds in the direction of ethics.[15] When the problem of other minds is couched in terms of the break between the inner and the outer, then what is amazing is the complacency of self-knowledge in the face of such doubts. If the discontinuity between the self and the other is seen as a gap between mind (inner) and words (outer), then such a gap discloses a discontinuity within the self as well, and announces an essential possibility that words might "fail" the speaking subject.

Cavell argues, therefore, that reading Wittgenstein's notion of language in terms of traditional skepticism encounters a series of difficulties: first, such a reading still keeps the theory of meaning squarely within the bounds of the knowing subject; second, it misunderstands the role of language in social praxis; and, finally, it can imply erroneously that for Wittgenstein the issue of the identity of concepts remains unproblematic. Thinking about language in terms of the traditional picture of skepticism tends to misconstrue the discontinuities within linguistic practices and intersubjective relations as the lack of correspondence *between* language and the world, subject and object. Cavell suggests that this interpretation not only erases the intersubjective character of language but also covers over the deeper consequences of the revision of skepticism Wittgenstein's philosophy enables.

The central difficulty of Wittgenstein's philosophy of language lies not in the gap between existence and identity but in the mode by which the intersubjective linguistic criteria establish meaning. Wittgenstein gives us a sense of this difficulty when he insists that the meaning of a word cannot be "grasped" immediately, but becomes understood only when "the overall role of the word in language is clear," that is, on the basis of relations with other elements of language [*PI*, #30]. As Henry Staten argues, for Wittgenstein isolated terms do not contain meaning within themselves but acquire signification only when they are used in specific contexts—that is, when they constitute linguistic practices. Such an understanding of language is closely related to structuralist linguistics insofar as in both cases the meaning of the word is not determined on the basis of reference to the object or to an inner subjective process but through relations with other words. This is the point Cavell stresses as well: "'Wittgensteinian criteria do not relate a name to an object, but various concepts to the concept of that object.' . . . They establish the position of the concept of an 'object' in our system of concepts" [*CR*, 76]. Yet, even though meaning in both cases is relational, Wittgenstein does not articulate a general system of linguistic rules (a structuralist code) that would regulate specific uses, but determines meaning on the basis of linguistic practices themselves.[16]

What a skeptical suspicion registers here (and misconstrues as the problem of the existence of the world) is that the focus on diverse uses of the word destroys the traditional concepts of identity and the unity of meaning. Cavell explains this dissatisfaction as follows: "'But *the* meaning of a word is *one thing*, not a lot of scattered things pointed to in various contexts'" [*CR*, 76]. Again, Wittgenstein anticipates this objection and exposes what kind of misleading assumptions about language lie behind it: "there are *countless* . . . different kinds of use of what we call 'symbols', 'words', 'sentences'. And this multiplicity is not something fixed, given once for all; but new types of language, new language-games, as we may say, come into existence, and others become obsolete and get forgotten" [*PI*, #23]. This emphasis on "countless" uses of the word and on the temporal character of meaning challenges a familiar assumption that the meaning of a word is 'one thing', and that it can be unified under a concept and expressed as a timeless essence. The focus on the recurrence of a word, on the contrary, points out that meaning cannot be grasped immediately but needs to be explained by unfolding different uses in different contexts. What the displacement from the subjective to the intersubjective character of language reveals is the irreducible temporal detour of meaning—this is what Cavell calls projection of the word, and, as I will indicate in subsequent chapters, what Derrida thematizes as iteration, and Benjamin as transmissibility. The necessity of such a temporal unfolding in turn problematizes the distinction between the particular and the general.[17] Thus, what Wittgenstein's notion of projection questions—and this point will be absolutely crucial in Cavell's revision of skepticism—is the very model of knowledge understood as the subsumption of particulars under universals. Although for Wittgenstein the meaning of a word is more general than its particular use (and that is why it lends itself to a repetition), this generality cannot be articulated in advance (as a concept or as a rule) apart from listing the specific instances in which the word is deployed. As Cavell emphasizes, such an irreducibly temporal mode of the explanation of meaning is supposed to make us "dissatisfied with the idea of universals," to make us "see that concepts do not usually have, and do not need 'rigid limits' so that universals are neither necessary nor even useful in explaining how words and concepts apply to different things" [*CR*, 187–88].

The fact that the generality of words cannot be defined in terms of universals brings about not only a crisis of identity but also a crisis of the linguistic norm. The threat of skepticism links the temporal unfolding of meaning with difference rather than identity, indeed, with the scattering rather than the gathering of sense. It implies that there is "no one thing in common," no unity underlying all these countless uses of the word but, in Wittgenstein's words, "a complicated network of similarities overlapping and criss-crossing" [*PI*, #66]. Comparing divergent uses of the word to a thread made out of fibre twisted on fibre, Wittgenstein remarks that "the strength of the thread does not reside in the fact that some one fibre runs through its whole length, but in the overlapping of many fibers" [*PI*, #67]. However, when overlapping similarities do not articulate the unity of meaning, "one thing in common," then concepts of everyday language seem to lose their identity and precision. "Uncircumscribed," unbounded, and "blurred," the concepts and words of ordinary language are marked by ambiguity— ambiguity that stems from our inability either to fix meaning to specific contexts or to determine the totality of possible contexts in advance. As Cavell argues, "there is no 'everything' to be said. For we haven't been asked, or asked ourselves *everything* either; nor *could* we, however often we wish that were possible" [*CR*, 184]. The temporal projection announces, therefore, on the one hand, the impossibility of totalizing meaning, and, on the other, the perpetual threat of deviation—of stepping outside the bounds of linguistic norms.

Since the temporal detour posits meaning as incomplete and ambiguous, it also opens a threat of deviation with the same gesture with which it establishes linguistic norms. Linking repetition with difference, the trajectory of linguistic projections cannot be regulated by concepts or rules.[18] Such, in Cavell's terms, are the consequences of "the fierce ambiguity" of ordinary language:

> Why haven't we arranged to *limit* words to *certain* contexts, and then coin new ones for new eventualities? The fact that we do not behave this way must be at the root of the fierce ambiguity of ordinary language, and that we won't behave this way means that for real precision we are going to have to get words *pinned* to a meaning through explicit definition and limitation of context [*CR*, 180].

The temporality of projection suggests that the possibility of speaking within and outside linguistic norms stems essentially from the same capacity of language—which means that the boundaries between what counts as inside (that is, what remains the same) and what as outside (that is, what is different) linguistic norms are particularly fluid and open to revision. To anticipate Cavell's further argument, let me say that the fear of deviation, which is as essential to language as the conditions of its stability, will constitute the appeal to community as a way to fix the boundaries of these linguistic norms.

Cavell's last point is that the discontinuous temporality of projection creates a profound anxiety about the competence of the subject and the efficiency of pedagogy. The potentially unlimited range of uses of words implies that the interminable process of learning at no point assures the mastery of the speaking subject. As Cavell argues, we have to learn how to use words in new contexts without the assistance of rules, and, to a certain degree, without the help of conventions, just as we learn, for instance, to use the word "feed" in such ordinary expressions as "to feed the lion," "to feed pride," "to feed the baby," and "to feed the meter" [*CR*, 181–183]. The multiplicity of uses perpetually tests and questions the mastery of the speaking subject because our knowledge of language is not limited merely to "learning" a set of definitions but involves the capacity to follow the recurrence of the word, to "know" how to continue with this word in new circumstances, to know how to go on [*CR*, 78].

Yet, can this anxiety about the efficiency of pedagogy be confined to a crisis of subjectivity?[19] What if we read this anxiety, in the way for instance Homi Bhabha does in his analysis of nationality, as an indica-

tion of the profound conflict between the temporality of linguistic projection and the ends of pedagogical instruction?[20] Given the fact that
linguistic criteria, in and of themselves, do not secure a continuous
reproduction of culture, we have to consider the constitutive role of
pedagogical instruction in the reproduction of "forms of life."
Although Cavell claims to read Wittgenstein as a philosopher of culture, he never addresses the social function of pedagogy implied by
the numerous examples of instruction in *Philosophical Investigations*.
Because he all too quickly retreats into a discussion of the crisis of the
subject, Cavell never even considers what sort of implications the
incompatibility between linguistic projection and ends of pedagogy
might have for the transformation of cultural life.

Instead of cultural change, the fear that we might not know how
to go on, that we, like Beckett's characters, might get stuck or become
lost in the "complicated network" of language games, brings about an
overwhelming sense of the paralysis of the speaking subject. Always
one step behind the movement of language, the subject has lost not
only its primacy as the source of meaning but also the capacity to
retrieve the alien origin of signification in retrospection. In a gesture
similar to a certain kind of modern writing, Cavell situates his speaking subject on the verge of the abyss: "We begin to feel, or ought to, ter-
rified that maybe language (and understanding, and knowledge) rests
upon very shaky foundations—a thin net over an abyss" [*CR*, 178].
This is indeed a *serious* reckoning with the possibility of skepticism.
And yet, one needs to question both the pathos and the implicit purpose of this catastrophic outcome. Why does Cavell, just before he
shifts the terrain and finds the means of recovery from skepticism,
confront us for a moment with nothing short of a disaster? It is as if the
very possibility of a cure and recovery from skepticism depended
upon the capacity to feel the seriousness of this potential catastrophe.[21]

Revision of Skepticism: Acknowledgment, Community, and the Aesthetics of Ordinary Speech

If thinking about the conjunction of language and skepticism means
finding oneself, eventually, suspended on a "thin net over an abyss,"
then the possibilities of "going on," proceeding further with this problematic, become increasingly more difficult. As I suggested earlier,
Cavell's text will pursue simultaneously the two different responses to
this impasse of the subject revealed by the skeptical interpretation of
linguistic difficulties. One of them, a more radical and more difficult

path, will lead to a provocative reinterpretation of skepticism itself and to a rethinking of the intersubjective character of signification. The second response is much more predictable and familiar. Focusing on the threat that the possibility of skepticism represents, it will seek to recover from it, to unify meaning, and to secure what Kafka calls ironically "the ground under our feet." Significantly, community is the point where these two paths intersect—where the task of the revision of skepticism merges with the ethos of the recovery from its threat. By bringing into relief the limits of the subject-centered understanding of language, this tension between revision and recovery, I argue, reveals in turn the unresolved conflict between alterity and community in Cavell's work. In order to find a way out of this conflict—in order to harmonize the signification of alterity with the larger context of community—Cavell will appeal to the aesthetics of ordinary language.

The main point of Cavell's revision of skepticism is to articulate the difference between the familiar skeptical thesis negating the possibility of knowledge and the so called truth of skepticism—what we might call its affirmative moment. Cavell suggests that both skepticism's understanding of itself and its philosophical refutations take it for granted that the significance of skepticism is limited to its negative thesis, which expresses the impossibility of knowledge. Therefore, a different interpretation of skepticism would not only have to alter its self-understanding but would also have to step outside the parameters defining its struggle with philosophy: "I take (2) [a sense of skepticism that we can never know with certainty of the existence of something or other] to be a piece of what I think of as skepticism's picture of itself, its self-understanding. A formidable criticism of skepticism—as of any serious philosophy—will have to discover and *alter its understanding of itself*" [CR, 37–38, emphasis added]. Such a "formidable criticism" radicalizes the meaning of failure by disclosing a surplus of signification emerging from the very paralysis of subject-centered rationality.

To alter the philosophical understanding of skepticism means to question, first of all, the structure of exemplarity operative in the skeptical "recital." The typical trajectory of a skeptical argument leads from a particular case of dissatisfaction with knowledge to a general conclusion that we can never know anything with certainty. Cavell points out that the problem is not with the skeptical conclusion but with the epistemologist's examples, which while referring to specific ordinary objects (pieces of wax, tomatoes, etc.), are construed as the best cases representing the optimal conditions of knowledge in general, and therefore already set the mechanism of exemplarity in motion. The importance of such an exemplary case can be expressed as follows: "if I know *anything*,

I know *this*" [*CR*, 429]. Because a particular claim is taken to be representative of knowledge in general, the progression from a local failure to the total negation of knowledge is a foregone conclusion.[22] What is amiss with the structure of the skeptical argument, according to Cavell, is the "apparent assumption that our knowledge of the world as such is at stake in the examination of the particular claim to know" [*CR*, 46]. This assumption amounts in fact to the total obliteration of the particularity and singularity of the object or of the other person. Drawing on Wittgenstein's interventions into the paradigm of knowledge defined as subsuming particulars under universals, Cavell demonstrates that there is no meaningful linguistic context in which such a totalizing claim about the possibility or impossibility of knowledge can be made.[23] Let us recall that the idea of the totality of knowledge or meaning is incompatible with Wittgenstein's notion of temporal projection, where none of the particular applications of the word can be converted into the best case representing all of its possible uses. Based on the critique of exemplarity (and the opposition of the general and the particular on which it rests), Cavell's intervention here is directed against the ideal of the totality of knowledge presupposed by both the skeptical argument and its philosophical refutation. Incapable of thinking the particular and the temporal, both skepticism and its refutation belong to the totalizing thinking about universals.

If the skeptic reads a specific case of failure in an exemplary fashion as a collapse of the totality of knowledge, Cavell interprets it as an interruption of that totality. In Cavell's revised description, particular cases of dissatisfaction with knowledge and language do not negate the totality of knowledge as such, but reveal instead a surplus of signification—a strange "truth" that our *basis* in the world and in the human community is not (entirely) that of knowing, and therefore, is not a basis at all in the traditional epistemological sense (i.e., serving the purpose of legitimating a particular knowledge claim). We can now articulate the difference between the negative thesis and the "truth" of skepticism in more precise terms: if the thesis of skepticism negates the possibility of knowledge as such, the "truth" of skepticism reveals that our relation to the world and others cannot be reduced to totalizing cognition, representation, or logical necessity. Consequently, in place of the negation of the totality of knowledge, Cavell's reappraisal of skepticism points to an outside or a beyond of that totality. By interrupting the totality of knowledge, the truth of skepticism allows us to grasp a certain outside of reason, and, consequently, an outside of philosophy. To paraphrase Adriaan Peperzak's insight about a parallel revision of skepticism at work in Levinas's ethics, we might say that Cavell's interest in revising skepticism is motivated by the search for ways of thinking and speaking "beyond the order of well-founded and self-assured *logos*," that is, beyond philosophy itself.[24] Thus, the very recognition of "the claim of reason" is simultaneously intertwined in Wittgenstein's philosophy of language with the acknowledgment of the other of reason.[25]

Such a recognition of the other of reason changes the significance of failure: the moment of failure is interpreted as an interruption of the totality of knowledge, or as a shift which opens a different "region" of thinking:

> What the thesis [of skepticism] now means is something like: Our relation to the world as a whole, or to others in general, is not one of knowing, where knowing construes itself as being certain. So it is also true that we do not *fail* to know such things [*CR*, 45].

Although on some level "we do not fail to know" it, the philosophical refutation of skepticism is blind precisely to the difference between the negativity of the overt thesis of skepticism and the affirmation of its truth. By bringing this difference to light, Cavell's revision of the skeptical argument performs the "shifting of the weight" from a dissatisfaction with knowledge to a displacement of knowledge. What the truth of skepticism registers—and what its philosophical refutation forgets—is both the limitation of knowledge and a need for its supplement (to use Derrida's term), as if our articulations of what counts as knowing were too narrow.

I would like to suggest that Cavell's supplement of philosophical reason takes the form of three interrelated displacements: from logical thinking to indeterminate judgment; from subjective rationality to intersubjective relations; and, finally, from propositional form to ordinary patterns of communication. Aiming to recover both the particularity and sociality of thinking, Cavell's investment in judgment here is similar to Hannah Arendt's interpretation of the social implications of Kant's *Critique of Judgment*: "the faculty of judgment deals with particulars, which 'as such, contain something contingent in respect of the universal,' which normally is what thought is dealing with."[26] Cavell's turn to judgment is already implied in his revision of skepticism: if both the classical skeptical argument and its philosophical refutation obliterate the particular by subordinating it to the totality of knowledge, the truth of skepticism gives a new prominence to judgment as the mode of thinking about the particular. Departing from the universal validity of knowledge secured by logical argumentation, the focus on judgment (which taints knowledge with contingency) underscores the relations among the judging members of the community—hence the emphasis on judgment not only preserves the particularity of the object or the other person but also reveals the irreducibly intersubjective character of knowledge. Specifically, for Cavell that means that the quest for the epistemological grounding of knowledge is supplanted by the appeal to the communal/linguistic context of knowledge: "the focus upon judgment takes human knowledge to be the human capacity for applying the concepts of a language to the things of a world" [*CR*, 17]. Thus, the "truth" of skepticism brings about a recognition that knowledge itself makes sense only within the frame of what Wittgenstein calls "our forms of life" [*Lebensform*]. The necessary linguistic consequence of the communal framework of knowledge is a turn away from the logical analysis of discourse (which, with its privileging of the propositional form and logical rigor, is abstracted from everyday communication) to an analysis of more ambiguous, ordinary language at work in intersubjective praxis.

Cavell's revision of skepticism suggests that in the absence of any other foundation of truth, the meaningfulness of language could rest only on the exchange among its speakers and the social conventions governing this exchange. As Charles Bernstein eloquently puts it, "we are initiated by language into a socious, which is for us the world. So that the foundations of knowledge are not so much based on a preexisting empirical world as on shared conventions and mutual attunement."[27] Following Wittgenstein, Cavell especially resists here the Platonic gesture of grounding the discursive community upon a philosophical foundation.[28] Cavell's engagement with skepticism discloses therefore the fact that the project of providing an epistemological validation for the community is not only unsatisfactory but misses the point, because the appeal to social exchange does not function as a foundation of knowledge but rather as a condition of judgment.[29]

One of the more significant consequences of Cavell's emphasis on this sociality of judgment is the shift from truth to value.[30] Contesting the separations between the domains of reason—truth and value, knowledge and morality, "is" and "ought"—Cavell suggests that the representation of "what is" is not only inseparable from what it is called but also from "what it counts as for us." The renegotiation of the distinctions between truth and value opens another scene of contestation (to which we will turn shortly), this time between philosophy and literature. Cavell's redefinition of knowledge is meant to bring to the fore the fact that "the idea of valuing" is "the other face of asserting" [*CR*, 94], that truth about the world is inseparable from an interpretation of this world in terms of social values. Knowledge, therefore, is not merely an accumulation of true propositions about the world but also a reflection of the values and judgments of a community of speakers—values embedded in what Wittgenstein calls, the forms of life:

> what we seem headed for is an idea that what can comprehensibly be said is what is found to be worth saying. This explicitly makes our agreement in judgment, our attunement expressed through criteria, agreement in valuing. So that what can be communicated, say a fact, depends upon agreement in valuing, rather than the other way around [*CR*, 94].

To posit what we say as the basis of knowledge is to undercut the neutrality and disinterestedness of knowledge—that is, to acknowledge the necessary risk that the appeal to 'our' agreements and convictions as the ground of truth might dissolve the strict distinction between rationality and opinion, or even worse, between reason and social prejudice.[31] As Cavell writes, "it is an examination that exposes one's convictions . . . ; so it requires a breaking of one's sense of necessity, to discover truer necessities . . . . Which means that I have to experiment in believing what I take to be prejudices, and consider that my rationality may itself be a set of prejudices" [*CR*, 21].[32]

To posit "the agreement in valuing" as the framework of knowledge is to reconceive it in the context of what Cavell calls the "aesthetics" and the "economics" of speech. It means to think of meaning and knowledge in terms of subjective desire (aesthetics) and intersubjective linguistic exchange (economics): "If we formulate the idea that valuing underwrites asserting as the idea that interest informs telling or talking generally, then we may say that the degree to which you talk of things, and talk in ways, that hold no interest for you . . . is the degree to which you consign yourself to nonsensicality" [*CR*, 95]. This aspect of Cavell's work implies that judgments of value underwriting the concept of truth do not reflect a strict hierarchy but derive from subjective desires, and that these desires themselves are embedded in the exchanges among speakers. Cavell's emphasis on exchange, desire, and interest underscores the fact that common values are not fixed and unalterable but are, precisely, open to exchange, negotiation, and the games of seduction.[33] At this point, Cavell departs from the Enlightenment ideal of the separate domains of reason and points to a proximity between aesthetics, philosophy, and psychoanalysis, all of which engage in different ways the question of how desire and exchange among diverse interests regulate meaning.

If, by departing from propositional discourse, the "truth" of skepticism reveals the intersubjective character of knowledge and language, we need to ask what notion of intersubjectivity is operative in Cavell's work. *The Claim of Reason* stresses two different moments of linguistic exchange—the alterity of the other person and the being together of the speakers in the discursive community—without explaining, however, how these two moments relate to each other. Consequently, Cavell articulates the "other of reason," presupposed and revealed by language, in two different ways. On the one hand, the "outside" of reason is figured as an acknowledgment of the irreducible alterity of the other person; on the other, as the mutual attunement among the speakers in a discursive community. I am going to argue, however, that there is a profound tension between these two insights and that Cavell eventually attempts to resolve this disparity by assimilating alterity into a vision of communal unity. That is why, despite the emphasis on the positive signification of the "truth" of skepticism, Cavell's work is still haunted by the threat of the other of reason. This persistent threat of skepticism, like a recurring ghost of the other, uncovers a more radical signification of alterity incommensurate with the notion of a unified community, which Cavell's work locates as the "basis" for communication.

Let me start with the idea of acknowledgment, which stresses the fact that the subject's exposure to the other is irreducible to questions of knowledge, cognition, comprehension. As Cavell writes, "A 'failure to know' might just mean a piece of ignorance, an absence of something, a blank. A 'failure to acknowledge' is the presence of something, a confusion, an indifference, a callousness, an exhaustion, a coldness."[34] The difference between knowledge and acknowledgment, which the "truth of skepticism" allows us to grasp, implies that the relation to the other does not represent merely an epistemological problem but involves a necessity of response (for example, when the other is in pain). Gerald Bruns has argued for some time now that there is a profound affinity between Cavell's idea of acknowledgment and Levinas's face-to-face encounter with the other. In the context of philosophical interpretations of Wittgenstein's and Cavell's work, Bruns's intervention is crucial because it allows us to shift the discussion from the issue of the subject's place in the community (which corresponds to the private/public language debate) to the signification of alterity in the context of diverse language games and the community of speakers. As he argues, acknowledgment "disrupts our self-possession by forcing us out of the mode of knowing into that of answering."[35] This disruption of self-possession suggests a lack of reciprocity between the self and the other. Consequently, the encounter between the self and the other is not a

symmetrical relationship that could be grasped in an adequate representation or regulated by linguistic criteria. The implied asymmetry is
precisely what makes acknowledgment irreducible to knowledge of the
other, since knowledge is predicated on reciprocity expressed in the
idea of truth as adequation. To illustrate this contrast, Cavell claims that
"the alternative to my acknowledgment of the other is not my ignorance
of him but my avoidance of him, call it my denial of him" [CR, 389]. The
alternative to the acknowledgment of alterity, in other words, is indifference and refusal of responsibility rather than a failure of knowledge.

Yet, important as this ethical moment in Cavell's work is, the question remains as to how such a non-reciprocal relation to the other,
revealed by the truth of skepticism, is to be reconciled with the second
aspect of the linguistic exchange, namely, the community of speakers,
or whether the exposure to the other is compatible with the notion of
social exchange at all. As Cavell consistently argues, "the philosophical
appeal to what we say, and the search for our criteria on the basis of
which we say what we say, are claims to community" [CR, 20]. But
what sort of understanding of the linguistic community is presupposed
by the public character of language, and how is this being in common
to be reconciled with the acknowledgment of alterity? Put differently,
how is the ethical moment of acknowledgment to be sustained within
the economics and the aesthetics of speech? Throughout this essay I
have been repeating after Cavell phrases like "we," "ours," "for us,"
and it is time now to confront the question of who "we" are. When
Cavell considers the other side of the linguistic exchange—the belonging together of speakers within a community—he consistently stresses
the continuity between the subject and the discursive community,
between the "I" and others, rather than an asymmetry between the
speakers. This continuity and reciprocity is reflected not only in the
persistence of the pronoun "we" but also in the definition of linguistic
exchange as *agreement*, which is based on Wittgenstein's idea of the
agreement in judgment. This particular ideal of community based on
intersubjective agreements conflicts with a non-reciprocal relation to
alterity expressed in the idea of acknowledgment. Since the encounter
with the other, revealed by the truth of skepticism, cannot be contained
in the vision of communal unity, this alterity is viewed as a threat from
which we need to recover. If the truth of skepticism reveals the notion
of linguistic response culminating (and perhaps breaking down) in the
non-reciprocal encounter with the other, the notion of the recovery
from skepticism posits the other as a threat. Not surprisingly, the recovery from skepticism is intertwined with a regulation of linguistic
exchange—a regulation that will assure that the threat of alterity is subsumed into social harmony.

It is the mode of this regulation of the diverse language games that will concern us here. Assuming that even the revised significance of skepticism can be a cause of dis-ease, Cavell posits this regulation as a version of the "talking cure"—something on the order of a psycho-analysis of philosophy. And it is Cavell's interpretation of the thera-peutic mode in Wittgenstein's philosophy that is at once most interest-ing and most problematic. We have to say from the outset that the process of recovering from skepticism is by no means identical with its refutation, at least not with the classical form of refutation—namely a negation of the skeptical thesis that we do not know the existence of the world or others with certainty [*CR*, 45]. It will, rather, consist in a spe-cific interpretation of the nature of the exchanges among speakers, of the conventionality of language, and above all, of the *sensus communis*, which is posited as a means of unification rather than a cause of the fur-ther dispersion of meaning.

Since recovery from skepticism does not result from philosophical refutation, nor from the appeal to community as a rational ground of truth, it becomes clear that this therapeutic *sensus communis* cannot be confused with a rational community (underlying, for instance, Habermas's notion of communicative rationality), where the consen-sus in question is mediated by a concept, a rational argument, or com-munication. As Cavell's reinterpretation of skepticism makes it clear, the commonality of this *sensus* is not assured by logical necessity, based on the rules of reason. Rather, the appeal to community affords merely "an anthropological, or even anthropomorphic, view of neces-sity; and that can be disappointing; as if it is not really *necessity* which he has given an anthropological view of. As though if the a priori has a history it cannot really be the a priori in question" [*CR*, 118–119]. To play on Cavell's references to the psychoanalytic cure, perhaps what is at stake here is an unconscious *communio*—a *sensus* unaware of itself, an unintelligible sense bespeaking the other side of reason.

Furthermore, this unintelligible sense of community is also dis-tinct from the political community, where the idea of social consensus is mediated by the notions of the social contract, norms of action, or ideology. By separating *sensus communis* from politics, Cavell also deemphasizes the questions of power, conflicts, and complex negotia-tions among competing interests. Unconstrained by any external necessity or force, and therefore presupposing a community formed by free and equal subjects, *sensus communis* in question here precedes the operations of power and violence. In fact, any evidence of force or violence in language will be thought by Cavell on the model of a fall or deformation of an original state of affairs. Acknowledging a certain similarity to the idea of a political consensus, Cavell stresses nonetheless the difference between the unity of community he wants to pre-suppose and the political community evoked in the idea of the social contract: "it is an old, if unestablished feeling, that the mutual mean-ingfulness of the words of a language must rest upon some kind of connection or compact among its users; and that the classical locus of philosophical investigations of this idea of a compact lies in the dis-cussions of the social contract supposed to have established the politi-cal community" [*CR*, 22]. Although the theories of language (and Saussurian linguistics is a classical example here) frequently concep-tualize the belonging together of the speakers after the model of the social contract, for Cavell the connection between the speakers is not achieved by social contracts or conventional norms but involves a spontaneous agreement to "speak for others" and to allow them to speak for oneself. In Cavell's interpretation, consensus rests on a notion of representative speech, manifesting the unmediated reci-procity among the speakers.

This sense of representative speech allows Cavell to restore the continuity between a subjective experience and a social reality: "Rousseau's discovery is less a discovery of new knowledge than a discovery of a mode of knowledge, a way to use the self as access to the self's society" [*CR*, 26]. If the acknowledgment of the other dis-rupts the self-possession and knowledge of the subject, the appeal to community restores the confidence and assurance of the self (let us say, it privileges the Emersonian over the Levinasian aspect in Cavell's thinking). That is why Cavell's appeal to community does not conflict with personal confession: "those capable of the deepest personal con-fession (Augustine, Luther, Rousseau, Thoreau, Kierkegaard, Tolstoy, Freud) were most convinced they were speaking from the most hid-den knowledge of others" [*CR*, 109]. In place of the subject's exposure to the other, the idea of recovery places an emphasis on finding one-self, on finding one's own proper and, at the same time, representative voice in the community of speakers.

If the *sensus communis* Cavell posits as the cure for skepticism is neither rational nor political, perhaps it can be explained by a recourse to aesthetics. Not limited to the question of desire, the "aesthetics" of ordinary speech performs more work in Cavell's argument than he is willing to acknowledge—in fact, it provides a bridge between the sig-nification of alterity and the signification of community. This surrepti-tious aestheticization of speech and community is particularly evident in the way Cavell interprets Wittgenstein's idea of our "agreements in judgments" as the spontaneous *attunement* (*Stimmung*) in the way the speakers use language. Mediated neither by social contracts (and, by extension, neither by conventions, institutions, or writing) nor by concepts and rational will, the agreements in judgments remain undetermined, occurring, paradoxically, prior to any judgment. In order to retain a sense of community which, although not determined by the rules of reason, remains nonetheless in harmony with the claim of reason, and to rescue thus the endangered idea of rationality (by linguistic projections and by the emphasis on alterity), Cavell has to claim that agreements in judgments do not emerge from the complicated network of linguistic and pedagogical exchanges but instead precede and enable these exchanges. Let me suggest that this spontaneous unification of speakers and language games manifests the aesthetic quality similar to the Kantian judgment of taste—it displays the lawfulness without a law, the synthesis without a concept, the unity without a rule. As Kant writes, "I say taste can be called *sensus communis* with more justice than sound understanding can, and that the aesthetical judgment rather than the intellectual may bear the name of a sense common to all . . . . We could even define taste as the faculty of judging of that which makes *universally communicable*, without the mediation of a concept, our feeling in a given representation."[36] As a spontaneous harmony, the agreement in judgment does not emerge from a common history, social practices, contracts or conventions, because it is not the sort of agreement that can be negotiated, produced or reproduced through language. Rather, the unmediated aesthetic agreement—a natural accord, one would want to say, and Cavell will eventually say so—is presupposed as an antecedent to the work of criteria and social exchanges. It is perhaps not surprising that Cavell refers to the aesthetic unification of the manifold language games, because his analysis of skepticism has established that neither concepts nor conventional norms can regulate the lines of linguistic projection. In the wake of the crisis of exemplarity and the breakdown of conceptual regulation, aesthetics performs the work of spontaneous synthesis prior to any rule or concept. If the revision of skepticism discloses *sensus communis* as the other of reason, the aesthetic interpretation of community assures us that this unintelligible sense is nonetheless complimentary to reason. Thus, in the last resort, the recovery from skepticism depends on the fine aesthetic "tuning" of speakers.

Yet, this aestheticization of the community also implies a certain displacement of aesthetics from the topography of the subject to the topography of the intersubjective language games. The spontaneous synthesis of *attunement* does not display the ideal proportion of the subjective faculties (the free play of imagination and understanding), but manifests the unmediated consonance of the speakers themselves. In such a communal space, the manifold voices gather themselves into one harmonious chorus. Unlike the asymmetry implied in the acknowledgment of the other, the spontaneous balancing act—unmediated, yet as harmonious as in music, as precise as in measurement, and as systematic as in calculation—subsumes the signification of the other into the mutual "attunement" of speakers:

> The idea of agreement here is not that of coming to or arriving at an agreement on a given occasion, but of being in agreement throughout, being in harmony, like pitches or tones, or clocks, or weighing scales, or columns of figures [CR, 32].

To manifest itself, *sensus communis* does not even require a contemplation of a beautiful object, because it itself is akin to the work of art—in this densely metaphorical passage, attunement is figured as a musical concert of pitches and tones. Undetermined by any conventional standard, such a musical harmony rests on the inner unity of the social body, which in the last resort is expressed in the figure of listening with the same ear: "I am proposing that our access to belief is fundamentally through the ear, not the eye" [CR, 391]. This concatenation of tones and the tuning of ears not only suggests the internal unity of the linguistic community but also implies a rhetoric of temporality quite different from the temporal character of linguistic projections. What is at stake in this metaphorical play is the synchronization of voices, their harmonization in time. If the interminable unfolding of meaning opens the irreducible temporal gap between the subject and linguistic projections, the aesthetics of *attunement* masters this temporal difference, makes up for the delays and postponements, and gathers all the dispersed voices into the fullness of the present.

I will have something more to say about the fate of the social body unified through the figure of the ear in the context of Kafka's parables on translation and Beckett's monstrous bodily inscriptions. But something of that fate is already announced in Cavell's figurative language, which, in its attempt to secure the innate unity of the communal body, turns it into something inorganic and mute. What does it mean, for instance, to compare the spontaneous harmony of the community to clocks, mathematical figures, and weighing scales?[37] This excessive play of comparison not only disrupts the promised similitude but also collapses the indeterminate aesthetic agreement into the very means of determination. There is nothing intimate about the equation between "columns of numbers" and nothing "amazing" about the balance of weighing scales. All these figures make the internal vocal unity of the community indistinguishable from the external determination of relations. It is not the case that Cavell could have chosen a better metaphor—according to his own interpretation of figurative language, metaphors are suspicious precisely because they pressure and disrupt common agreements. The performance of the figurative language in this passage already prefigures Cavell's more explicit theoretization of metaphor. Metaphors, and we will return to this later, fail to provide a cure for skepticism because such a cure is itself an unacknowledged allergic reaction to alterity.

This particular use of aesthetics not only unifies community as a spontaneous harmony of voices but also allows Cavell to reinterpret the significance of linguistic form, in particular, to eclipse the conventionality and grammaticality of the form of life. The attempt to separate "communal agreements" from the arbitrariness, artificiality, and contingency usually implied in the term of convention is the key issue in Cavell's interpretation of Wittgenstein's "forms of life": "our ability to use language as depending upon agreement in 'forms of life' (#241). But forms of life . . . are exactly what have to be 'accepted'; they are 'given'" [*CR*, 30]. Cavell complains that the leading interpreters of Wittgenstein, including Kripke, make him "too conventional" and, consequently, diminish the importance of the natural in language: "the typical emphasis on the social eclipses the twin preoccupation of the *Investigations*, call this the natural . . . . The partial eclipse of the natural makes the teaching of the *Investigations* much too, let me say, conventionalist."[38] To distance himself from the conventionalist interpretations of form and grammar, Cavell views the spontaneous agreement as more akin to an internal nature of human life than to conventional criteria:[39] "They [conventions] are, rather, fixed by the nature of human life itself, the human fix itself" [*CR*, 110]. Cavell's reduction of grammar to "human fix" eventually translates itself into the "biological" interpretation of forms of life: "I give the formulation about forms of life having to be accepted, being the given, its biological direction—emphasizing not *forms* of life, but forms of *life*" [*DD*, 42–43].

With such an organicist understanding of the forms of life, Cavell can divorce convention from the contingencies of social practice or history:[40]

> We are thinking of convention not as the arrangements a particular culture has found convenient, in terms of its history and geography, for effecting the necessities of human existence, but *as those forms of life which are normal to any group of creatures we call human* . . . . Here the array of "conventions" are not patterns of

life which *differentiate* human beings form one another, but those exigencies of conduct and feeling *which all humans share* [CR, 111, emphasis added].

Separated from history and social practice, the internal unity of social life seems to maintain itself spontaneously, free from any regulation, be it discursive or political: "we are not asked to accept . . . a particular fact of power but the fact that I am a man" [DD, 44]. What we are asked to acknowledge in Cavell's interpretation of community, therefore, is not only the social character of language and the constitutive role of the forms of life but also a particular vision of the social, articulated on the model of an involuntary inner purposiveness characteristic of nature or of the beautiful work of art. As Lyotard remarks about such aesthetic regulation, "the idea is thus that of an 'interior' purposiveness, which isn't voluntary, nor conceived of, nor interested in any way, but which is natural to mind . . . . And that is why art at its basis belongs to nature, and why . . . nature is at bottom art."[41]

Presumably, Cavell assimilates the aesthetic agreement in forms of life to the natural rather than the conventional character of language in order to underscore the fact that linguistic conventions are not external but constitutive of communal and subjective identities, and that it is, therefore, impossible to change them *without* disrupting the pattern of social life. And yet, this attempt to naturalize convention (in contrast to, say, making nature conventional) seems to eliminate altogether the possibility of change or of critical intervention into the patterns of communal life. As J. M. Bernstein argues, "this is an image of given community, of a passive *sensus communis*, of like-mindedness without history, of like-mindedness that is given rather than created . . . . Unless the passive *sensus communis* were open to deformation and reformation it would represent a principle of nature in opposition to culture, thereby contradicting the median role that the *sensus communis* is designed to fill."[42] By divorcing attunement from the institutional and political operations of power, Cavell hopes that his biological interpretation of forms of life will prevent the possibility of such uncritical conformism and "political or social conservatism" [DD, 44], but it is more accurate to say that aesthetics, assimilated to organicism, merely conceals this possibility and thereby betrays ideological complacency.[43]

By absorbing "form" into "life," Cavell's aesthetic interpretation of *sensus communis* contains and counteracts the disruptive effects of the grammatical understanding of form—namely, the divergences and discontinuities of meaning registered by skepticism. Thus, instead of deploying the radical linguistic insights to rethink the very notion of being in common, Cavell appeals to the aesthetic unity of community in order to contain the instability of ordinary language. The acceptance of the common forms of life, spontaneously harmonized, is supposed to close off the series of linguistic discontinuities that Cavell's discussion of grammar emphasized, that is, to restore a clear distinction between deviations and so called normal uses of the word: "The coincidence of soul and body, and of mind (language) and world *überhaupt*, are the issues to which Wittgenstein's notion of grammar and criteria are meant to speak . . . . In Wittgenstein's view the gap between mind and the world is closed, or the distortion between them straightened, in the appreciation and acceptance of particular human forms of life, human 'convention'" [*CR*, 108–109]. It is possible to argue, however, that these disruptive effects of form are precisely what preserves the place of the other against an enclosure within the immanence of community. Consequently, the philosophical ambition to counteract linguistic "deviations" betrays perhaps a desire to enclose the other within a socio-linguistic totality. Such enclosure of alterity is once again accomplished by a metaphoric turn which translates the fluid boundaries between the inside and the outside of language games—between "normal" and "deviant" ways of speaking—in terms of the absolute divide between life and death. As a result of this metaphoric logic, interiority and communal identity represent a living space, whereas exteriority and alterity become deadly, a form of menace: "The signs are dead; merely working them out loud doesn't breathe life into them; even dogs can speak more effectively" [*CR*, 84].

With alterity occupying the place of deadly exteriority, it is not surprising that the threat of otherness is eventually described as a fear of exile, or as a loss of the sense of dwelling in the world. When the signification of radical alterity is assimilated to the idea of exile, however, then this reduction bespeaks a sense of nostalgia for the original unity, or the primordial dwelling. The interconnection between skepticism and nostalgia in Cavell's work reveals community as always already endangered—as a common being already lost and therefore in need of recovery. As Jean-Luc Nancy argues, such a nostalgic feeling is constitutive of the thought of community in Western philosophy: "But it is here that we should become suspicious of the retrospective consciousness of the lost community and its identity . . . at every moment in its history, the Occident has given itself over to the nostalgia for a more archaic community that has disappeared, and to deploring a loss of familiarity, fraternity and conviviality."[44] Within this conception of community, the impact of alterity and of linguistic dissemination is figured as a secondary and unfortunate accident, the negative consequences of which have to be reversed by returning dispersed words and speakers to their original home:[45]

> Wittgensteinian criteria are appealed to when we "don't know our way about", when we are lost with respect to our words and to the world they anticipate. Then we start finding ourselves by finding out and declaring the criteria upon which we are in agreement [*CR*, 34].

> It would a little better express my sense of Wittgenstein's practice if we translate the idea of bringing words back as *leading* them back, shepherding them; which suggests not only that we have to find them, to go where they have wandered, but that they will return only if we attract and command them . . . . The lives themselves have to return [*DD*, 35].

The task of bringing words home, of *shepherding* them—this communal and linguistic odyssey—is the only possibility of linguistic and cultural change Cavell envisions. Yet, since any substantial change in signification cannot result from a social or political intervention (and Cavell himself admits that this can be translated into a case of political conservatism), recovery must involve an internal change, coming forth from within the organism itself. The return to the original dwelling, then, becomes a reenactment of the moment of origination itself—a repetition of birth: "The rhetoric of humanity as a form of life...standing in need of something like transfiguration—some radical change, but as it were from inside, not *by* anything; some say in another birth" [*DD*, 44].

Cavell's focus on the passive acceptance of "our form of life," on the return to our original home, misses, I argue, a competing emphasis in *Philosophical Investigations* on the possibility of imagining/conceiving "innumerable" other forms of life [*unzähliges Andere*]. When Wittgenstein's famous statement—"to imagine a language means to imagine a form of life" (*eine Sprache vorstellen heisst, sich eine Lebensform vorstellen*) [*PI*, #19]—is read with the emphasis on imagining/picturing different forms of life, then it does not suggest a compliant acceptance of the forms of life as always already given, but discloses a possibility of alternative discourses and alternative communities. This possibility of transformation is even further strengthened by Wittgenstein's numerous examples of failed instructions, which alerts us to the breakdown of the pedagogical machinery and to the subsequent interruption of cultural continuity. What these moments of failed instruction suggest is that "the internal unity" of community is continually produced and reproduced within the pedagogical framework. Although

Cavell himself unwittingly acknowledges the possibility of a cultural transformation when he considers the incompatibility between linguistic projections and the aims of pedagogical instruction, he refuses to elaborate the political implications of this conflict for the social and cultural change. By confusing the role of pedagogy with the spontaneous acceptance of the given forms of life, Cavell, in fact, increases the pedagogical efficiency and eliminates the cultural discontinuities Wittgenstein's text allows for.

As an alternative to Cavell's interpretation of "forms of life," I would like to refer to Drucilla Cornell's notion of "recollective imagination" and its transformative role in the reproduction of community. Such an acknowledgment of the recollective imagination allows us to account not only for the constitutive character of community and the force of pedagogical will, but also for the transformation of "our forms of life."[46] By linking repetition of intersubjective criteria to difference, Cornell's focus on transformative imagination circumvents both the positivistic reduction of linguistic criteria (to self-evident norms simply being there) and, I would add, the aesthetic interpretation of such criteria as spontaneous agreements expressing the harmony of human nature. Furthermore, by intervening into the aestheticization of forms of life, the notion of transformative imagination can open for us a different role of aesthetics in ordinary language. No longer required to bridge the gap between the signification of alterity and linguistic community, such an aesthetics preserves the place of the other in intersubjective relations and thereby redefines what "life in common" means. Let me add what should be rather obvious: the desire to imagine forms of life differently might be motivated not merely by dissatisfaction with the finitude of knowledge but also by a pervasive suspicion that "our" agreements erase the signification of alterity from the linguistic exchange—and that this violent exclusion might be as systematic, deep, and intimate as our agreements are. Cavell himself worries about this possibility of exclusion of alterity without acknowledging it, and that is why he is uneasy about the air of conservatism in Wittgenstein and in his own writing, that is why he desires to divorce forms of life from the operation of power, which in the end leaves him emphasizing life rather than form—life without language, that is.

Moments of Excess: Alterity, Metaphor, Modernism

Cavell's argument registers only two possible responses with respect to the shared forms of life: they are either acknowledged or repudiated but not open to radical transformation. Cavell accepts the act of criticism only insofar as it is linked to the *internal change* of forms of life, or to interior transformation, which only reassembles the unity of language and community after its dispersion on the outside.[47] Cavell's notion of criticism is in fact a conservation of the original essence of the project rather than its transformation: "This is why deep revolutionary changes can result from attempts to *conserve a project*, to take it back to its idea, keep it in touch with its history" [*CR*, 121, emphasis added]. What will allow us to contest this project of conservation is the emphasis on the discontinuous repetition of forms of life implied in Cavell's discussion of metaphor and modernism. In contrast to the aesthetics of attunement, which indeed does conserve the essence of communal project, I would like to elaborate here an alternative notion of aesthetics corresponding to the acknowledgment of alterity. In so doing, I will focus on what the idea of attunement fails to accommodate, and, therefore, what it situates in the proximity of skepticism: the claims of alterity and the effects of figurative language. Since in Cavell's argument the signification of otherness and metaphor present similar "dangers" to common speech, it is possible to argue that figurative language preserves the place of alterity within the economics of speech and, by the same token, opens for us an alternative understanding of aesthetics in Cavell's project.

Without this alternative sense of aesthetics, Cavell's emphasis on spontaneous attunement absorbs alterity within the immanence of the social space. Unlike the thought of Levinas, for whom otherness always shatters the totality and mutuality of discourse, Cavell's work articulates alterity within the vision of representative speech—within the economy of the common and the shared. In this vision, both the subject and the other have the exemplary status as 'a representative human,' as a member of the group, and this status within the community enables their mutual acknowledgment as well: "But if I am to have my own voice in it, I must be speaking for others and allow others to speak for me. The alternative to speaking for myself representatively . . . is not: speaking for myself privately. The alternative is having nothing to say, being voiceless, not even mute" [*CR*, 28]. In other words, the alternative to representative speech lies not in the signification of alterity but in the muteness of the subject. Yet, when mutual acceptance becomes a necessary condition of speech, the thought of alterity is erased altogether from the linguistic exchange among the speakers: "What I withhold myself from is my attunement with others—with all others, not merely the one I was to know" [*CR*, 84–85]. Even though Cavell stresses the precariousness and groundlessness of this attunement, he nonetheless gives priority to the common, shared, and native rather than to the different, other, or foreign. Subsumed within the immanence of community, alterity can appear only as a secondary modification within those patterns of discourse "which all humans share." Moreover, since the shared and the common participate in the economy of "normalcy" and "naturalness" ("it is a view in which the idea of *normality*, upon which the strength of criteria depends, is seen to be an idea of *naturalness*" [*CR*, 122]), difference and alterity are valorized as manifestations of monstrosity.

With the emphasis placed on coincidence and on the shared forms of life, it is not surprising that the signification of radical alterity can announce itself only as a recurring threat of skepticism or madness. Consider, for instance, how the ethos of normalcy characterizes the significance of difference: "I expressed this significance a moment ago by saying that such people do not live in our world. Whether, in such a case, we can still respond to them as *persons, remains problematic*" [*CR*, 90]. Cavell is eloquent on the subject of the practical difficulties of such a "case" and amazingly silent on its ethical and political consequences. Any case of disagreement or difference produces anxiety because it raises the question of whether alterity can be thought within the common and the shared without being compromised. The following sentence by Cavell captures this sense of apprehension particularly well: "this meant not that normally (usually) a statement made on the basis of a criterion is true, but that it is true of *the normal inhabitants of our world*, of anything we recognize as part of our world" [*CR*, 168, emphasis added]. Radical difference is threatening not so much because it undercuts the process of normalization and undermines the established ways of speaking but because it demonstrates that certain speakers are excluded from the "normal" inhabitants and their world. As the operations of exclusion reveal, the concatenation of values such as normalcy, naturalness, and humanity is inseparable from violence.[48]

The complicity between the "spontaneity" of the aesthetic synthesis and violence inherent in normalization is marked in Cavell's argument through the recurring rhetoric of linguistic "intolerance." The fact that deviation in linguistic usage is a possibility internal to the functioning of language makes this admission of "intolerance" as the price of communal unity even more unavoidable:

> But though language—what we call language—is tolerant, allows projection, not just any projection will be acceptable, i.e., will communicate. Language is equally, definitively, intolerant—

as love is tolerant and intolerant of differences, as materials or organisms are of stress, as communities are of deviation, as arts or sciences are of variation [*CR*, 182].

Both the "outer" variance and "inner" constancy are necessary if a concept is to accomplish its tasks—of meaning, of understanding, communicating, etc. [*CR*, 185].

Both of these passages admit that if meaning is determined on the basis of linguistic practices rather than on the basis of reference or general rules, the theory of meaning must be open to the possibility of "difference" and "variance." But a certain intolerance to difference immediately articulates it as unbearable "stress," or "deviation." For the same reason, the second quotation presents the divergence in meaning as outer and constancy as inner, even though the very distinction between the inner and the outer is problematized through the use of quotation marks. This hierarchy of inner and outer, constant and different, links the stability of meaning to normalcy and alterity to deviation.

The unavoidable linguistic and communal dissonance or discord implicates the "unmediated" aesthetic synthesis in the mediation of pedagogy and operations of power—it suggests that the ideal of mutual attunement does not occur spontaneously but is prepared in advance by pedagogical machinery. One of its most powerful effects is the process of normalization and exclusion. Cavell, however, avoids further deliberation on this disturbing conjunction of language, community, and power. By speaking of the intolerance of love, organisms, communities, and arts in the same sentence, Cavell implicitly links intolerance with the natural limits of endurance rather than with the discursive operations of violence or the effects of pedagogy. As was the case with linguistic conventions, the questions of intolerance, and the potentially political rhetoric that accompanies them, are eventually assimilated to the obvious facts of human nature—that is, facts that do not require further explanation: "Underlying the tyranny of convention is the tyranny of nature" [*CR*, 123]. Such a persistent naturalization of political rhetoric (which, nonetheless, escalates from "intolerance" to "tyranny") is a rather familiar effect of ideology. This naturalization of intolerance is particularly disturbing when we consider highly contested cases of linguistic difference—cases calling into question the "tyranny" of sexist or racist language—instead of Cavell's trivial examples of abnormal linguistic behavior (as, for instance, a man calling his hamsters into a dentist's office). In such contexts, we might feel compelled to reverse Cavell's aphorism and claim that "underlying the tyranny of nature is the tyranny of conventions."

Yet, the signification of alterity is not the only danger that befalls the spontaneous unity of social attunement. What is equally inimical to common sense is the very rhetoric of ordinary language, in particular, the unavoidable figurative aspect of language games. What interests me here is whether a serious attention to figurative language can open for us a less violent understanding of aesthetics, no longer required to harmonize reason with its other or to naturalize intersubjective agreements. Cavell's description of figurative language not only reveals the areas of language usage that are not dominated by collective agreements but also suggests that our mutual attunement in language is put into question in these areas. By subverting the values of the common and by intensifying disjunctions in our "normal" ways of speaking, metaphor preserves the radical signification of alterity within economy of language. As Cavell himself remarks, figurative language represents a sort of dilemma which can be explained neither in terms of the aesthetics of attunement nor in terms of the epistemology of skepticism.

Because figurative language has the ambiguous status of both the exceptional case and the general condition of signification, it cannot be excluded from the normal ways of speaking, the way the figure of the other can be set aside from "the normal inhabitants of our world." In the context of his prior discussion of the projection of the word, Cavell has to admit that "the condition of metaphor is the *same* as the possibility of language *generally*" (emphasis added). Furthermore, the crucial stages in Cavell's own argument—for instance, attunement, exile, shepherding—are articulated by means of metaphors. If the figurative transfer of the word reveals the same condition of meaning as the projection of the word in general, how can it be treated as an exceptional and restricted case of linguistic usage? I noted earlier that Cavell had considerable difficulty maintaining the generality of our mutual attunement, where generality meant "those exigencies . . . which all humans share." Now he confronts the opposite problem—the task of restricting metaphor to the exceptional case of linguistic practice. But the only way Cavell can avoid saying "all language is metaphorical" is to call metaphor "unnatural." Although such a qualification intends to stress a secondary status of figurative language in comparison with "the normal" lines of projection, it also suggests that metaphor disrupts the assimilation of form into nature and therefore recalls and intensifies the erased effects of "grammar":

> The phenomenon I am calling "projecting a word" is the fact of language which, I take it, is sometimes responded to by saying that 'All language is metaphorical'. Perhaps one could say: the possibility of metaphor is the same as the possibility of language generally, but what is essential to the projection of a word is that it proceeds, or can be made to proceed, *naturally;* what is essential to a functioning metaphor is that its "transfer" is *unnatural*—it breaks up the established, normal directions of projection [*CR*, 189–190].

As this passage implies, figurative language strains the limits of our attunement, *breaks up* the established ways of speaking, turns our "native" tongue into something foreign. Cavell's description of metaphor suggests certain qualities of literary language in general, in particular, its capacity to function outside the closure of established conventions and to intensify the heterogeneity of discourse. Instead of accepting Cavell's interpretation of literary language as a secondary and unnatural linguistic practice, we might consider it as a case of generalized projection, extending the use of language beyond shared conventions and common agreements. Although Cavell calls metaphor "unnatural," it might be more precise to say that metaphor not only questions the hierarchy of natural and unnatural, normal and abnormal, but also reveals that "nature" and "norm" in Cavell's discourse are produced by (forgotten) metaphoric turns.

This analysis of figurative language is remarkably similar to the way Cavell describes the talk of strangers: both ways of using language are somehow out of tune with the normal inhabitants of "our" world. As this similarity suggests, metaphor undoes the aesthetic unification of community and reveals the signification of alterity always already inhabiting linguistic exchange. In the light of this undoing, the unity of the community loses its spontaneity and naturalness and appears instead as an effect of pedagogical machinery. Figurative language, or what we might call the rhetoric of ordinary speech, disrupts the simultaneity of attunement and inscribes the temporality characteristic of linguistic projections into intersubjective relations. The temporality of figurative transfer suggests, therefore, that the signification of other does not belong to the order of the present but, as Cavell writes, to the "unimaginable" future or improper past. This temporal breach in the communal unity transports *sensus communis* beside itself, and eventually, outside the realm of reason. It is not by accident, therefore, that Cavell's valorization of metaphor so closely resembles his valorization of difference and alterity. And this proximity between the figure and otherness inadvertently situates Cavell, together with such diverse theorists of poetic language as de Man or Kristeva, against the Aristotelian tradition, which takes metaphor to be an expression of the analogy of Being.

In the context of the above description of metaphor it is somewhat less surprising that a philosopher who devotes as much attention to the relation between literature and philosophy as Cavell does puts more emphasis on the function of the literary character rather than on the *character* of literary language. After all, this evasion of figurative language is dictated by the claim of reason itself and the demands of pedagogy.[49] By disrupting the immanence of the community, or worse, by contesting the boundaries between the inside and the outside, metaphor deepens the disparity between reason and alterity:

> What makes metaphor unnatural is its occasion to transcend our criteria; not as if to repudiate them, as if they are arbitrary; but to expand them, as though they are contracted . . . . And metaphor transcends criteria not as if to repudiate our mutual attunement but as if to pressure this attunement (under which pressure certain of our attunements with others will fail; but with certain others the attunement will be intensified and refined) . . . (This realm is neither outside nor inside language games).[50]

According to Cavell, the force of metaphor puts the mutuality and the commonness of speaking and speakers into question by revealing the heterogeneity on which they rest. By being neither inside nor outside linguistic games, metaphor signifies here a perpetual possibility of displacement, reminding us that the boundaries of linguistic norms are fluid and open to revision. Consequently, it renders suspect all the oppositions on which the project of recovery from skepticism rests— the distinctions between the inner and the outer, home and exile, life and death, the natural and the unnatural. By dislocating these oppositions, the rhetorical character of ordinary speech disrupts the immanence of community and re-marks the transcendence (it provides, as Cavell says in the above quotation, an occasion for *transcendence*) of alterity within the horizon of shared speech. As such, metaphor radicalizes the signification of the outside of reason by pointing that it can no longer be harmonized with the claims of reason.

This particular function of figurative language is obfuscated, however, when figurative language is interpreted as a sign of skepticism. Both approaches to language are "unnatural" for Cavell but not in the same way. What makes skepticism (here Cavell does not talk of the "truth of skepticism" but of its own self-understanding) unnatural is the fact that it repudiates the notion of attunement altogether and, consequently, treats all criteria as arbitrary. What makes metaphor "unnatural" is the way it exceeds the common and the shared aspects of language. The proximity between the metaphorical and the skeptical is rooted in the way they criticize the idea of attunement by calling it either "arbitrary" or "contracted." In both cases the idea of the shared and native tongue, the common being of the community, is put into question. In the case of figurative language, however, this disruption of commonality does not bespeak merely a dissatisfaction with the limitation of language but involves an intervention. In place of therapy, metaphor undoes the operation of pedagogy and reminds us of the forgotten "truth" of skepticism: it re-turns us to the signification of alterity.

These remarks about figurative language are extended to the aesthetics of modernism, an aesthetics which Cavell likewise associates with a "slackened conviction in a community" [*CR*, 109–110]. The ambivalence about figurative language is addressed to modern literature in general:

> In the modern neither the producer nor the consumer has anything to go on (history, convention, genre, form, medium, physiognomy, composition...) that secures the value or the significance of an object apart from one's wanting the thing to be as it is [*CR*, 95]

Cavell's analysis of modernism points to a certain vacillation in modern art between "a slackened conviction in a community" (and, therefore, a break from "our conventional agreements") and a renewal of our agreements through establishing new conventions. When the belief in the community has been "slackened," Cavell posits the subjective desire of the artist or the autonomy of the work of art as the only "value" of modernist aesthetics. Cavell argues that when the work of art departs from the notion of community based on "shared agreements," it isolates itself from the economics of speech altogether, and therefore remains in complicity either with subjectivism or aestheticism. Consequently, the aesthetics of speech (limited in this case to subjective desire or artistic autonomy) would be the only value left to protect the text from turning into a compilation of deadly signs. Repudiating linguistic norms, modern aesthetics, according to Cavell, relinquishes its hold on the "economics of speech," that is, on language in its social dimension.

Although Cavell's argument suggests an analogy between skepticism and the autonomy of the work of art (insofar as both destroy the conviction in a community), his ambivalence about modernist aesthetics suggests a somewhat different understanding of modernism:

> What happens if this conviction [in community] slackens? As in Kafka and Beckett;.... In such straits, perhaps you write for everybody and nobody; for an all but unimaginable future; in pseudonyms, for the anonymous; in an album, which is haunted by pictures and peopled with voices. But what happens if you are not a writer; if you lack *that* way of embodying, accounting for, a slackened conviction in a community, and of staking your own (in imagination, in a world of works)? [*CR*, 109–110]

I would like to dwell for a while on this strange figure of "the haunted album" as an allegorical moment displaying the predicament of modernism and its mode of writing. In the context of Cavell's reading of *Philosophical Investigations*, this figure should remind us of Wittgenstein's own description of his text as "an album": "thus this book is really only an album" [*PI*, v]. In his "Preface" to *Philosophical Investigations*, Wittgenstein dramatizes his failure to produce a book in which "thoughts should proceed from one subject to another in a natural order and without breaks" [*PI*, v]. In contrast to the aesthetics of a book and its premise of organic wholeness, the figure of an album suggests an incomplete and fragmentary itinerary: "this compels us to travel over a wide field of thought criss-cross in every direction" [*PI*, v]. Wittgenstein's description of the aesthetics of the text, remarkably similar to the formal features of literary modernism, anticipates and reflects his discussion of the complex topography of diverse language games, a topography which also accommodates the sense of dispersion "in every direction". It is all the more remarkable in this context that the itinerary of Wittgenstein's "investigations" at no point conveys Cavell's idea of an aesthetic recuperation of the original unity of language. In the face of the dispersion of language, this album does not provide a reassuring narrative of "shepherding" words home, of returning speakers and language to their original *Heimat*. If "Preface" conveys nonetheless an idea of a journey—a certain displacement of both the subject and language—it is a journey without the return to the original unity and without a final destination. In the absence of such recuperation of the unity and the commonality of language, the haphazard route of Wittgenstein's writing betrays a fatal affinity to modernist aesthetics insofar as it too can be accused of a "slackened conviction" in the community.

Testifying to the dispersion of language, the figure of the album does not, however, merely manifest the impersonality or anonymity of discourse, always in excess of both the subjective intentions and the communal essence. As Cavell's passage unwittingly acknowledges, the figure of "an album haunted by pictures and peopled with voices" not so much accounts for a slackened conviction in community as it embodies a signification of alterity within intersubjective praxis. Presented as an unknown, anonymous and alien voice—"everybody and nobody" and yet not a member of a common body—the other in this passage turns the idea of language as the "house of being" not necessarily into a prison-house but rather into a "haunted" house. If we juxtapose for a while Cavell's description of modernism, evoked here in the figure of a haunted house or a haunted text, with his earlier discussion of attunement as the spontaneous agreement among the speakers, it becomes clear that modernist aesthetics does not provide a bridge between the signification of alterity and the signification of community. Thus, the greatest "shortcoming" of modern aesthetics is that it no longer performs the therapeutic function of synthesizing the manifold of voices without the mediation of rules or conventional norms. Refusing to harmonize the other of reason with the ends of reason, such a "haunting" aesthetics nonetheless makes claims upon reason itself. In contrast to Cavell's presumption that the other is but an intimately familiar tone, always already synchronized with the communal chorus, the "haunted text" preserves the signification of the other as an irreparable discord in the communal "ear."

The noncoincidence of alterity with the common sense and with the sense of being in common is even further emphasized in Cavell's text through the rhetoric of temporality. Disrupting the spontaneous synchronization and orchestration of attunement, modernist aesthetics suggests that the other does not belong to the order of the present but, as Cavell writes, to the "unimaginable future" or to the "haunting" past. This temporal breach in the most intimate and inner communal chorus exposes the fragile *sensus communis* to external forces it can no longer assimilate or retrieve. Beseeched and haunted, the *sensus* is transported beside itself, in fact, outside the realm of sense. This expropriation of the most intimate and proper of all senses suggests that the aesthetics of modernism, renouncing the therapeutic function of attunement, resembles something like the aesthetics of the uncanny.

Could it be that Cavell's ambivalence about modernism responds, far more precisely than his discussion of attunement, to the dangerous claims that the signification of alterity makes upon both literature and philosophy? Thus, we might risk the hypothesis that what is rehearsed in the figure of the "haunted album" is the otherwise missing elaboration of the aesthetics of acknowledgment.

My readings of the selected modern texts in the second part of this book will resume Cavell's question: "what happens if this conviction [in community] slackens?" I will argue that the "haunting" texts Cavell situates in the vicinity of skepticism extol neither the value of the private desires of the artist nor of the autonomy of the work of art but explore instead different ways of belonging together and different modes of linguistic exchange. The textual explorations of those marginal "regions of words' use" that cannot be explained by the appeal to "our agreements" criticize the very concept of community as a place of recovery, as a common place, as a place uniformly ours. These marginal voices confront us with what Derrida calls a spectral community—a community always already haunted by what it cannot accommodate. As my readings of Kafka, Beckett, and Gombrowicz intend to show, such texts explore precisely those aspects of literary language, otherness, and heterogeneity that the idea of "mutual attunement" obscures or conceals. Although at odds with the notion of common agreements, these texts redefine the very notion of the "economics" of language, so that it no longer amounts to the order of the same. By rejecting the idea that linguistic and communal differences could be accounted for in the context of the economic calculations of losses and recoveries, these texts deploy the rhetoric of failure in order to suggest a different economy, to which we might refer, after Derrida, as a "general economy of writing". In order to get a sense of how "haunting" such an economy might be, we need only to recall Samuel Beckett's words: "try again fail again. Fail better."

* * *

In the end, I would like to suggest that Cavell's inquiry into the intersection between skepticism and language opens up possibilities of interpretation that his own philosophy does not fully develop. His revision of language in the light of skepticism advances the notion of projection—the temporal unfolding of meaning—which indicates that speaking within and outside language games stems essentially from the same capacity of language. Cavell's revision of skepticism in the light of this vision of language allows him to shift the paradigm of signification from the subject to the discursive community. Yet, the ethos of recovery from the disease of skepticism (and the threat of modernism, I would add) not only narrows down the range of projections to the so-called normal uses of the word but also restricts possible interpretations of being in common to "our agreements." Such a recovery erases the signification of the other from the unified social body and figurative language from the normal ways of speaking. And yet, the very difficulties that figurative language, modern texts, and alterity pose for Cavell inaugurate important questions for the theory of language and the theory of modern literature. First of all, what would a revision of skepticism, no longer restricted by the task of recovery, amount to? What would the unavoidable moments of linguistic deviation tell us about the economics and aesthetics of ordinary speech? How can we articulate a function of literary language within this unrestricted economy of speech? And finally, how can Cavell's radical insights into the temporality of linguistic projection enable us to revise the very notion of discursive community? These questions open the framework for my reading of Derrida's philosophy and for the interpretations of literary texts that follow.

NOTES

1. For a brief but lucid discussion of the shift from epistemology to the philosophy of language, see Julia Annas and Jonathan Barnes, *The Modes of Skepticism: Ancient Texts and Modern Interpretation* (Cambridge: Cambridge UP, 1985), 4–6.

2. This is the point Stephen W. Melville emphasizes in his reading of Cavell: "The moment we approach the skeptic no longer by thinking to refute him, but by asking *how* he can say *that,* the ground shifts beneath the traditional arguments." *Philosophy Beside Itself: On Deconstruction and Modernism* (Minneapolis: U of Minnesota P, 1986), 22.

3. For diverse discussions of deconstruction in the context of skepticism see, for instance, Charles Altieri, *Act and Quality: A Theory of Literary Meaning and Humanistic Understanding* (Amherst: U of Massachusetts P, 1981), 26–28; Jay Cantor, "On Stanley Cavell," in *Raritan* 1 (1981): 50–51; A. J. Cascardi, "Skepticism and Deconstruction," in *Philosophy and Literature* 8 (1984): 1–14; Michael Fischer, *Stanley Cavell and Literary Skepticism* (Chicago: U of Chicago P, 1989), 1–9, 30–35; Eugene Goodheart, *The Skeptic Disposition in Contemporary Criticism* (Princeton: Princeton UP, 1984).

4. Jürgen Habermas, *The Philosophical Discourse of Modernity,* trans. Frederick G. Lawrence (Cambridge: The MIT P, 1992), 295.

5. This focus, dictated by the limitations of my essay, does justice neither to the range of Cavell's interests (which include, in addition to philosophy, literature and film) nor even to his sources of philosophical inspiration (which include, in addition to Wittgenstein, Emerson, Heidegger, and Freud). Still, I will claim that the main aspects of his philosophy of language and skepticism are most fully elaborated in the context of his reading of Wittgenstein's *Philosophical Investigations*.

6. Rogers Albritton, "On Wittgenstein's Use of the Term 'Criterion'," in *The Journal of Philosophy* 56 (1959): 845–857; Norman Malcolm, "Wittgenstein's *Philosophical Investigations*," in *The Philosophical Review* 63: (1954): 530–59; both articles are reprinted in George Pitcher, ed., *Wittgenstein: A Collection of Critical Essays* (Garden City, N.Y.: Doubleday, 1966).

7. Stanley Cavell, *The Claim of Reason: Wittgenstein, Skepticism, Morality, and Tragedy* (Oxford: Oxford UP, 1979), 7. Subsequent references to this work will be marked parenthetically, preceded by *CR*.

8. Wittgenstein's *Philosophical Investigations* has produced rich secondary literature. For helpful accounts of skepticism and the theory of language in the later Wittgenstein, see for instance, Saul A. Kripke, *Wittgenstein on Rules and Private Language* (Cambridge: Harvard UP, 1982) and P. F. Strawson, *Skepticism and Naturalism: Some Varieties* (New York: Columbia UP, 1985), 14–21, 69–92. For a recent elaboration of the implications of the later Wittgenstein for literary theory, see for instance, the special issue of *New Literary History*, entitled *Wittgenstein and Literary Theory*, 19 (1988): 209–440.

9. Henry Staten, *Wittgenstein and Derrida* (Lincoln: U of Nebraska P, 1984), 66

10. Ludwig Wittgenstein, *Philosophical Investigations*, trans. G. E. M. Anscombe (New York: Macmillan, 1953), #1. Subsequent references to this edition will be cited parenthetically, preceded by PI.

11. For the account and reformulation of the private language argument, see Kripke, *Wittgenstein on Rules and Private Language*, 54–113.

12. This appeal to linguistic practice is sometimes viewed as a "pragmatic turn" but this is not the direction of Cavell's argument. For a discussion of the pragmatic turn as a way to "validate theoretical knowledge through praxis-oriented considerations" see Nicholas Rescher, *Skepticism: A Critical Reappraisal* (Totowa, NJ: Rowman and Littlefield, 1980), 58–85.

13. Cavell elaborates the relation between the Kantian a priori forms of understanding and Wittgenstein's grammar as the conditions of possible knowledge in "The Availability of Wittgenstein's Later Philosophy," in *Wittgenstein: The Philosophical Investigations*, ed. George Pitcher (Notre Dame: U of Notre Dame P, 1968), 176.

14. For a concise discussion of language games as "our frame of reference," see P. F. Strawson, *Skepticism and Naturalism*, 16–21.

15. Gerald Bruns has persuasively argued that there is a deep affinity between Cavell's notion of acknowledgment and the Face of the Other in the ethics of Emmanuel Levinas. See, for instance, his "Stanley Cavell's Shakespeare," in *Critical Inquiry* 16 (1990): 619–620.

16. For a discussion of this difference, see, for instance, Henry Staten, *Wittgenstein and Derrida*, 79–81.

17. As Robert Mankin points out, "we could not conceive of language if particular and general did not operate at once." Robert Mankin, "An Introduction to *The Claim of Reason*," in *Salmagundi* 67 (1985): 75.

18. For a discussion of the limits of rules and skepticism in later Wittgenstein, see Saul Kripke, *Wittgenstein on Rules and Private Language Argument*, 7–55.

19. On the issue of learning language in Wittgenstein, see Strawson, 76–82.

20. Homi K. Bhabha, "DissemiNation: Time, Narrative, and the Margins of the Modern Nation," in *Nation and Narration*, ed. Homi Bhabha (London: Routledge, 1990), 291–321.

21. Richard Rorty interprets this seriousness as a turn from epistemology to Kantian romanticism and Sartrean existentialism—in other words, a turn from "perceptual error to romance." "From Epistemology to Romance: Cavell on Skepticism," in *Review of Metaphysics* 33 (1981) 759–74.

22. As Cascardi points out, Cavell's revision of skepticism deploys Wittgenstein's insight that "there is no (reasonable) context in which to project our general claims of knowledge." A. J. Cascardi, "Skepticism and Deconstruction," 7–11.

23. For further analysis of Cavell's critique of exemplarity see, Barry Stroud, *The Significance of Philosophical Skepticism* (Oxford: Claredon P, 1984), 255–264.

24. My reading of Cavell is indebted at this point to Adriaan Peperzak's brilliant interpretation of the functions of skepticism in Levinas's ethics. See his "Presentation," in *Re-Reading Levinas*, ed. Robert Bernasconi and Simon Critchley (Bloomington: Indiana UP, 1991), 54–59.

25. As Albrecht Wellmer remarks about the implications of Wittgenstein's philosophy, "when we speak of the meaning of a linguistic expression, this "identity" of meaning must be provided with an index of non-identity—not only as regards the relation between language and reality but also as regards the relation between speaker and speaker." Wellmer likewise argues that this analysis of meaning leads to a discovery of the "Other of reason": "the discovery of a quasi-fact which precedes all intentionality and subjectivity." Albrecht Wellmer, "On the Dialectic of Modernism and Postmodernism," in *Praxis International* 4 (1985): 352.

26. Hannah Arendt, *Lectures on Kant's Political Philosophy*, ed. Roland Beiner (Chicago: The U of Chicago P, 1982), 13. The main difference between Arendt and Cavell is that for Arendt the intersubjective deployment of judgment has far-reaching political consequences—the issue that Cavell largely ignores.

27. Charles Bernstein, "The Objects of Meaning: Reading Cavell Reading Wittgenstein," *Content's Dream* (Los Angeles: Sun and Moon P, 1986), 172.

28. In P. F. Strawson's words, linguistic conventions do not constitute a foundation but rather a framework within which doubts, validations, or repu-

diations of knowledge can occur. "It is quite clear that Wittgenstein does not regard these propositions, or elements of the belief-system, as foundations in the traditional empiricist sense, i.e., as basic reasons . . . for the rest of our beliefs. The metaphor of a scaffolding or framework, within which the activity of building or modifying the structure of our beliefs goes on, is a better one." P. F. Strawson, *Skepticism and Naturalism*, 16.

29. The fact that Cavell's analysis of language does not provide a firm epistemological grounding for the discursive community situates his project in anti-foundationalist tradition in epistemology. As Roger Shiner remarks, Cavell's appraisal of skepticism intends to show that "our form of life, our knowledge of and responses to the world and each other, are all in a certain genuine sense *groundless.*" Roger A. Shiner, "Canfield, Cavell and Criteria," in *Dialogue* 22 (1983): 267.

30. For a lucid discussion of Cavell's claim to community, see Stanley Bates's review of *The Claim of Reason* in *Philosophy and Literature* 4 (1980): 266-273.

31. Cavell's emphasis on economics and aesthetics of speech questions the Enlightenment ideal of a complete dissociation of public reason from communal prejudices and conventions—the ideal which Cavell, together with many other critics of the Enlightenment, would consider to be itself a myth. For an excellent discussion of the critique of the Enlightenment in the context of postmodern theories, see Drucilla Cornell, *The Philosophy of the Limit* (New York: Routledge, 1992), 1–39; and Jürgen Habermas, *The Philosophical Discourse of Modernity*, 106–130.

32. Such a concept of knowledge and language is also not far from the Nietzschean idea of truth as "an estimation of value." Take, for instance, Cavell's suggestion that we should look at Heidegger's "The Word of Nietzsche: 'God is Dead'" in order to find out in what sense Nietzsche's metaphysics is "a metaphysics of value" [CR, 96]. Unlike Nietzsche, Cavell wants to distance his project on the one hand from a possibility of nihilism and on the other from pursuing connections between value, contingency, and power. For much more radical consequences of dissolving truth into value see Gianni Vattimo, *The End of Modernity: Nihilism and Hermeneutics in Postmodern Culture*, trans. Jon R. Snyder (Baltimore: The Johns Hopkins UP, 1985), 19–50. See also Snyder's excellent introduction to this edition, vi-xix. For Vattimo, the proximity of truth and value lies at the core of the project of nihilism, which is concerned with unmasking all systems of truth as systems of belief and persuasion.

33. The most consistent theory of value articulated on the basis of social exchange and desire is presented in Barbara Herrnstein Smith, *Contingencies of Value: Alternative Perspectives for Critical Theory* (Cambridge: Harvard UP, 1988).

34. Stanley Cavell, *Must We Mean What We Say: A Book of Essays* (New York: Charles Scribner's Sons, 1969), 264.

35. Gerald L. Bruns, "Stanley Cavell's Shakespeare," 619.

36. Immanuel Kant, *Critique of Judgment*, trans. J. H. Bernard (New York: Macmillan, 1951), 137–38. My critique of Cavell is indebted to Lyotard's inter-

pretation of the status of the community in the judgments of taste. Jean-François Lyotard, *"Sensus Communis,"* trans. Marian Hobson and Geoff Bennington, in *Judging Lyotard,* ed. Andrew Benjamin (New York: Routledge, 1992), 1–25.

37. The inorganic and instrumental character of the metaphor of attunement was suggested to me by my colleague, Kathy Psomiades.

38. Stanley Cavell, "Declining Decline," in *This New Yet Unapproachable America: Lectures after Emerson after Wittgenstein* (Albuquerque, New Mexico: Living Batch Press, 1989), 41. Subsequent references to this essay will be marked parenthetically as *DD.*

39. See for instance Roger A. Shiner, "Canfield, Cavell and Criteria," 262–264.

40. Cavell's solution given to skepticism resembles Hume's naturalism, which claims that Nature implanted certain beliefs, like beliefs in bodies, which we have to take for granted in our thinking. The point of similarity is that Cavell also tends to naturalize that which has to be presupposed as the framework of inquiry. On the conjunction between skepticism and naturalism in Hume and Wittgenstein, see Strawson, *Skepticism and Naturalism,* 10–21.

41. Lyotard, *"Sensus Communis,"* 18–19.

42. J. M. Bernstein, *The Fate of Art: Aesthetic Alienation from Kant to Derrida and Adorno* (University Park: Pennsylvania State UP, 1992), 102–103.

43. At this point, I think, Seyla Benhabib's recent critique of communitarianism can be addressed to Cavell's interpretation of the social forms of life (which is not to say that Cavell's philosophy can be called communitarian): "communitarians often seem to conflate the philosophical thesis concerning the significance of constitutive communities for the formation of one's identity with . . . a morally conformist attitude." Seyla Benhabib, *Situating the Self: Gender, Community and Postmodernism in Contemporary Ethics* (New York: Routledge, 1992), 74.

44. Jean-Luc Nancy, *The Inoperative Community,* ed. Peter Connor, trans. Peter Connor et al (Minneapolis: U of Minnesota P, 1991), 10.

45. Henry Staten's critique of Wittgenstein's commentators who interpret his project as a "philosophic *nostos,* bringing language home" can be very well applied to Cavell's idea of attunement. See Henry Staten, *Wittgenstein and Derrida* , 74–79.

46. Drucilla Cornell, *Transformations: Recollective Imagination and Sexual Difference* (New York: Routledge, 1993), 12–30

47. I would like to mention at this point that Jean-Luc Nancy's interpretation of discursive community attempts to think of being in common without compromising the alterity of the other person. Nancy's criticism of the notion of community which reduces being in common to "a common being" or to a communal essence is particularly applicable to Cavell's discussion of community. See *The Inoperative Community,* xxxvii–xl.

48. For the discussion of power operating through discourse see Michel Foucault, "The Discourse on Language," in *The Archeology of Knowledge and The*

Discourse on Language, trans. A. M. Sheridan Smith (New York: Pantheon Books, 1972), 215–220.

49. In his critique of Cavell's avoidance of the problematic of figurative language, Robert Mankin links the "extraordinary" use of language in literature to "the forcing element in all conventions." "An Introduction to *The Claim of Reason,*" 66–89.

50. Stanley Cavell, *In Quest of the Ordinary: Lines of Skepticism and Romanticism* (Chicago: U of Chicago P, 1988), 147–148. For a critical discussion of Cavell's understanding of metaphor, see Robert Mankin, "Introduction to *The Claim of Reason,*" 66–89.

3

Rhetoric of Failure and Deconstruction[1]

When Christopher Norris feels compelled to protest that "there is no excuse for the sloppy misreading of Derrida that represents him as some kind of transcendental solipsist who believes that nothing 'real' exists outside the written text," he inadvertently confronts the consequences of one of the most pervasive themes in the reception of deconstruction, namely, skepticism.[2] Despite the enormous influence of Derrida's work, and despite the numerous studies devoted to his writings, one still hears accounts of the deconstructive enterprise as a contemporary form of skepticism, as a "fetish of discontinuity,"[3] or as "a negative formalism" of sorts that reduces our relation to the world merely to the "undecidability" of writing. Indeed, for many critics a fleeting acquaintance with Derrida's texts only confirms their worst suspicions: his relentless "undoing" of the principles and norms of Western thinking, his incessant uncovering of aporias and contradictions, his notorious focus on "undecidables," and, in particular, his deconstruction of the representational view of language, not to mention the style of his own writing—all these disconcerting features seem to question the validity of knowledge with a rigor verging on obsession. In fact, deconstruction has been called a paradigmatic example of "a skeptical methodology of literary analysis"[4] or "the skeptic disposition in contemporary criticism."[5] The most sustained and relatively recent arguments to this effect are presented, for instance, in Michael Fischer's study *Stanley Cavell and Literary Skepticism* and in Christopher Butler's book *Interpretation, Deconstruction and Ideology*. Although I focus here primarily on the work of Derrida, this "affinity" to skepticism has been with equal frequency explored in connection with Paul de Man, Stanley Fish, or J. Hillis Miller. In the words of one of the critics, "the real opponent of deconstruction is the theorist who denies this skepticism as I have done."[6]

Because the problematic of skepticism is so frequently associated with the most fundamental misreading of Derrida's work, deconstructive critics usually dismiss the whole discussion out of hand. Yet such a cursory dismissal of the issue of skepticism not only fails to explain why Derrida's work so consistently provokes these kinds of misreading but also, and more importantly, disregards the way in which his philosophy engages and deconstructs the skeptical argument. Thus, we miss the opportunity to explain the function of the rhetoric of failure in Derrida's texts, and the relation of this rhetoric both to the critique of rationality and to the affirmative force of deconstruction.

In order to explain how Derrida's work engages the problematic of skepticism, I will contrast two very different ways of broaching the problem of skepticism within deconstruction: the first path, followed by many of Derrida's critics, dismisses the critical force of poststructuralism by assimilating it into the "classical" skeptical challenge which philosophy knows how to refute; the second path, initiated by Levinas's response to Derrida, implies just the reverse—that the ethical consequences of Derrida's critique of logocentrism and the philosophy of the subject are perhaps incomprehensible without a prior reappraisal of skepticism. Depending on the way it is articulated, the relation between deconstruction and skepticism can serve, therefore, two different purposes. In the first case, the problem of skepticism sets up the contrast between the traditional picture of language as a reliable means of representation at the disposal of the subject, and the deconstructive view, in which language relinquishes this representative function and therefore leaves the subject without any relationship to the external world. Focused on the issue of whether or not language refers to external reality, this discussion does not question the centrality of the knowing subject in any decisive way. In Levinas's case, however, skepticism is appealed to in order to articulate the difference between language understood within the parameters of subjectivity and language conceived as an exposure to the other. For Levinas, the very contrast between representation and exposure to the other opens a possibility of thinking language beyond the confines of subject-centered rationality.

The difference between these two ways of articulating the connection between deconstruction and skepticism is crucial, I argue, for understanding the place of Derrida's thought in the context of post-modernity. Thus, what is at stake in reexamining the issue of skepticism is not only a matter of settling a controversy within a reception of deconstruction but also an inquiry into the consequences and dilemmas of the postmodern critiques of rationality. One of the most powerful criticisms addressed to deconstruction in particular, and to the post-modern critiques of reason in general, is the Habermasian claim that the postmodern thought is caught in what he calls a performative contradiction—that is, in the inevitable aporia of the totalizing critique of reason destroying its own foundation: "The totalizing self-critique of reason gets caught in a performative contradiction since subject-centered reason can be convicted of being authoritarian in nature only by having recourse to its own tools."[7] This aporia, which for Habermas illustrates the often unacknowledged impasse of postmodern thought generally, is not so different from the contradiction characteristic of the skeptical position. Both skepticism and postmodernism would be examples of a totalizing critique which, by questioning all philosophical positions, undercuts its own legitimacy. Indeed, Habermas himself suggests this similarity between the aporias of postmodernity and skepticism by arguing that the critical unmasking of subject-centered rationality leads to a pessimistic and skeptical attitude or even to a renunciation of philosophy for anthropological, psychological, historical, or literary methods.[8]

For Habermas, the postmodern critique of modernity not only is incapable of legitimating its project but ultimately fails to overstep the bounds of subject-centered rationality it claims to overcome. According to Habermas, deconstruction as well as postmodern thinking in general negates the paradigm of the subject in an abstract manner but does not provide any alternative in its place. By privileging Derrida's critique of Husserlian phenomenology over his engagement with Levinas, Habermas can argue that "even Derrida does not extricate himself from the constraints of the paradigm of the philosophy of the subject."[9] This is the case because "Derrida does not take as his point of departure that nodal point at which the philosophy of language and of consciousness branch off, that is, the point where the paradigm of linguistic philosophy separates from that of philosophy of consciousness and renders the identity of meaning dependent upon the intersubjective practice . . ."[10]

Following the perspective opened by Levinas's response to Derrida, I am going to argue that the critical reappraisal of skepticism within deconstruction provides an answer to both of the Habermasian objections. First, by focusing on the rhetoric of skeptical discourse,

Levinas reinterprets the moment of contradiction as the temporal difference between two irreducible modes of signification. Second, this double model of signification reenacted in the skeptical thesis demonstrates precisely where Derrida's philosophy separates itself from the philosophy of the subject by elaborating structures of language that enable the address and signification of the other. In the context of Derrida's writings on communication and community, it becomes clear, however, that the signification of alterity in Derrida's thought does not lead to a new paradigm of reason based on intersubjective understanding and mutual consensus which Habermas wants to propose as an alternative both to subject-centered rationality and its postmodern critiques. Rethinking the place of skepticism in Derrida's philosophy of language can open, therefore, an alternative both to the aporias into which the critique of subject-centered rationality falls and to the new paradigm of rationality based on intersubjectivity.

Unmasking Deconstruction: Skepticism in Disguise?

Predictably, the question of skepticism was raised immediately after Derrida's famous lecture "Différance," presented to the "Société française de philosophie" in 1968, and has been "inappropriately" repeated ever since in the form of either lengthy philosophical arguments or common sense opinions that seem to be so obvious that they do not require justification. The very persistence of this theme is certainly not accidental, because the charges of "skepticism" recapitulate in an exemplary way the most frequent criticisms addressed to Derrida's work in general[11]—the "crisis" of reference and representation, the indeterminacy of meaning, the lack of autonomy or unity of the text, and finally, the lack of any social or political stakes behind the demystifying rigor of deconstruction.[12] Because of this exemplary weight, the issue of skepticism raised during the discussion following the "Différance" lecture is turned very quickly into a test of Derrida's philosophical credentials. Formulated by a representative voice of philosophy,[13] the question of skepticism allows the audience to convert the disconcerting novelty of deconstruction into a form of something very familiar: "What happens is that, on the one hand, in your paper we see new dimensions; they are indisputable: *différance*, the trace . . . . And then, there are some traditional things, and I wonder how strictly you have separated them out. *It is at this point that we can situate the definite question*, connecting the two perspectives: is your philosophy, which is in the process of being born, a *form of skepticism* or is it indeed a philosophy in the sense of a philosophy that bears a content?" [emphasis added].[14] Evoked as a decisive touchstone, the issue of skepticism is supposed to clarify Derrida's relation to philosophy, or even more, to decide whether his thought, which is "in the process of being born," is a legitimate child of philosophical tradition.

Such trials of philosophical legitimation have been staged numerous times in the reception of Derrida's work. No matter how ingenious, most of the attempts to unmask deconstruction as an unacknowledged expression of skepticism operate within the post-Kantian epistemology without inquiring into the ways deconstruction is precisely a critique of that tradition. Based on the claims of consciousness to the accurate representation of the external world, this tradition, as Richard Rorty points out, continues to shape modern philosophy of language.[15] It is hardly surprising, therefore, that the charges of skepticism are quite predictable and familiar: time and again we have heard that the skepticism of deconstruction destroys any sense of correspondence between language and the objects in the world; that Derrida's critique of representation and linguistic reference leads to a crippling version of linguistic immanence, which leaves the speaking subject without any relationship to the external world. The related issues of the indeterminacy of meaning and the so-called free play of the signifier are usually interpreted as a consequence of the destruction of the referential grounding of language—once language is cut off from a correspondence to the external world, then there is nothing internal, no privileged signified or signifier, to secure the stability of meaning: "It is thus a skepticism concerning reference that makes it at all too plausible for Derridans to propose an alternative meaning or use for the text. If language use lacks the stability of Kantian correspondence, then it may indeed be seen as perpetually self-referring, or as simply disseminating meanings."[16] Despite its superficial rhetoric of freedom (as in the "free play of the signifier") or despite its exaggerated investment in pleasure,[17] such an endless dissemination of meaning in conjunction with a critique of representation in fact implies the exact opposite, namely, the entrapment of consciousness in the sphere of textuality: "No appeal from text to world is allowed. We are trapped within the text and within our own interpretation of it" [emphasis added].[18] Such, in the end, is the dramatic conclusion of the philosophical narrative that casts deconstruction in the role of "perhaps the most widespread cultural skepticism yet known."[19]

We get a different version of the same story when the text itself is viewed as the external object and its deconstructive interpretation as a repetition of the skeptical inquiry ending in a doubt about the existence of the world. Claiming to extend the implications of Cavell's work on skepticism into literary theory, Michael Fischer has advanced the following argument: "I want here to argue that this deconstructive probing of texts parallels external-world skepticism, as represented by Cavell. The literary theorist questioning the textual object resembles the traditional epistemologist meditating on the piece of wax, tomato, envelope, or desk that necessarily occupies this form of skepticism."[20] Before one could address Fischer's argument, one would have to ask whether the analogies between texts and tomatoes, or between reading and perception, are appropriate in the first place.[21]

According to Richard Rorty, such misreadings of deconstruction have their origin in a certain confusion of philosophical genealogies. The implication of Rorty's argument is that to accuse Derrida of skepticism is to put him in the wrong philosophical camp, so to speak—that is, precisely, to confuse deconstruction with post-Kantian language philosophy, with its privilege of the subject and its concern with truth as the accuracy of representation. Focused on the relation between the subject and the object, on the correspondence between representation and the represented, between words and things, skepticism operates within the field of subjective reason, which deconstruction, with its critique of logocentrism, calls into question. Skepticism accepts this ideal of knowledge even if its relentless questioning demonstrates that the conditions of knowing cannot be fulfilled or that the criteria for certainty cannot be met *within* the epistemological enterprise. As Cascardi succinctly observes, "traditional skepticism, in its adversarial but complementary relationship to classical epistemology, has accepted certain ideals of knowledge as setting the parameters of the debate, whereas the deconstructionist wants to call into question those very bounds."[22] Since deconstruction questions the very parameters of the Kantian philosophy of the knowing subject, it can no longer be contained within the tradition of skepticism, even though Derrida's critique of representation makes it very tempting to do so: "One can easily conclude . . . that Derrida conceives his work as purely negative—deconstructing the metaphysics of presence in order to leave the texts bare, unburdened by the need to represent."[23] For Rorty, it makes more sense to align deconstruction with the post-Hegelians and their notion of truth as a historical artifact emerging from intersubjective interpretation, or rather, from an endless process of the "reinterpretation of our predecessors' reinterpretation": "To understand Derrida, one must see his work as the latest development in this non-Kantian, dialectical tradition—the latest attempt of the dialecticians to shatter the Kantians' ingenuous image of themselves as accurately representing how things really are."[24]

Although this double distinction between the two philosophical traditions—not only between post-Kantian formalism and post-Hegelian historicism but also implicitly between the subjective and "intersubjective" conceptions of language—remains useful, Rorty's own placement of Derrida remains problematic.[25] Although Rorty has no problems with the negative part of Derrida's project, that is, with the "debunking of Kantian philosophy generally," he cannot account for the 'productive,' affirmative side of deconstruction. This inability to articulate the affirmative role of deconstruction stems from a wrong diagnosis of what is at stake in Derrida's critique of Kantian philosophy, and specifically, from the confusion of representation with responsibility, and of alterity with intersubjectivity. What Rorty sees at the core of Derrida's 'debunking' is the notion that "language has responsibilities to something outside itself, that it must be 'adequate' to do its representative job."[26] Because Rorty limits the question of responsibility to the task of representation (which he rejects), he sees responsibility, or the affirmative force of deconstruction, simply as an attempt to save some residues of representation. This constructive side of Derrida is "unfortunate" and "nostalgic" because, although it deconstructs the concept of representation, it still preserves some relation to exteriority (based on the notion of the trace). That is why Rorty is more comfortable with the "negative" notion of deconstruction as textual immanence than with the "constructive, bad side of Derrida's work." What is problematic in this reading is that responsibility remains confined to the philosophy of the subject and is not understood, as Derrida and Levinas would have it, as an indication of the relation to the other. Thus Rorty's critique of Derrida's affirmative side repeats exactly the error he sees in the usual misreading of the negative side of deconstruction: he fails to divorce the issues of responsibility, and exteriority from the philosophy of the subject and to reinterpret them in the context of the relationship to the other (the relationship, which only imprecisely can be called "intersubjective"). Nonetheless, by calling attention to the configuration of representation, responsibility, and exteriority, Rorty's essay provides a compelling diagnosis of the stakes in the discussion of deconstruction and skepticism. In the wake of his discussion, we are left with two unanswered questions: first, whether a critique of representation necessarily relinquishes all responsibilities to something outside language; and second, how responsibility can be articulated apart from the task of representation.

The specific sense of responsibility emerging from Derrida's work cannot be addressed at all when the parameters of the discussion are drawn around the issues of correspondence, linguistic reference, mimetic representation, and the knowing subject. Whether Derrida's work is seen as an affirmation of pure textuality or as a manifestation of skepticism, we see the same unexamined assumption that deconstruction espouses the notion of non-referential language. It makes little difference whether Derrida's privileging of the Saussurian notion of the differential nature of meaning is interpreted as an affirmation of writing or as a linguistic version of skeptical doubt, because in both cases deconstruction is invariably reduced to textual immanence. Take, for instance, Jay Cantor's attempt to characterize deconstruction as a version of classical skepticism:

> Deconstruction is a version of skepticism which attacks the claim of consciousness that it has at its disposal a language that is representative of the world or even of itself. Signifiers cannot, deconstructive writers argue, be adequately, reliably, aligned with signifieds. Caught up in that play of differences which is the structuration of language, signifiers can never successfully reach out to their referents . . . . Deconstruction is a classical skeptical argument, recast using linguistic metaphors. What in the skeptic's argument is called *the world*, is here called *referents or signified* . . . . We cannot have them with the certainty that is meant to be provided by the foundational epistemologists' principles of adequation between representation and represented.[27]

Cantor's dissatisfaction with Derrida follows very closely the pattern identified by Stanley Cavell in the context of certain misreadings of Wittgenstein—the temptation to read linguistic difficulties in terms of skepticism ends predictably in the assertion of the gap between the world and language at the disposal of solitary consciousness. Although Derrida's critique challenges the very foundational principle "of adequation between representation and represented" and all its corollary notions of the reliability, certainty, or perfect alignment between signifieds and signifiers, names and objects, the question remains, whether such critique necessarily reenacts "a *classical* skeptical argument."

I will argue in greater detail why this is not the case; for now, let me point out that the seemingly inevitable conclusion that deconstruction is a form of skepticism is reinforced by a peculiar rhetoric of linguistic incarceration. Let us notice the frequency of dramatic phrases like "caught up in that play," "can never successfully reach out," "we cannot have them," etc. Such rhetoric creates the impression that Derrida's critique of naming as a one-to-one correspondence between words and things, or his critique of the identity of meaning, forecloses the subject's access to the "outside" of language, whether this outside goes under the name of the world, the real, other people, history, etc. Either endlessly postponing our entry to the world, or dissolving the notion of the world altogether into a web of signifiers, the linguistic predicament of deconstruction appears to many as a form of imprisonment. This conviction about the erasure of the world, or any other form of exteriority, is widely shared by the proponents and opponents of deconstruction alike: "And for the deconstructionist, as for the skeptic, there comes a point at which the world drops out. It is converted not into a dream or an hallucination, but into a 'free-play of signifiers.'"[28] From here it is only a step to the common conclusion that rigorous deconstruction of the closure of metaphysics ends up in the even worse enclosure of textuality. After all, does not Derrida himself claim that "there is nothing outside the text" ("*Il n'y a pas de hors-texte*") [*OG*, 158]?[29]

If, indeed, deconstructive criticism only brings about an overwhelming sense of entrapment in the sphere of textuality, then it appears as a futile enterprise, no matter how rigorously it is performed and no matter how much pleasure it gives its practitioners:

> The radical demystification of language by deconstructive reason—the absolute revelation of language as the unsayable (*as language for which there is nothing to reveal*) by its rigorous rationality—becomes a determining and deterministic presupposition that paradoxically, and against its original intention, locks thinking (and the men and women who practice it) into a textual space—the "scene of writing"—without exit, and thereby makes human beings prisoners . . .[30]

If the skepticism of Descartes left him imprisoned in a solipsistic consciousness, the skepticism of deconstruction, according to this reading, merely shifts the terrain of imprisonment from consciousness to language itself. Since the rhetoric of linguistic imprisonment is meant to dramatize an overwhelming paralysis of the speaking subject, this reception of deconstruction (as a form of skepticism) implicitly confirms the Habermasian claim that deconstruction merely exhausts the paradigm of subjective reason without proposing a different alternative in its place. Now it seems that by merely questioning whether the relationship to the outside of language can be expressed in terms of adequation or correspondence, the demystifying rigor of Derrida's thinking is incapable of articulating the problem of exteriority as such.

In his response to such misreading, Derrida repeatedly argues (especially in *Positions*)[31] that his problematization of reference does not lock us in the immanence of the linguistic system but, on the contrary, aims to pose the question of the outside in a far more radical way than the principle of adequation allows:

> I never cease to be surprised by critics who see my work as a declaration that there is nothing beyond language, that we are imprisoned in language; it is, in fact saying the exact opposite. The critique of logocentrism is above all else the search for the "other" and the "other of language." Every week I receive critical commentaries and studies on deconstruction which operate on the assumption that what they call "post-structuralism" amounts to saying that there is nothing beyond language, that we are submerged in words—and other stupidities of that sort. Certainly, deconstruction tries to show that the question of reference is much more complex and problematic than traditional theories supposed. It even asks whether our term "reference" is entirely adequate for designating the "other.". . . But to distance oneself thus from the habitual structure of reference, to challenge or complicate our common assumptions about it, does not amount to saying that there is nothing beyond language.[32]

In this passage, Derrida articulates the limit of the representational function of language as alterity, as the *otherness* of the world rather than as the *dissolution* of the world. Speaking for many readers of Derrida, Christopher Norris finds this argument "ingenious but finally unconvincing," and the whole debate—"a familiar kind of epistemological dead-end."[33] What Norris misses here, however, is that Derrida's critique of adequate representation does not merely "complicate" linguistic reference but shifts the entire paradigm of language: from the one based on the centrality of the speaking subject to the one based on "the search for 'the other' and 'the other of language.'"

Derrida's "search for 'the other' and 'the other of language'" clarifies in an important way both the proximity and difference between deconstruction and skepticism. Derrida admits certain affinities to skepticism insofar as he perceives skepticism to be one of the possible modes of attention to difference and to the limit of philosophy. Yet, he insists, the skeptical questioning of philosophical truth still remains an internal and immanent inquiry that respects the goals of knowledge. If Derrida wants to distance himself from skepticism, it is because his critique of rationality oversteps the bounds of the philosophy of the subject within which skepticism is still articulated: "But is it not quite clear that the questioning of truth does not develop *within* philosophy? Within philosophy, empirical or skeptical discourses are incoherent and dissolve themselves, following a well-known schema. Nonetheless, the moments of empiricism and skepticism have always been moments of attention to difference . . . . One can see the empirical or skeptical moments of philosophy as moments when thought meets the philosophical limit and still presents itself as philosophy. That, perhaps, is the only weakness of skeptical or empiricist philosophy."[34] Whereas skepticism remains an immanent questioning of knowledge, Derrida's critique, in its search for the other of reason, surpasses the bounds of rationality. Departing from the model of correspondence between objects and thinking, or things and words, Derrida's work is oriented toward what has been *excluded* from the horizon of reason. As Derrida claims, "my central question is: from what site or non-site can philosophy as such appear to itself as other than itself, so that it can interrogate and reflect upon itself in an original manner? Such a non-site or alterity would be radically irreducible to philosophy. But the problem is that such a non-site cannot be defined or situated by means of philosophical language."[35] Rejecting the model of an internal criticism of reason, Derrida searches for an "aside" of thinking, from which to interrogate philosophy itself. The outcome of this interrogation does not lead, however, to a new legitimation of a philosophical position but uncovers instead a "non-philosophical site," a certain "u-topos" of ethics. Levinas's discussion of skepticism addresses precisely the problem Derrida identifies here— namely, the problem of how to describe the ethical signification of alterity irreducible to philosophy by means of philosophical language.

In the aftermath of the polemics surrounding deconstruction and skepticism, we need to rethink more carefully how the problem of otherness complicates the skeptical vision of language cut off from any relationship with exteriority. Because this u-topos of alterity, according to Derrida, cannot be contained within the philosophy of the subject, deconstruction, like skepticism, articulates a limit to representational language and to knowledge based on accurate representation. However, the figuration and function of this limit in deconstructive criticism is fundamentally different from the skeptical repudiation of knowledge. Skepticism articulates the internal limit of philosophical reason as a deficiency, or a failure of knowledge, and therefore, as a deplorable loss of mastery. If deconstructive practice is also attentive to the limits of thought, it is not because they present obstacles or deficiencies that should be overcome, but because they disclose strategic places where exteriority and alterity could surface. This is one of the reasons why deconstruction, even when it deploys the rhetoric of failure, does not share the skeptical mood of disaster, loss, or catastrophe. As Barry Stroud concludes in his study of Cartesian skepticism, skeptical discovery is truly devastating—it paralyzes and corrodes all possibilities of thought and language: "the consequences of accepting Descartes's conclusion as it is meant to be understood are truly disastrous. There is no easy way of accommodating oneself to its profound negative implications."[36] Yet, the deconstructive interpretation not only does not approach the limit of thought as the precipice of a disaster, but it embraces it as an opening of "unheard-of" possibilities. The function of the limit changes from a lamentable repudiation of knowing to a disclosure of otherness. As Drucilla Cornell has recently argued, "to reach the limit of philosophy, is not necessarily to be paralyzed. We are only paralyzed if we think that to reach the limit of philosophy is to be silenced . . . . The dead end of aporia, the impasse to which it takes us, promises through its prohibition the way out it seems to deny."[37]

Levinas and Derrida: Skepticism and the Signification of Alterity

Although interpretations of deconstruction as a *classical* skeptical argument note accurately the attention to the failure of knowledge or representational language in Derrida's texts, they miss the fact that such failure functions not only as a theme but also as a rhetoric, implying a model of language transgressing the bounds of the philosophy of the subject. Consequently, these interpretations overlook the double signification such rhetoric produces: that it discloses both a risk and a promise, paralysis and possibility, negativity and affirmation, impasse and transgression. By ignoring this double signification, one also disregards the positive importance of exteriority and otherness in Derrida's work and ends up with the idea of language as a prisonhouse—a notion of language deprived of any responsibilities to its outside. What our discussion of the reception of deconstruction demonstrates, therefore, is that although an affirmative moment in Derrida's philosophy still announces itself through a failure of subjective reason, the classical version of skepticism is quite incapable of explaining the double signification this moment entails. In order to comprehend what I am calling here "a rhetoric of failure" in Derrida's texts, we need to broach the significance of skepticism for deconstruction in an entirely different way.

A good place to start such inquiry is provided by the exchange between Derrida's philosophy and Levinas's ethics. The relationship between deconstruction and Levinasian ethics is pertinent here for several reasons. Although in his important essay, "Wholly Otherwise," Levinas contests the skeptical reading of deconstruction as a "prison-house of language," he nonetheless stresses the importance of skepticism in Derrida's work, albeit in a manner radically different from the usual objections raised by Derrida's critics. Like many other critics of philosophical modernity, Levinas associates Western rationality and its models of signification with the privilege of presence and consciousness: "the present of the theme, where the one and the other enter into signification or become significations, is correlative with a subject which is a consciousness."[38] Rethinking the place of skepticism in this context not only focuses on the exhaustion of subject-centered reason but also on its displacement. As Robert Bernasconi suggests, the case of skepticism provides Levinas a model or an analogy to think about the incompatible significations generated in language at the moment it addresses the other.[39] In this sense, Levinas, in his provocative and frequently quoted statement, can claim that "language is already skepticism" [*OB*, 170]. Consequently, both in Levinas's and Derrida's work, the revision of skepticism provides a way to dissociate language from the philosophy of the subject, which has dominated the discourse of modernity at least since Kant.

What is important to stress about Levinas's reading of Derrida, is a curious displacement of the importance of skepticism—it is raised as a crucial linguistic problem in the context of the ethical, rather than the epistemological, implications of deconstruction. This suggests that for Levinas, as for Cavell, skepticism not so much negates the possibility of truth as questions its primacy as a philosophical concern. As Bernasconi suggests, for Levinas "neither philosophy nor truth find their ultimate justification in themselves" but have to be subordinated to the ethical relation to alterity.[40] Yet what is much less frequently emphasized is that this displacement of the primacy of the subject and truth stems from Levinas's critique of the internal relation between rationality and domination. Let me add that an absence of a similar critical attention to the operations of power in Cavell's writings points to the main difference between Cavell's and Levinas's revision of skepticism. In this context it is important to recall that ethics for

Levinas opens a radical questioning of the subject's will to knowledge, in particular the phenomenological model of knowledge, "where thought remains an adequation with the object."[41] Exposing the inherent connection between knowledge and power, Levinas, like many other critics of modernity, claims that by annulling the difference between the represented and its representation, the knowing subject both grasps and constitutes the object on his/her own terms, and, therefore, deprives it of its alterity: "It is a hold on being which equals a constitution of that being."[42] Knowledge exercises power by neutralizing alterity and by encompassing it within the totality of the conceptual or linguistic system. In order to disrupt the violent assimilation of alterity to the order of representation, consciousness, or language understood as a system of signs, Levinas insists on the radical exteriority of otherness. All the crucial terms in Levinasian thought— "beyond," "excess," "transcendence," "infinity," or "trace of the other"—both perform and preserve this exteriority against the closure of a phenomenological or linguistic system.[43] Consequently, if Levinas insists on the lack of correspondence, or the lack of coincidence, between representation and the represented, it is not because of the failure of knowledge but rather because of the unacknowledged complicity of rationality and power implied in its success. Levinas's indictment of the violence of rationality motivates his turn from the philosophy of the subject to an ethics based on respect for alterity.

Exploring the ethical potential of deconstruction in his 1973 essay "Wholly Otherwise," Levinas raises the issue of skepticism in order to account for the temptation to read Derrida as a skeptic and to show what such a reading covers over when it is limited to epistemological concerns. As if anticipating Habermas's objections to Derrida, Levinas suggests that the temptation to read deconstruction as skepticism arises, indeed, from an apparent contradiction in the deconstructive enterprise: on the one hand, deconstruction reveals "significations which do not have to comply with the summation of Knowledge," but on the other, it has to express these significations within a logocentric conceptuality, that is, in a language very much committed to the "summation of Knowledge." This performative contradiction is analogous to the contradiction which philosophy has always been eager to detect in the skeptical position. As the classical refutation of skepticism points out again and again, by denying the possibility of truth, the skeptical thesis negates all possible philosophical theses, including its own. The inherent self-contradiction in the skeptical position seems to mirror the predicament of deconstruction and, as Habermas argues, the aporias of the postmodern totalizing critiques of rationality. Certainly, Levinas's ethics is also implicated in a "risk" of such a contradiction:

> Discourse in the course of which, amidst the shaking of the foundations of truth, against the self-evidence of present lived experience . . . Derrida still has the strength to say "is it certain?" as if anything could be secure at that moment and as if security and insecurity should still matter.
>
> One might well be tempted to infer an argument from this use of logocentric language against that very language, in order to dispute the produced deconstruction: a path much followed by the refutation of skepticism, but where, although at first crushed and trampled underfoot, skepticism got back up on its feet to come back as the legitimate child of philosophy.[44]

Obviously, for Levinas the analogy between skepticism and Derrida's philosophy does not serve to "dispute" deconstruction but rather to stress the ethical stakes implied in the "risk" of contradiction. The very "incoherence" of skepticism furnishes an example of a heteronomous position that is both inside and outside philosophy, that both respects and subverts philosophical language (the Greek language, as Derrida calls it). On the one hand, both Levinas and Derrida call skepticism a legitimate child of philosophy because its fundamental question concerns the possibility of truth: skepticism "remained in love with the truth, even if it felt incapable of embracing it." This skeptical love of truth, like Orphic song, is strongest at the moment when it proclaims the loss of the beloved. Stanley Cavell would add that skepticism remains a legitimate child of philosophy because even its doubt recognizes the claim of reason: in order to invalidate the possibility of knowledge, the skeptical argument has to prove first that its objections express *reasonable* doubts—a task Descartes performs, for instance, in his first Meditation. But on the other hand, the legitimacy of skepticism ends when it is forced to announce its conclusions in a self-contradictory discourse and then refuses to heed the voice of philosophical reason pointing out these contradictions. As Robert Bernasconi succinctly puts it, "in *what* it says, in its said, skepticism cannot avoid being a philosophy. But by virtue of its refusal to abide by the refutation it has received, skepticism shows disdain for the *logos* which it itself employs."[45] For Levinas, this incoherence of skeptical discourse, which reveals the hybrid position of skepticism with respect to the philosophical tradition, raises the question about how to articulate the shift from the logic of contradiction to the heteronomous mode of signification.

In a way similar to Cavell's approach, Levinas's reappraisal of skepticism does not concern the arguments and counter-arguments traded between skepticism and philosophy but the unique model of signification reenacted in skeptical discourse. What is at the very core of Levinas's analysis is a shift from the logical contradictions in skeptical discourse to its rhetoric. In order to see in skepticism the possibilities of a displacement of subject-centered reason, one needs to pay attention not only to the logic of the skeptical argument (which is refutable) but also to its rhetoric, in particular, the rhetoric of temporality. For Levinas, the moment which philosophy interprets as contradiction in fact enacts a double signification, announcing not only a failure of knowledge but also a radical interruption or displacement of philosophical reason. Levinas claims that even though incommensurate, these two moments of discourse cannot be called contradictory because they are no longer simultaneous. In Levinas's interpretation, the logical error of contradiction in the skeptical position needs to be re-read as the rhetoric of temporality, or what Levinas calls irreducible diachrony:

> But, in following this path, one would risk missing one side of the signification which this inconsequence bears. One would risk missing the incompressible nonsimultaneity of the Said and the Saying, the dislocation of their correlation . . . As if simultaneity were lacking from the two significations, so that the contradiction broke the knot that tied them together. As if the correlation of the Saying and the Said was a diachrony of that which can't be brought together.[46]

Let us notice that the shift from the logic of non-contradiction to the rhetoric of temporality not merely dramatizes the instability of meaning but, more importantly, discloses the ethical rather than epistemological significance of that instability. Reread from the ethical perspective, skepticism illustrates an insurmountable dislocation (both temporal and spatial) of two different significations, or what Levinas calls the Said and the Saying. The Said represents the unity and systematicity of propositional discourse, aiming at synchronizing and establishing relations between different terms. Encompassing the order of representation with its ideal of the correspondence between object and subject, things and language, the Said belongs to the order of subject-centered reason. The Saying, which interrupts and transcends the order of the Said, preserves the ethical relation to alterity, the non-thematizable exposure of the subject to the other. What emerges from this familiar, for Levinas's scholars, contrast between the Saying and the Said is a rather surprising, and frequently overlooked, interpretation of rhetoric. Irreducible to "referential aberration," Levinas's turn to rhetoric reveals a disjunction between the epistemological and the ethical, or between the negative and the affirmative, significance of linguistic instability.

This incommensurate signification of the Saying and the Said has been expressed in Levinas's earlier work ("The Trace of the Other") through the figures of Ulysses and Abraham. The myth of Ulysses illustrates for Levinas the main paradigm of the philosophy of the subject in which consciousness closes the circle of its own identification by representing the other to itself. In opposition to this paradigm, Levinas proposes an encounter with alterity as an Abrahamic movement without return: "*A work conceived radically is a movement of the same unto the other which never returns to the same.* To the myth of Ulysses returning to Ithaca, we wish to oppose the story of Abraham who leaves his fatherland forever for a yet unknown land."[47] By creating an "irremissible disturbance" in the order of thought, the ethical encounter with the other dislocates the position of the subject and the order of discourse: "The relationship with another puts me into question, empties me of myself."[48] In the face-to-face relation with the other, consciousness no longer coincides with itself, no longer returns to its point of departure or completes the circle of its identification.[49] As Jill Robbins argues, "the opposed itineraries of Odysseus and Abraham can evoke, respectively, the circular identification of egological life versus a radical going out toward the other, a negative that is recuperable versus a negative that is not recuperable, the return to a *site* of the Same versus a departure from the site of the Same, indeed a departure from all sites."[50]

When read with an eye to the incommensurate moments of discourse, the problem of skepticism, to which Levinas devotes the final section of *Otherwise Than Being or Beyond Essence*, can provide a powerful example of a similar displacement of subject-centered reason. Despite persistent philosophical refutation, the return of skepticism implicitly demonstrates that these two moments of discourse—the Said and the Saying, representation of the other and exposure to the other—cannot be brought together in "a knot" of contraction. As Levinas explains, "this return of the diachrony refusing the present makes up the invincible force of skepticism" [*OB*, 169].

In a manner similar to Cavell, Levinas suggests therefore that the signification of skepticism is not absorbed by its explicit negative thesis (the order of the Said), that the "truth" of skepticism (its Saying) is incommensurate with "the truth whose interruption and failure its discourse states" [*OB*, 168]. In this double reading of the skeptical position, the failure or impossibility of knowledge is intertwined, though not simultaneous, with the ethical affirmation of otherness:

> Skepticism, which traverses the rationality or logic of knowledge, is a refusal to synchronize the implicit affirmation contained in saying and the negation which this affirmation states in the said. The contradiction is visible to reflection, which refutes it, but skepticism is insensitive to the refutation, as though the affirmation and negation did not resound in the same time [*OB*, 167–8].

What both Cavell and Levinas claim, therefore, is that the philosophical understanding of skepticism does not extend beyond the negation expressed in its thesis, and therefore misses not only the moment of affirmation but also the rhetorical model of language deployed in skeptical argument. And both imply that in order to register the double signification announced in skeptical language, one would have to interrupt the confines of the philosophy of the subject. The main difference between Cavell and Levinas lies perhaps in the way they understand this implicit moment of affirmation—attunement in the first case and ethical Saying in the second.

This revised picture of skepticism changes, according to Levinas, its role in the history of philosophy. Although skepticism has always been one of the perennial epistemological issues, in the twentieth century the refutation of skepticism has constituted one of the main parameters of the definition of epistemology as the theory of knowledge.[51] As W. D. Hamlyn puts it, epistemology "must be set against a general skepticism concerning the matter in question. *To be called upon to justify the possibility of knowledge or of certain kinds of knowledge makes sense only on the supposition that it or they may not be possible.*"[52] Levinas's interest in skepticism, however, neither endorses the skeptical position nor treats it as an occasion to legitimate his own theory of knowledge. On the contrary, Levinas's reappraisal of skepticism intends to displace the primacy of the epistemological quest for the legitimation of knowledge in order to reveal the prior ethical responsibility for the other. Levinas suggests, therefore, that philosophy has misread, or disregarded, the formidable challenge of skepticism: not merely an internal epistemological difficulty, skepticism questions the very priority given by philosophy to the questions of truth, knowledge, and the subject: "The permanent return of skepticism does not so much signify the possible breakup of structures as the fact that they are not the ultimate framework of meaning" [*OB*, 171]. Consequently, the implicit affirmation in skepticism points to the transcendence of the philosophy of the subject, to the outside which cannot be recuperated within the coherence of rational discourse. By refusing to acknowledge this moment of affirmation, "the history of Western philosophy has not been the refutation of skepticism as much as the refutation of transcendence" [*OB*, 169].

How does this reappraisal of skepticism bear, according to Levinas, on our assessment of deconstruction, and, especially, on the function of the rhetoric of failure within deconstructive discourse? The parallel that Levinas draws between the ethical significance of skepticism and Derrida's deconstruction reveals a double discourse in which the *representation* of the other is put into question by the *response* to the other. To think of the relation between deconstruction and skepticism in this way is to attend first of all to the double signification of the interruption of linguistic totality: to its affirmative and negative moments, to diachrony and synchrony, to transcendence and immanence, to the impossibility of knowledge and the possibility of alterity. In remarking the diachronic dislocations in the texts it reads, deconstruction, in a manner parallel to skepticism, attends to "the interruptions of the discourse found again and recounted in the immanence of the said . . . conserved like knots in a thread tied again, the trace of a diachrony that does not enter into the present, that refuses simultaneity" [*OB*, 170]. Derrida's essay "Tympan" is a revealing example of such an analysis of the interruption of philosophical discourse. Serving as an introduction of sorts to the collection *Margins of Philosophy*, and recalling some of the concerns Derrida addresses to Levinas in "Violence and Metaphysics," "Tympan" might be called Derrida's own "essay on exteriority," since it examines how the question of a radical exteriority necessitates a drastic revision of the available models of textuality. Far from advocating "the text without exit," Derrida advances here an idea of textuality open to and emerging from a ceaseless exchange with exteriority. What is important in the context of the debate on deconstruction and skepticism, is that Derrida not only addresses the problem of exteriority as one of the most pressing issues in deconstruction but also accuses philosophy of "failing" to respond to it: this "failure" of response is, paradoxically, coextensive with the "success" of a philosophical knowledge of the other.

In order to arrive at a different relation between the text and otherness, however, one needs to interrogate first the dominant logic of exteriority formulated within philosophical conceptuality because, after all, "exteriority and alterity are concepts which by themselves have never surprised philosophical discourse. *Philosophy by itself has always been concerned* with them" [*T*, xiii]. Despite this concern, or perhaps because of it, philosophical discourse has always insisted upon the mastery of alterity; it has approached the limit of thought only to dispose of it: "Therefore it has appropriated the concept (of the other) for itself; it has believed that it controls the margin of its volume and that it thinks its other" [*T*, x]. The question arises, therefore, whether it is possible to demarcate a signification of exteriority and otherness that would not be absorbed in advance by a philosophical determination of alterity. It is a crucial question that Derrida also addresses to Levinas's ethics.

What Derrida thematizes in "Tympan" is, in fact, the main concern of *Margins of Philosophy* as a whole and most of his writings as well: an inquiry into how the coherence of discourse is produced at the expense of otherness and whether this coherence can be dislocated in order to allow for a different relation with exteriority. Derrida argues that by thinking the other as its own proper margin or its proper referent, philosophy organizes its discourse in such a way that it is never surprised or disturbed by its outside: it is "a discourse that organizes the *economy* of its representation, the law of its proper weave, such that its outside is never its *outside*, never surprises it, such that the logic of its heteronomy still reasons from within the vault of its autism" [*T*, xvi]. The philosophical determination of the concept of exteriority occurs according to the complex logic of *tympanum*—a reference, among other associations, to the protective membrane in the ear, balancing external pressures and maintaining an equilibrium between the outside and the inside. By giving priority to the subject, philosophy, according to Derrida, organizes its discourse on exteriority within a certain field of listening, a certain deceptive receptivity, which in the end makes every external interruption resonate within its own voice. At the same time, "tympanum" is a printing device which allows for the proper alignment of the margins and reproduction of the text. The complicity between the auditory and the visual function of tympanum—between listening and representing the other—allows for a delineation of the margin as the proper limit of discourse. In the extreme "autism" of subject-centered reason, its outside is never an outside, because it is either projected from within or else mastered through representation. Therefore, the question that Derrida poses is whether it is at all possible to arrive at a different figuration of marginality—marginality no longer conceived as the proper limit of thinking but as the trace of alterity resisting the appropriation of reason:

If philosophy has always intended, from *its point of view*, to maintain its relation with the nonphilosophical . . . *that constitute its other*, if it has constituted itself according to this purposive *entente* with its outside, if it has always intended to hear itself speak, *in the same language*, of itself and of something else, can one, strictly speaking, determine a nonphilosophical place, *a place of exteriority or alterity* from which one might still treat of *philosophy?* Is there any ruse not belonging to reason to prevent philosophy from still speaking of itself . . . ? [*T*, xii, emphasis added]

Constituted from within the philosophical discourse, exteriority, or the place of the other, functions either as a reserve at the disposal of thought or else is articulated in negative terms as an empty and mute space: "a negative about which there seems to be nothing to do, a negative without effect in the text *or* a negative working in the service of meaning" [*T*, xxiv]. The other as the proper margin of philosophy appears either as a blank space that can receive and reproduce the inscription of thought ("without mark, without opposition, without determination, and ready, like matter, the matrix, the *khōra* to receive and repercuss type" [*T*, xxvii]) or as negativity recuperated within the dialectical production of meaning.

Such a conceptual determination of exteriority is calculated to secure the possibility of thinking the other. But, in a crucial reversal of usual epistemological priorities, Derrida claims that the very conditions of thinking entail the impossibility of radical alterity. In a mode similar to the Levinasian critique of metaphysics, Derrida maintains that thinking the other as one's own proper limit amounts, precisely, to "missing it":

To *insist* upon thinking *its other:* its proper other, the proper of its other, an other proper? In thinking it *as such*, in recognizing it, one misses it. One reappropriates it for oneself, one disposes of it, one misses it, or rather one misses (the) missing (of) it, which, as concerns the other, always amounts to the same [*T*, xi–xii].

This critique of the philosophy of the subject mirrors uncannily some of the charges levelled against Derrida's own texts. However, if interpretations of deconstruction as a form of skepticism maintain that the deconstructive critique of representation leaves it without a relation to exteriority (exteriority usually understood in this case as a stable referent arresting the play of signification),[53] Derrida claims that one misses the exteriority of the other precisely by recognizing and representing it. We might say at this point that skepticism is one mode of registering the fact that one misses the other, one mode of acknowledging the opacity of the other with respect to the appropriating movement of thought. Although skepticism registers a lack of continuity between the inside and the outside, between the subject and the other, this realization remains entirely negative—it concerns itself only with the possibility or impossibility of knowledge and not with an ethical response to alterity. To treat alterity merely as an obstacle to knowledge is still to avoid the encounter with the other.

How is it possible, however, to interrupt "philosophy's field of listening" in order to maintain the exteriority of the other? In a mode parallel to Levinas's discussion of the affirmative signification of skepticism, Derrida proposes a different mode of articulating exteriority. Neither a blank space ready for an inscription of thought nor an unfortunate obstacle to knowledge, such exteriority is affirmed as a trace of otherness: "beyond the philosophical text there is not a blank, virgin, empty margin, but another text, a weave of differences of forces without any present center of reference" [*T*, xxiii]. In "Différance," Derrida explicitly credits Levinas for elaborating the 'concept' of the trace in relation to irreducible alterity. What cannot be represented within the volume of the Book, or volume of truth, is precisely the fact that the margin/other writes or grafts itself.

In this context, Derrida's analysis of supplementarity is one of the most compelling examples of the effects of marginality and alterity already at work within the interiority of meaning. By developing the structure of the supplement through his reading of Rousseau in *Of Grammatology*, Derrida shows that "other and the other of language" is not a blank negative space but that it writes itself and impinges upon the integrity of meaning. Focusing on the way Rousseau (in *The Essay on the Origin of Languages*) denounces the "dangers" of this intrusion, Derrida contrasts the negative valorization of exteriority with what he calls the logic of supplementarity:[54]

> There *must* (*should*) *have* been plenitude and not lack, presence without difference. From then on the dangerous supplement, scale or harmony, *adds itself from the outside as evil and lack* to happy and innocent plenitude. It would come from an outside which would be simply the outside. This conforms to the logic of identity and to the principle of classical ontology . . . but not to the logic of supplementarity, which would have it that the out-

side be inside, that the other and the lack come to add themselves as a plus that replaces a minus, that what adds itself to something takes the place of a default in the thing, that the default, as the outside of the inside, should be already within the inside, etc. [*OG*, 215].

According to the logic of identity, any addition from the outside must be interpreted either as a "lack," or minus, appending itself to an original plenitude (whether this plenitude represents, as in Rousseau, nature, speech, or self), or as a compensatory plus needed only to fill an unfortunate deficiency. Derrida's play on the pluses and minuses indicates that in either case the other would be subordinated to what Levinas calls "the economy of the same." Derrida argues, however, that in Rousseau's text pluses and minuses do not add up; that they do not achieve the final balance. Consequently, Derrida elaborates the structure of supplementarity (which he identifies with the functioning of language in general [*OG*, 149]) not only to demonstrate that the other as supplement assumes two contradictory significations—both plus and minus, surplus and compensation—but also to underscore the fact that alterity disturbs the economy of identity and proper meaning. Because of this disturbance, the supplement receives an ambiguous valorization: as an imprint of exteriority, it seems both therapeutic and dangerous, necessary and superfluous. By refusing Rousseau's explicit gesture of interpreting this disturbance in a skeptical way as a degradation or decline afflicting the integrity of language and culture, Derrida also shows that in Rousseau's text this seemingly "external" supplement becomes in fact a *condition* of meaning in general—meaning is always already affected by the other. Derrida's re-valuation of what is represented in Rousseau's text as decline, loss, or a deficiency of language is analogous to Levinas's interpretation of the double-sided signification of the skeptical argument. Derrida's reappraisal of the seemingly negative valorization of the supplement—either as an external lack or as a corrupting "substitute that enfeebles" the original energy of language—aims to affirm the traces of exteriority and otherness incommensurate with the logic of identity.

In "Plato's Pharmacy," Derrida associates even more explicitly the complex operations of the supplement with an "allergic reaction" to otherness. In Plato's *Phaedrus*, it is the power of written discourse that figures as an ambiguous external addition to thought and memory, and therefore its influence is represented as both a cure and a poison (both significations are implied in the Greek word *pharmakon*). This devaluation of writing is itself a symptom of a larger system of signification which opposes the value of the interior to the exterior, the intimate to the alien, the living to the dead, the subject to the other. As "pharmakon," writing consistently evokes fears of death, poison, or disease because it is associated with otherness rather than with the expression of the living soul: "Just as Rousseau and Saussure will do in response to the same necessity, yet without discovering *other* relations between the intimate and the alien, Plato maintains *both* the exteriority of writing and its power of maleficent penetration, its ability to affect or infect what lies deepest inside" [*PP*, 110]. Consequently, the word "pharmakon"—like the word supplement in Rousseau's texts— is not only caught in the contradictory chains of signification but also describes how the formation of these chains occurs in response to exteriority and alterity.[55]

Always suspect as coming from the other, writing evokes a defensive response—it provokes allergic reactions. A defensive reaction to an alien body, allergy functions in Plato's text not only as a figure of a disease but also as a paradigm of the subject's relation to alterity: "The natural illness of the living is defined in its essence as an *allergy*, a reaction to the aggression of an alien element . . . . This schema implies that the living being is finite . . . : that it can have a relation with its other, then, in the allergic reaction, that it has a limited lifetime . . . . The immortality and perfection of a living being would consist in its having *no relation at all with any outside*" (second emphasis mine) [*PP*, 101]. Suffered as a disease, the "unfortunate" necessity of responding to the other, like the necessity of writing, announces the finitude and mortality of the subject—the relation to the other becomes a measure of the fall from ideal perfection, autonomy, and self-sufficiency. Therefore, as Derrida writes, in Plato's text only "God has no allergies" [*PP*, 101]. Figured as an unfortunate necessity, as the imperfection and mortality of human beings, the relation to the other reveals the inescapable limits of the subject. Yet, because this figuration of alterity is so entirely negative, subjects and communities predictably search for the means of escaping from this "unfortunate" predicament, for the miraculous cure absolving them from the obligation of a response. Whenever the other evokes allergic reactions, therapeutic methods are soon invented. As we have learned from Cavell's argument (but we can see a similar gesture in Plato's text as well), the appeal to community can always function as such a successful therapeutic measure.

Community and Communication

Derrida's detailed reading of the *Phaedrus* elaborates the effects such allergic reactions to alterity have on the formation of the Platonic concepts of memory, logos, paternity, speech, and truth.[56] I would like to focus, however, specifically on how such allergic response to alterity shapes the notion of discursive community—the topic elaborated in the final sections of "Plato's Pharmacy." What interests me here is whether discursive community can provide a cure to the threat of skepticism, in the manner suggested, for instance, by Stanley Cavell, or whether it can constitute an alternative paradigm of reason replacing the philosophy of the subject, in the way elaborated by Jürgen Habermas. By insisting that the impasses of modernity can be overcome only when "the paradigm of the knowledge of objects" is replaced by "the paradigm of mutual understanding between subjects capable of speech and action," Habermas claims that Derrida's philosophy remains caught up in "the abstract negation of the self-referential subject" and, therefore, is incapable of providing an alternative to subject-centered reason.[57] Derrida's work, however, deconstructs the very opposition between "discursive community" and the philosophy of the subject by showing what these two symmetrically opposed paradigms have in common—an allergic reaction to alterity. If the paradigm of intersubjectivity and community is limited to mutual reciprocity and understanding between subjects, then this paradigm, and the ideal of communication underlying it, is incapable of articulating and sustaining the relation to alterity as an irreducible dimension of being in common.

The concern with the role of community was an important subtext of Derrida's interpretations of Rousseau and Lévi-Strauss, long before this topic received critical attention from other post-structuralist writers like Blanchot or Nancy, with whom it is more frequently associated. In *Of Grammatology*, Derrida argues that both Rousseau and Lévi-Strauss share the same nostalgia for the lost community of authentic speech: "The ideal profoundly underlying this philosophy of writing is therefore the image of a community immediately present to itself, without difference, a community of speech where all members are within earshot" [*OG*, 136]. The ideal community, and we have seen a repetition of this classical theme in Cavell's argument, is primarily a community listening with the same ear—an intimate social wholeness enclosed within the natural range of the voice. As the metaphor of the collective body implies, community defined in terms of internal unity secures a direct and immediate contact between its members: "Self-presence, transparent proximity in the face-to-face of countenances and the immediate range of the voice, this determination of social authenticity is therefore classic: Rousseauistic but already the inheritor of Platonism . . ."[*OG*, 138]. And yet, the community that gathers its members into a single body and assimilates its plural ways of speaking into a single collective voice is predicated upon an effacement of differences. Thought with nostalgia for what has already been lost, or as an utopian project yet to be accomplished, such community is intertwined with the privilege of voice and presence.

In "Plato's Pharmacy," perhaps more explicitly than elsewhere, Derrida suggests that this determination of communal authenticity is inseparable from linguistic and political violence. Violence is in fact the other side of nostalgia. Derrida argues here that indeed the "floating indetermination" or "undecidability" of meaning produced by the exposure to alterity and exteriority represents a threat not only to logic but also to community defined in terms of presence and the proximity of speakers to each other. To restore the principle of self-identity, both in its logical and communal sense, "it is thus necessary to put the outside back in its place. To keep the outside out. This is the inaugural gesture of 'logic' itself, of good 'sense' insofar as it accords with the self-identity of *that which is*" [*PP*, 128]. In order to reveal the sociopolitical implications of this "inaugural gesture" of logic, and in order to link this constitution of the "good" sense together with a formation of "common" sense, Derrida dwells on the complicity between the ambivalent valorization of the *pharmakon* in Plato's text and the traditional figure of the scapegoat (*pharmakos*, the word which in fact Plato does not use). The restoration of the integrity and immanence of the communal space, just as is the case with the restoration of proper sense, calls for the sacrificial exclusion of the figure of the other. The strange unity of these two gestures of exclusion, both of which belong to the order of the allergic reaction the living organism undergoes in relation to its outside, reestablishes a clear division between the inside and the outside (the model of every conceptual opposition), between the pure and the impure:

> The city's body *proper* thus reconstitutes its unity, closes around the security of its inner courts, gives back to itself the word that links it with itself within the confines of the agora, by violently excluding from its territory the representative of an external threat or aggression. That representative represents the otherness of the evil that comes to affect or infect the inside by unpredictably

breaking into it. Yet the representative of the outside is nonetheless *constituted* . . . in the very heart of the inside [*PP*, 133].

As this passage makes clear, the appeal to communal unity indeed restores the proper sense and the logic of self-identity but at a price of political and discursive violence. The philosophical appeal to community, especially when it is intended to provide a cure for skepticism, is inseparable from the violent exclusion of otherness from the social body—this is where the complicity between *pharmakon* (cure) and *pharmakos* (scapegoat) is most powerful and dangerous. Reconstituting the immanence of the community, such a violent "expulsion" of the parasite is intertwined with a refusal of transcendence and otherness. By demonstrating how this violent refusal of transcendence operates on both discursive and social levels, Derrida not only refuses to endorse "textuality without exit" but explicitly argues that the deconstruction of linguistic immanence has to be extended to the ideals of social immanence constitutive of communal unity.

In a manner similar to Levinas, Derrida suggests, therefore, that the recuperation of the unity of meaning is not accomplished by means of logic alone but involves a political and pedagogical decision. Derrida's insistence on the complicity between *pharmakon* and *pharmakos* anticipates a question posed with such poignancy by Levinas: "Are the rendings of the logical text mended by logic alone? It is in the association of philosophy with the State and with medicine that the break-up of discourse is surmounted. The interlocutor that does not yield to logic is threatened with prison or the asylum or undergoes the prestige of the master and the medication of the doctor" [*OB*, 170]. The rhetoric of skepticism as a communal threat can summon divergent powers to secure the recovery of a (common) sense and a sense of being in common: logic, politics, medicine, and pedagogy collaborate in the production of such a cure. Unlike Cavell, Levinas argues that the perennial return of skepticism reminds us not so much of the fragility of human knowledge but "of the, in a very broad sense, *political character of all logical rationalism*, the alliance of logic with politics" [*OB*, 171, emphasis added]. As Levinas and Derrida in different ways argue, the appeal to discursive community as the means to recuperate meaning (or as a cure from skepticism) is always possible because philosophical discourse has already been constituted within the confines of the agora. Underscoring the complicity between truth and violence, Derrida's reading of the *Phaedrus* in the context of the rite of the *pharmakos* emphasizes precisely this point. It is not surprising, therefore, that Derrida should refer to Levinas's ethics as the most powerful thematization of this complicity between "light and power," between truth and suppression of otherness: "Incapable of respecting the Being and meaning of the other, phenomenology and ontology would be philosophies of violence. Through them, the entire philosophical tradition, in its meaning and at bottom, would make common cause with oppression and with the totalitarianism of the same. The ancient clandestine friendship between light and power, the ancient complicity between theoretical objectivity and techno-political possession" [*VM*, 91].

That Derrida rejects the appeal to communal unity as a safeguard against skepticism or failure is bad enough; yet, what is worse, he proposes to generalize the possibility of failure in order to undo the classical notion of communication that usually underlies theories of community and intersubjectivity. As we have seen, the Platonic and Rousseauistic theme of communal unity and authenticity is determined in terms of oral communication among the speakers present to themselves and to each other. In the well-known essay "Signature Event Context," Derrida returns to this ideal of intersubjective communication—and to its relation to skepticism, failure, and the exclusion of alterity. This essay has achieved a certain notoriety because it initiated Derrida's debate with the speech act theory—and, consequently, this dispute has determined the context in which it is usually interpreted.[58]

I would like to suggest, however, that Derrida's focus on the possibility of failure in communication, thematized so directly in this essay, has larger ramifications. It can be interpreted as a critical intervention into the philosophical thematization of community in terms of a mutual understanding and a consensus among speakers. Derrida's generalization of failure in communication undercuts both the notion of a homogenized community without difference and the idea of language based on such community.

As Derrida repeatedly argues, theories of discursive community and intersubjectivity, even though they present themselves as alternatives to the philosophy of the subject, deploy in fact a traditional notion of communication: "oral communications destined to be understood and to open or pursue dialogues within the horizon of an intelligibility and truth of meaning, such that in principle a general agreement may finally be established" [*SEC*, 310]. Consequently, the notion of intersubjective communication is still articulated according to the main premises of the philosophy of the subject and its privileging of consciousness, presence, and voice. It is this notion of communication, submitted to the ideal of truth, that becomes the focus of a deconstructive reading in "Signature Event Context." What is at stake in Derrida's generalization of failure is, therefore, "the break with the horizon of communication as *the communication of consciousnesses or presences*, and as the linguistic or semantic transport of meaning" [*SEC*, 316, emphasis added]. In order to "break" with the metaphysics of the subject, Derrida articulates a different mode of the linguistic exchange—or what he describes here as "iteration". If the concept of communication implies a uniform social space, a symmetrical relationship between the sender and addressee, and an origin of meaning in subjective intention, iteration links any linguistic exchange to an encounter with the other. Consequently, this generalized possibility of failure in communication becomes the "positive condition of possibility" for linguistic exchange divorced from the paradigm of subjectivity.

In his polemics with Austin, Derrida points out that the theory of performative utterance not only acknowledges the possibility of failure, risk, or "infelicity" as something unavoidable in communication, but, at the same time, treats this possibility as accidental, and therefore, irrelevant to a discussion of language. This simultaneous acknowledgement and disavowal of the risk in communication is bound to the fact that the analysis of ordinary speech is meant to provide an answer to epistemological skepticism, which, according to Austin, disregards how the ordinary questions about knowledge function in everyday circumstances.[59] In Derrida's words:

> Austin's procedure is rather remarkable, and typical of the philosophical tradition . . . . It consists in recognizing that the possibility of the negative (here, the *infelicities*) is certainly a structural possibility, that failure is an essential risk in the operations under consideration; and then, with an almost *immediately simultaneous* gesture made in the name of a kind of ideal regulation, an exclusion of this risk as an accidental, exterior one that teaches us nothing about the language phenomenon under consideration [*SEC*, 323].

Specifically, failure means here the inability of the speaker's intention to determine "the totality of his locutionary act" [*SEC*, 322]. It points to a breakdown of dialogue, to the lack of reciprocity between the speakers, and in the end, to the lack of their common agreement.

In a manner similar to Cavell's interpretation of Wittgenstein, Derrida proposes, then, to take the possibility of failure seriously—as a risk that reveals something essential about the nature of communication and linguistic community:

Therefore, I ask the following question: is this general possibility [of risk in communication] necessarily that of a failure or a trap into which language might *fall,* or in which language might lose itself, as if in an abyss situated outside or in front of it? . . . In other words, does the generality of the risk admitted by Austin *surround* language like a kind of *ditch,* a place of external perdition into which locution might never venture, that it might avoid by remaining at home, in itself, sheltered by its essence or *telos?* Or indeed is this risk, on the contrary, *its internal and positive condition of possibility* (emphasis mine)? [*SEC,* 325, Derrida's emphasis, unless otherwise indicated].

Here, I think, we see most clearly Derrida's proximity to and difference from skepticism: it is undeniable that Derrida's interpretations of philosophical and literary texts not only pay close attention to their "failure" but also insist on generalizing this possibility. Failure and skepticism, however, do not merely present for Derrida symptoms of the exhaustion of subject-centered reason but also ways to disassociate language and communication from that paradigm. That is why, in a reversal of the skeptical position, Derrida asks a crucial question, namely, whether what appears as failure within the philosophical paradigm of the subject is not a condition of possibility of a different structure of communication, text, signification.

By turning a generalized possibility of failure into a condition of possibility, Derrida advances the notion of linguistic exchange which systematically links any transfer of meaning to alterity. He calls this exchange iteration (*iter* comes from Sanskrit *itara* "other"): "everything that follows may be read as the exploitation of the logic which links repetition to alterity" [*SEC,* 315]. In the classical concept of communication, meaning has its origin, or source, in the subject, and the successful transport of meaning is secured by the symmetrical relationship between speakers in a dialogue. That this is still the case even in the theory of the performative utterance is evident, for instance, in the preference that Austin gives to first person utterances in the active voice. As Derrida argues, "this conscious presence of the speakers or receivers who participate in the effecting of a performative, their conscious and intentional presence in the totality of the operation, implies teleologically that no *remainder* escapes the present totalization" [*SEC,* 322]. The fact that the subjective intention totalizes the entire field of communication *without remainder* indicates that intersubjective communication is merely an extension of the philosophy of the subject and, consequently, fails to conceptualize what the encounter with the other entails for the theory of communication. As a way of intervention, Derrida's emphasis on failure separates the process of communication from subjective intention precisely because the subject does not constitute the other as the recipient of its message but, in the Levinasian sense, is exposed to alterity prior to any intention to communicate.

Such an emphasis on the irreducible heterogeneity in communication displaces the traditional paradigm of intersubjectivity, thought in terms of an exchange between addressee and recipient. In contrast to the privilege given to subjective intention, Derrida argues that a non-symmetrical linguistic exchange entails an absence of the subject: "By all rights, it belongs to the sign to be legible, even if the moment of its production is irremediably lost . . . (even if it) is abandoned to its essential drifting"[*SEC*, 317]. Because the text carries the possibility of a radical separation from its origin, it can be "grafted" into different contexts, presented to other recipients, function differently for different audiences.[60] Derrida suggests that this force of separation, which creates "an essential dehiscence in the subject," and transports the subject outside itself, is a performative effect *par excellence*. This performative force, however, is no longer determined by the subjective intention to signify, but by the very structure of the address to the other—the address, which, as Levinas reminds us, puts the subject radically into question. Elsewhere, Derrida argues more explicitly that the condition of all performatives lies in the address to the other whom the subject "does not constitute and to whom it can only begin by asking."[61] One can hear in this, perhaps, a certain solidarity between Derrida's description of linguistic exchange in which the subject no longer coincides with itself and the Levinasian address to the other as an Abrahamic movement without return.

Derrida's emphasis on heterogeneity and alterity structuring both the social field of communication and the text itself does not mean, however, that the transmission of meaning can be arrested at the moment of its reception by some empirical addressee, but on the contrary, implies the absence of the recipient: "A writing that was not structurally legible—iterable—beyond the death of the addressee would not be writing." "It must be repeatable—iterable—in the absolute absence of the addressee or of the empirically determinable set of addressees" [*SEC*, 315]. How are we to understand this "absolute absence" of the recipient—does it not contradict all that we have said about Derrida's rereading of failure as a disclosure of otherness? Although Levinas is preoccupied with the face to face encounter with a specific other and Derrida with the textual inscriptions of this encounter in general, we can see a certain parallel between Derrida's interpretation of the absolute absence of the recipient and the Levinasian articulation of the irreducible diachrony revealed in the encounter between the other and the same. In both cases the emphasis falls on the fact that the other cannot be thought on the model of presence (even in terms of absence as a modification of presence). What is implicitly suggested here is that the other can no longer occupy the position of a recipient of the message—cannot be reduced merely to a destination for a subjective intention. This radicalization of absence in the process of communication emphasizes therefore not only the asymmetry between the other and the self but also the fact that they do not belong to the same temporality.

By interpreting the evidence of failure as a condition of a response to the other, Derrida explores in "Signature Event Context" how alterity constitutes both the character of linguistic exchange and its performative force. Dissociated from subjective intention, the performative effect of language is articulated as a "force of rupture" or a "force of separation," which disrupts any sense of symmetry or analogy between speakers and, consequently, divorces linguistic exchange from the notion of intersubjective agreement. Although Derrida does not discuss it directly, the asymmetry between the self and the other, reenacted even in most everyday speech acts, has far reaching consequences for our understanding of intersubjectivity and discursive community. In particular, Derrida's discussion of iteration is incommensurate with a longing for communal unity, for "authentic" communication, and for the presence of speakers to each other. What Derrida's discussions of Plato, Rousseau, and Austin have in common is a critique of the discursive and social violence invariably associated with such nostalgia.

And yet, as Drucilla Cornell has argued, this critique of communal unity (a unity which provides a cure from skepticism) and immanence does not imply that the thought of discursive community is abandoned by Derrida.[62] Rather, Derrida suggests that if the concept of community is to be disengaged from the notions of immanence and totality, it has to embrace irreducible absence, division, and alterity as conditions of being in common. To the community of decision—that is, community constituted through violence and exclusion—Derrida opposes a more fragile community of the question: "A community of the question, therefore, within that fragile moment when the question is not yet determined enough for the hypocrisy of an answer to have already initiated itself beneath the mask of the question, and not yet determined enough for its voice to have been already and fraudulently articulated within the very syntax of the question" [*VM*, 80]. No

longer a cure (certainly not an answer) for skepticism, such community perhaps will avoid the pitfalls of nostalgia for impossible unity,
which, according to Derrida, shapes even such demystifying discourses as structuralism: "a sort of ethic of presence, an ethic of nostalgia for
origins, an ethic of archaic and natural innocence, of a purity of presence and self-presence in speech—an ethic, nostalgia, and even
remorse, which he often presents as the motivation of the ethnological
project . . . . Turned towards the lost or impossible presence of the
absent origin, this structuralist thematic of broken immediacy is therefore saddened, *negative*, nostalgic, guilty" [*SSP*, 292]. In a way evocative of Jean-Luc Nancy's deconstruction of the nostalgia shaping the
philosophical discourse of community in the West, Derrida opposes
this ethics of nostalgia to the ethics of responsibility.[63] In place of nostalgia for the immediate communion with others, a community of the
question submits the ideal of communion to responsibility for the violence and exclusion it entails.

Given the fact that the frequent interpretations of deconstruction
in terms of skepticism claim that its critique of representation leaves us
imprisoned within the immanence of textual space, Derrida's recur-
rent discussion of community, evident even in his early texts, might be
surprising. What I hope to make clear, however, is that Derrida's work
not only does not unburden language from all sense of social and
ethical responsibility but, conversely, intensifies it. As Levinas's
response to Derrida suggests, this sense of responsibility, irreducible
to the task of representation, reveals itself in the address to the other.
Skepticism, in this context, provides an example of a discourse in
which both the representation of the other and the expression of the
subject are put into question by the structure of this address. As we
have seen, this sense of responsibility informs not only Derrida's critique of textuality but also his deconstruction of social immanence.

"Hear Say Yes": Rhetoric, Skepticism, Modernism

In this section I would like to focus on Derrida's "investment" in modern aesthetics in order to articulate more clearly the significance of the
deconstructive models of rhetoric for the critique of social immanence.
In so doing, I hope to intervene into some of the misconceptions about
the place of both modernism and rhetoric in the Derridean project.
Derrida's writings on modern literature in general and on metaphor in
particular have often been perceived as attempts to valorize the disruptive and self-conscious language of the modern avant-garde over

both the pragmatic language of everyday practice and the philosophical language of theoretical knowledge. As Charles Altieri writes, Derrida's focus on rhetorical instability "summarize(s) his case on the inadequacy of models that base secure meanings on correspondence or phenomenological versions of presence. 'White Mythology' takes as its subject the possibility of making sharp philosophical distinctions between names, which denote single referents, and metaphors, which duplicate and contaminate any single direction for empirical inquiry."[64] Since for Derrida the instability of figures is not limited to literature but contaminates the entire philosophical conceptuality, for many critics of deconstruction this "dubious" privilege of rhetoric over logic entails a pervasive skepticism about the representational and communicative functions of language: "The result is that the basic ideas of philosophy (*theoria, eidos, logos,* and so on) may themselves be susceptible of philosophical reinterpretation: there is no reliable foundation or bedrock (to compound the metaphor) for our discourse."[65] As it is often argued, Derrida's reading of the forgotten metaphors in philosophical texts increases linguistic indeterminacy so that even appeals to the conventional agreements of speakers—which, if we recall, provided for Cavell the means of recovery from skepticism— merely smack of "ideological complacency."[66]

For many opponents of deconstruction, this "unfortunate" aesthetic turn not only violates the sound principles of philosophical argumentation but also destroys the social relevance of poststructuralist theory. By reducing philosophy to (modern) literature, Derrida seems to repeat, in the same stroke, the modernist withdrawal from social and political concerns. In a long "Excursus on Levelling the Genre Distinction between Philosophy and Literature," Habermas addresses both of these dangers in Derrida's work. According to Habermas, Derrida's contestation of the distinction between philosophy and literature has "disastrous" effects for both philosophy and social theory. On the philosophical level, Derrida's deployment of the rhetorical resources characteristic of modern literature is motivated, according to Habermas, by a desire to evade the aporias and contradictions of a "totalizing" critique of reason according to reason's own tools. Arising from the necessity of using logocentric language against itself, these aporias in the deconstructive project, as Levinas reminds us, are similar to the contradictions philosophy has always detected in the skeptical argument. In order to evade the dead end of contradiction into which Derrida's critique of reason falls, deconstruction, according to Habermas, makes an ingenious but ultimately ineffective turn to rhetoric and literature: "'deconstruction' of the philosophical tradition transposes the radical critique of reason into the domain of rhetoric and thereby shows it a way out of the aporia of self-referentiality."[67]

Yet what ultimately concerns Habermas in his critique of Derrida's displacement of the primacy of logic over rhetoric is not a distinction between philosophy and literature but a distinction between literature and everyday social practice. For Habermas, a much more dangerous implication of Derrida's analysis of rhetoric lies not in a somewhat naive belief that the rhetorical character of literary language can subvert the tradition of metaphysics but in the way literary discourse can undermine the capacity of ordinary language to produce intersubjective agreements. Suspecting that a violation of the hierarchy between logic and rhetoric undermines the autonomy of the work of art not only with respect to philosophy but also with respect to ordinary socio-linguistic practices, Habermas complains that Derrida deploys the disruptive models of textuality characteristic of the modern avant-garde to undercut the ordinary communicative practices. Let us recall that for Habermas this "danger" of "levelling of the genre distinction between philosophy and literature" is best exemplified by the work of Mary Louise Pratt, one of the most influential cultural critics of imperialism. Needless to say, this is an amazing diagnosis because Derrida's concern with rhetoric, in particular in the context of modernism, has been more often interpreted to result in a pure textuality cut off from any relation to social practice or in a new "ideology of the text" proclaiming a change in style to be equivalent to cultural intervention.[68] The surprising, and perhaps not intended, implication of Habermas's objections is that the rhetorical analysis of modern texts not only destroys the very concept of autonomous art, but also initiates a critique of the intersubjective model of social practice.[69] If Derrida's revision of the relation between rhetoric and logic undermines the autonomy of literature and overcomes its separation from social practice, then this "danger" is perhaps worth risking.

Ironically, Habermas's misreading of deconstruction suggests nonetheless deeper consequences of Derrida's concern with modern aesthetics than many deconstructive analyses themselves. Indeed, what is at stake here are the implications of the porous boundary between philosophy and literature not only for the history of metaphysics but also for our understanding of socio-linguistic practices. In order to pursue these implications, I would like to bring into proximity what is sometimes perceived as two antithetical articulations of the "other of reason": the textual emphasis on the excess of the rhetoricity of language questioning the self-evidence of truth, and the socio-ethical considerations of the claims of the other person in linguistic community. Any negotiation between these two inscriptions of the other of reason in turn requires a rethinking of the significance of rhetoric in Derrida's reading of modernist texts. In order to avoid hasty generalizing that Derrida's emphasis on rhetorical undecidability leads either to the negative epistemology of figurative language or to the endless recesses of linguistic self-reflection, it is important to elaborate more explicitly the ethical implications of rhetoric. As John Llewelyn puts it, it is a matter of the "crossing of responsibility . . . with the undecidable double bind."[70]

By underscoring the disjunction between the epistemological and ethical effects of figurative language, Derrida re-reads the rhetorical "abberation" as an inscription of the event and the performative address to the other. Irreducible to the negation of truth or to the vertigo of language reflecting only itself, the rift between the grammar and the figure, between the constative and the performative, stages a possibility of an event whose occurrence cannot be derived from, or anticipated by, the socio-linguistic norms and conventions. Understood as such an inaugural event, the surplus of rhetoric creates a rupture in the collective conditions of enunciation, and thus opens a passage toward the other beyond the present possibilities of signification. By suspending the capacity of grammar to calculate the unpredictable in advance, the figural instability of language, Derrida argues, allows for the coming of the unanticipated alterity—that is, for the experience of the other as "impossible."

In order to rethink the excess of rhetoric as an inscription of otherness, I would like to turn to Derrida's deconstruction of the philosophical concept of metaphor in "White Mythology," and to contest some of the usual readings of this famous essay. Although the main debate generated by this text revolves around the question of whether metaphor undercuts philosophical conceptuality or whether it remains subordinated to truth, this is not where the most radical intervention of "White Mythology" takes place. Rather, what Derrida points to is that the very affiliation of metaphor with truth implicates figurative language in the political and ethical violence—in the obliteration of alterity in social praxis. By deconstructing the metaphysical concept of metaphor, Derrida uncovers, therefore, the pervasive complicity between the philosophical genealogy of figure and the philosophical roots of ethnocentrism.

The affiliation of metaphor with truth has been brilliantly demonstrated, among other critics, by Rodolphe Gasché. As Gasché argues, it is a mistake to assume that Derrida deconstructs the language of philosophy and its ideal of representational knowledge by simply uncovering its metaphorical roots. Neither uncritically valorizing metaphor's subversive power nor linking metaphor to a failure of knowledge, Derrida, on the contrary, demonstrates that the philosophical concept of metaphor remains in the service of truth. According to Gasché, "Derrida's reformulation of the question of metaphor is concerned with the fundamental complicity between the philosophical determination of the concept of metaphor and the apparently subversive attempt to challenge philosophy on the grounds that its concepts are hidden tropes."[71] Consequently, the attempt to reveal the metaphorical origin of concepts (in the tradition of Nietzsche) is neither subversive nor skeptical in itself; more often that not it betrays a symbolist conception of language, based on the continuous derivation from sensory figure to conceptual generality:

> Metaphor, therefore, is determined by philosophy as a provisional loss of meaning, an economy of the proper without irreparable damage, a certainly inevitable detour, but also a history with its sights set on, and within the horizon of, the circular reappropriation of literal, proper meaning. This is why the philosophical evaluation of metaphor has always been ambiguous: metaphor is dangerous and foreign as concerns *intuition* (vision or contact), *concept* (the grasping or proper presence of the signified), and *consciousness* (proximity or self presence); but it is in complicity with what it endangers, is necessary to it in the extent to which the detour is a re-turn guided by the function of resemblance *(mimēsis or homoiōsis)*, under the law of the same [*WM*, 270].

Despite its ambiguous philosophical valorization, metaphor remains, according to Derrida, a metaphysical concept par *excellence*, "coordinated with the manifestation of truth" and with the production of knowledge. Indicating the extent to which rhetoric has been subordinated to logic, metaphor "remains in complicity with what it endangers" because the duplicity of the figure is determined according to the model of analogy, likeness, or imitation. As the classical definition of metaphor in Aristotle's *Poetics* makes clear, metaphoric transfer is not only defined in terms of analogy and resemblance but is systematically linked to the values of *logos, mimesis, homoiosis* (likeness).[72] Derrida argues that "everything, in the theory of metaphor, . . . seems to belong to the great immobile chain of Aristotelian ontology, with its theory of the analogy of Being, its logic, its epistemology" [*WM*, 236]. According to this philosophical determination, metaphor—not merely a superfluous poetic ornament—performs a cognitive function, which consists in the theoretical perception of hidden resemblances between diverse beings and in the calculation of the unpredictable. Despite a provisional loss of meaning reenacted in metaphor, metaphoric language remains in complicity with the task of representation and economic calculation.[73] Although considered less important, the pleasure in metaphor is, therefore, like the pleasure of knowledge or imitation—both are based on inferences, on "learning by resemblance, . . . [on] recognizing the same" [*WM*, 238]. Contrary to suspicions of skepticism, Derrida concludes that the philosophical concept of metaphor "as an effect of *mimēsis* and *homoiōsis*, the manifestation of analogy, will be a means of knowledge, a means that is subordinate, but certain" [*WM*, 238]. By gathering even diverse significations into a family of resemblances and similarities, metaphor operates within the economy of the same [*WM*, 240]. Although metaphorical language bears a disruptive potential, Derrida shows that philosophy in fact regulates and harnesses it for the production of knowledge.

Despite the detour of metaphoric transfer, during which meaning is separated from its referent and exposed to "wandering," the philosophical concept of metaphor remains subordinated to the value of the same rather than to the value of alterity. The metaphoric detour is only a provisional movement of expropriation, which, like Ulysses's journey, eventually returns to the domain of proper meaning. The provisional character of the metaphoric detour is aptly suggested by the figure of "the borrowed dwelling," which for Derrida refers to the movement of metaphorization as such: "The borrowed dwelling . . . it is a metaphor of metaphor; an expropriation, a being-outside-one's-own-residence, but still in a dwelling, outside its own residence but still in a residence in which one comes back to oneself, recognizes oneself, reassembles oneself . . . , outside oneself in oneself. This is the philosophical metaphor as a detour within (or in sight of) reappropriation, parousia, the self-presence of the idea in its own light" [*WM*, 253]. As Derrida shows, the philosophical determination of metaphor is structured around the opposition of the outside and the inside, the other and the same, the improper and the proper, loss and recuperation. The metaphorical trajectory traces a certain domain of exteriority, but the outside it marks is not radical enough either to resist the unification of meaning or to question what Derrida calls a topological and economical obsession with the idea of the locus/place.

What is significant, Derrida stresses, is the complicity between this recuperation of proper meaning and a certain trajectory of ethnocentrism. The philosophical concept of metaphor not only permits the recuperation of subjectivity but also identifies the "essence of man" with the Western rational subject: "This circulation has not excluded but, on the contrary, has permitted and provoked the transformation of presence into self-presence, into the proximity or properness of subjectivity to and for itself" [*WM*, 254]. The telos to which the metaphorical movement is subordinated is determined, therefore, in a double way: it is described, of course, as the proper meaning and the *parousia* of truth but also as a "property of man." The metaphorical trajectory promises not only a return to truth but also a recuperation of the essence of man. Defined as human (one's own) proper linguistic capacity, a metaphoric way of speaking does not disrupt the value of self-presence, but remains subordinated to the value of subjective identity and essence. And if subjectivity is disturbed provisionally by this linguistic transport outside itself, the movement of return is always secured through the function of analogy or resemblance, which maintains a continuity between the inside and the outside, origin and destination, the self and the other.

By showing similarities among differences, the metaphoric function of analogy performs the implicit unification and generalization of discourse[74] and, by extension, of speaking subjects. Maintaining the analogy between the self and the other, the process of metaphorization is inseparable from theories of intersubjectivity, communication, etc. Consequently, as Derrida argues, the metaphysical concept of metaphor is not only implicated in knowledge but also in the political and ethical questions accruing around the issues of difference and otherness.[75] When metaphoric language is determined as a "property of man," it is invariably linked to an overcoming of alterity, or to what Derrida calls the mastering of the "Oriental difference." In a discussion reminiscent of Levinas, Derrida suggests that the heliotropic odyssey of metaphor, always travelling from the East to the West, promises a sublation of the Jew by the Greek, of the Oriental by the Occidental. "The end of metaphor" is correlative with "the ends of ethnocentrism":

> This *return to itself*—this interiorization—of the sun has marked not only Platonic, Aristotelian, Cartesian, and other kinds of discourse...but also, and by the same token, the man of metaphysics. The sensory sun, which rises in the East, becomes interiorized, in the evening of its journey, in the eye and the heart of the Westerner. He summarizes, assumes, and achieves the essence of man, 'illuminated by the true light'. . . . This is the irrepressible philosophical desire to summarize-interiorize-dialecticize . . . the metaphorical division between the origin and itself, the Oriental difference [*WM*, 268-269].

In a certain economic condensation, metaphor announces and masters the difference between sensuality and intelligibility, the East and the West, man and woman—which brings us to the question of how the "irrepressible philosophical desire" to master the distance from the origin is implicated in power. When juxtaposed to the erasure of the "Oriental/sexual difference," the figure of "white mythology" no longer refers merely to the invisibility of rhetoric in philosophical discourse but rather congeals into what Derrida calls "the metaphor of domination." Marked by the connivance of the metaphorical and the philosophical in the obliteration of alterity, this figure of domination preserves the political myth of the essence of man. Far from being subversive, "white mythology" remains entrenched within both the philosophy and the politics of the subject—it allows the Western rational man to claim the essence of humanity and to cover over this violence by maintaining the calm neutrality of discourse.

It is this concatenation of values reproduced by the concept of metaphor—the same, similar, proper, general, and Western—that prompts Derrida to ask the decisive question: "Does not such a metaphorology, transported into the philosophical field, always, by destination, rediscover the same? . . . What *other* than this return of the same is to be found when one seeks metaphor?" [*WM*, 266]. The beginning of an answer emerges from Derrida's discussion of catachresis in "White Mythology." As a violent and forced trope constituting not so much a metaphorical sense but the secondary "proper" meaning of ideas, catachresis reveals that the proper sense has been produced by force: "What is interesting to us here, thus, is the production of a proper sense, a new kind of proper sense, by means of the violence of catachresis . . . " [*WM*, 256]. By establishing a link between figurality and performativity, catachresis uncovers that the proper sense represents not merely the meaning of being or the self-manifestation of the idea but is produced by linguistic displacement. Furthermore, its impropriety implicates this linguistic production of the proper in violence, and therefore, in the erasure of heterogeneity and differences—not only internal linguistic differences but also differences (to recall the crucial terms deployed by Derrida) between the self and the other, the inside and the outside, the West and the East.

If philosophy regulates the duplicity of figurative language according to the model of analogy or proportionality, to what extent can literature displace this model? Let us change, then, the terrain from the invisible "white mythology" of the metaphor in philosophy to its quite overt "mythology" in a literary text. Since Derrida interprets the philosophical determination of metaphor as a form of odyssey—as a provisional detour predicated upon a return to the proper meaning and the property of man—perhaps his explicit discussion of the odyssey *figure* in James Joyce's *Ulysses* will help illuminate a different function of rhetoric in modern literature. By juxtaposing "White Mythology" with "Ulysses Gramophone," I will discuss odyssey not only as an example of metaphor but also as a figure describing the movement of metaphorization as such.[76]

Derrida's discussion of the odyssey figure turns around the word "yes," the final word in Joyce's text and considered by him to be the most positive word in the language: "There is a question in *yes*, a request in *yes*, and perhaps, for it is never certain, an unconditional, inaugural affirmation of the word *yes* that cannot necessarily be distinguished from the question or the request" [*UG*, 54]. In contrast to the provisional negativity implied in the philosophical concept of metaphor—a negativity recuperated within the proper—can this tone of "inaugural" affirmation convey a sense of difference between the function of metaphor in literary and philosophical texts? Can such an "inaugural" event open a passage toward the other beyond the analogical assimilation of differences? At first, it seems hardly to be the case, since the final "yes" in *Ulysses* merely provides a closure to the "omnipotent Odyssean recapitulation" of meaning. As was the case with "White Mythology," Derrida shows that the odyssey figure in Joyce's text remains in complicity with a "'phenomenology of the mind' in the Hegelian sense of a 'science of the experience of the consciousness' and the great circular return, the autobiographic-encyclopedic circumnavigation" [*UG*, 32]. Although a literary text, Joyce's *Ulysses* is not very far from the philosophical ideal of the totality of knowledge: "ready to domesticate, circumcise, circumvent everything; it lends itself to and prepares itself for the encyclopedic reappropriation of absolute knowledge which gathers itself close to it, as Life does to Logos" [*UG*, 59]. Not surprisingly, Derrida calls Joyce "the most Hegelian" of modern writers. Both as a figure of narrative structure in Joyce's text and as a movement of metaphorization as such, the metaphor of the odyssey more than ever provides a continuity between philosophical and literary concerns with knowledge and truth. Not surprisingly, the final "eschatological" yes in *Ulysses* accomplishes a completion of the epic project predicated upon both the encyclopedic and autobiographical modes of knowledge.

Yet, although Derrida admits that literature, including modern avant-garde texts, has been shaped by philosophical conceptuality, he also argues that literary language can dislocate the order and the limits of philosophical discourse: "in literature... philosophical language is still present in some sense; but it produces and presents itself as alienated from itself, at a remove, at a distance."[77] *Ulysses*, for instance, does not merely affirm the encyclopedic ideal of knowledge and a figurative language subordinated to this ideal; it is also "haunted" by a different tonality of affirmation that contaminates its entire epic project. What allows Derrida to think the figure beyond the confines of analogy or resemblance, is the affirmation, and the risk of contamination associated with it, inherent in the performative address to the other. As Derrida argues, the affirmation of "yes" produces two, distinct yet inseparable, significations. On the one hand, such "yes," as a condition of monological and analogical discourse, enables a narcissistic positioning of the subject in language. Each time the subject commences or dreams of self-appropriation, it addresses itself through a "yes, I will." But on the other hand, the affirmation of "yes, I" is already redoubled and caught in a response to the other: it illustrates "the hetero-tautology of the *yes* implied in all *cogito* as thought, the position of the self, and the will of the position of the self" [*UG*, 64]. Even when the subject dreams of self-appropriation, such a dream is already contaminated by the trace of a different event—a trace, which escapes "an interiorizing anamnesis, a recollection of meaning" [*WM*, 269]. Incapable of closing the circle of self-identification, "*yes* indicates that the Other is being addressed" [*UG*, 63]. Since it does not have any specific semantic content, since it does not name anything, such a "yes" functions as a purely performative force, but is no longer restricted to first person utterances.[78] For that reason, Derrida calls "yes" pre-performative: "as a pre-performative force which, for example, in the form of 'I' marks that 'I' as addressing itself to the Other, however undetermined he or she is: 'Yes-I,' or 'Yes-I-am-speaking-to-the-other,' even if *I* is saying *no* and even if *I* is addressing itself without speaking" [*UG*, 62–63]. Neither a subjective initiative, nor an impersonal effect of linguistic operation, the address to the other does not produce the other's identity but rather opens a possibility of an inaugural event: it allows for the coming of the other by exhibiting the fragility of the closed grammatical structures.

How is Derrida's discussion of the performative force of this affirmation related to the process of metaphorization, implied in the figure of the odyssey? The affirmation of alterity and the risk of contamination performed by the "yes" are intertwined with a break in the great circular journey of the odyssey at the moment when the figure seems to be subordinated to the values of proper meaning and the "property of man": "In this final movement, I return then to the risk or the chance of this contamination by the *affirmation in laughter* of the Other, of the interference of an Elijah, that is to say of me, by the Other" [*UG*, 59–60]. In *Ulysses*, the possibility of such an event occurs—to give one of the most striking examples cited by Derrida—when the Greek model of the Odyssey and analogy is interrupted by an anticipation of the Hebrew prophet Elijah, whose coming has been advertised repeatedly in Joyce's text: "to contrive the break-in necessary for the coming of the Other, who might just happen to be called Elijah, if Elijah is the name of the unforeseeable Other for whom a place must be kept" [*UG*, 59]. Referring to the Jewish custom of keeping a place open for Elijah [*UG*, 50], and implicitly recalling Levinas's analysis of the welcome addressed to the Other, Derrida's emphasis on the instability of rhetoric is intertwined with an "unforeseeable" event of alterity.[79] The performative force of "yes" marks, therefore, a redoubling and a dissociation of the two strands of figurative discourse: the recuperation of the proper meaning and its unpredictable interruption.[80] If the odyssey remains a main figure organizing and unifying the composition of *Ulysses*, it is redoubled and interrupted by another figure it cannot contain—the figure of Elijah, yet another "synecdoche of Ulyssean narration, at once smaller and greater than the whole" [*UG*, 52].

As should be clear from the context, which dramatizes the relation between the Jew and the Greek, the rhetorical issues of analogy or difference, resemblance or otherness, are not merely formal or aesthetic concerns.[81] In an attempt to uncover the ethical implications of rhetoric, Derrida once again underscores the pervasive complicity between analogy and the "ends of (Western) man," between rhetoric and the philosophy of the subject, between aestheticism and ethnocentrism. It is not surprising, therefore, that Derrida's discussion of otherness in *Ulysses* from the outset resumes the differences between the Hellenic and the Hebraic, between the Occidental and the Oriental, differences that the philosophical concept of metaphor is supposed to master by inscribing them within the model of analogy and likeness: "Tokyo: does this city lie on the western circle that leads back to Dublin or to Ithaca?" [*UG*, 29]. Tokyo, Dublin, Ithaca—the disruption of analogy reveals that these locations no longer belong to the same circle, the same journey, the same itinerary of the Western traveller, who in the end, always returns to himself.

Nor do they speak with the same language. In Derrida's critique of ethnocentrism, the collapse of metaphoric analogy between the same and the other is linked to the Babelian proliferation of tongues. When figuration marks the asymmetry between the same and the other, it coincides with the possibilities and limits of translation.[82] Once the internal unity of discourse has been shattered by preserving the place of the other in its structure, the difference between languages, no longer subsumed by their similarity, starts to contaminate their internal purity as well. The other as the figure of the stranger calls into relief the difference between native and foreign tongues, marking both the necessity and impossibility of translation: "An act which in one language *remarks* the language itself, and which in this way affirms doubly, once by speaking it and once by saying that it has thus been spoken, opens up the space for a *re-marking*, which, at the same time and in the same double way, defies and calls for translation" [*UG*, 28]. As the example of *Ulysses* shows so well, the affirmation of "yes" addressed to the other resounds with the multiplicity of languages and discourses that defy unification. This Babelization of literary language marks the limit of both the philosophy of the subject and of intersubjective communication.[83]

What Derrida's deconstruction of the philosophical concept of metaphor and his analysis of the rhetorical force of literary language have in common is a focus on the non-thematizable exposure to the other and its inscription in language. Contrary to the numerous worries that such an apparent privileging of rhetoric over logic entails skepticism, Derrida's discussion of metaphor shifts the emphasis from the epistemological to the ethical effects of rhetoric. Derrida links the rhetorical instability of language to the force of affirmation, which precedes the usual opposition between the negative and the positive. Although he admits that such affirmation is capable "of destroying the very root of this competence, of this legitimacy" [*UG*, 50], at the same time he insists that this destruction or contamination of the order of discourse constitutes not only a threat but also "an opportunity": "For if there is the other, if there is a *yes*, then the Other no longer lets itself be produced by sameness or by the ego. *Yes*, the condition contained in all signatures and all performatives, addresses itself to the Other which it does not constitute, and to whom it can only begin by asking . . . " [*UG*, 63]. To think about the ethical significance of rhetoric, in the way I suggest here, is to complicate the usual take on the "positive force" of deconstruction, which more often than not has been articulated as a Nietzschean affirmation of becoming or as a celebration of textual play.[84] Derrida's reading of *Ulysses* suggests that the rhetorical affirmation of the other escapes the opposition between linguistic skepticism (which in the context of modern aesthetics is translated into the autonomy of the work of art) and the celebrations of textuality, the free play of signifiers, etc. Rather—and this is perhaps most clear in Derrida's analysis of literary texts—the affirmative force of deconstruction is inseparable from its profound sense of obligation. Although they belong to two different performative registers, the sense of play and the sense of responsibility are perhaps not incompatible but ceaselessly supplement each other, reminding us that Derridean affirmations, serious as they are, can also resound with laughter.

* * *

The contrast between two different ways of locating the inscription of skepticism within deconstruction illuminates the implications of Derrida's attempt to divorce the theory of language from the constraints of the philosophy of the subject. Operating within post-Kantian epistemology, the first type of interpretation sees in deconstruction merely a version of the "classical skeptical argument," and advances the claim that the deconstructive understanding of language is entirely formal and negative, that it destroys the principles of adequate representation and renounces all sense of responsibility to its outside—call it "the real world" or "history." In order to make sense of Derrida's claim that deconstruction is primarily a search for the "other" and "the other of language," I have turned to the alternative view represented by Levinas's reinterpretation of skepticism in the context of his non-epistemological ethics. Following Levinas's articulation of the linguistic model deployed in the skeptical argument, I have argued that Derrida's texts play on a double signification of the rhetoric of failure, emphasizing both the limits of the philosophy of consciousness and an implicit affirmation of alterity. Despite frequent confusions such rhetoric creates in the reception of his work, Derrida preserves this double signification as a refusal to synchronize otherness with the order of consciousness and the order of discourse. The contrast between these two ways of understanding skepticism and its relation to deconstruction allows us to articulate the point where Derrida's philosophy of language separates itself from the confines of the metaphysics of the subject. It is not only the case that Derrida's theory of language deconstructs the concept of the knowing subject by emphasizing the endless play of differences and signifiers, which exceed the efforts of consciousness to arrest meaning—it addresses the responsibility language bears to something other than itself and questions how this responsibility should be articulated. No longer exhausted, or even commensurate, with the task of representation or knowledge of the other, this responsibility is linked in Derrida's theory of language with the pre-performative force of the address to the other. By elaborating the scope of the responsibility tied to the signification of alterity, Derrida not only deconstructs the notion of linguistic immanence but also extends this critique to nostalgic visions of social immanence, constitutive of discursive community.

─────────────── **NOTES** ───────────────

1. The following abbreviations of Derrida's works are used in this chapter:
OG *Of Grammatology.* Trans. Gayatri Chakravorty Spivak. Baltimore: Johns Hopkins UP, 1974.
PP "Plato's Pharmacy." *Dissemination.* Trans. Barbara Johnson. Chicago: The U of Chicago P, 1981.
SEC "Signature Event Context." *Margins of Philosophy.* Trans. Alan Bass. Chicago: U of Chicago P, 1982.
SSP "Structure, Sign, and Play in the Discourse of the Human Sciences." *Writing and Difference.* Trans. Alan Bass. Chicago: U of Chicago P, 1978.
T "Tympan." *Margins of Philosophy.*
UG "Ulysses Gramophone: Hear say yes in Joyce" *James Joyce: the Augmented Ninth. Proceedings of the Ninth International James Joyce Symposium,* Frankfurt 1984, ed. Bernard Benstock (Syracuse: Syracuse UP, 1988), 27–75.
VM "Violence and Metaphysics." *Writing and Difference.*
WM "White Mythology: Metaphor in the Text of Philosophy." *Margins of Philosophy.*

2. Christopher Norris, *Derrida* (Cambridge: Harvard UP, 1987), 142.

3. Gerald Graff, *Professing Literature: An Institutional History* (Chicago: U of Chicago P, 1987), 242.

4. For a critique of this approach, see A. J. Cascardi, "Skepticism and Deconstruction," in *Philosophy and Literature* 8 (1984): 5.

5. Eugene Goodheart, *The Skeptic Disposition in Contemporary Criticism* (Princeton: Princeton UP, 1984). The list of similar examples is relatively long. For the most representative readings of deconstruction in terms of skepticism, see, for instance, Charles Altieri, *Act and Quality: A Theory of Literary Meaning and Humanistic Understanding* (Amherst: U of Massachusetts P, 1981), 26–28; C. Butler, "Deconstruction and Skepticism," in *Interpretation, Deconstruction and Ideology* (Oxford: Oxford UP, 1984); Jay Cantor, "On Stanley Cavell," in *Raritan* 1 (1981): 50–51; Michael Fischer, *Stanley Cavell and Literary Skepticism* (Chicago: The U of Chicago ᴾ, 1989), 1–9, 30–35; and S. J. Wilmore, "Scepticism and Deconstruction," in *Man and World* 20 (1987): 437–55. For a critique of this reception, see A. J. Cascardi, "Skepticism and Deconstruction," 1–14 and Christopher Norris, *Derrida,* 142–161.

6. S. J. Wilmore, "Scepticism and Deconstruction," 450.

7. Jürgen Habermas, *The Philosophical Discourse of Modernity: Twelve Lectures,* trans. Frederick G. Lawrence (Cambridge: MIT, 1992), 185.

8. Habermas sees the pessimistic skeptical attitude as one of the two possible outcomes of the postmodern critique of reason. The other strategy lies in an *Ursprungsphilosophie,* which proclaims "the possibility of a critique of metaphysics that digs up the roots of metaphysical thought without, however, itself giving up philosophy." *The Philosophical Discourse of Modernity,* 97.

9. Habermas, 166.

10. Habermas, 172.

11. A more receptive interpretation of deconstruction links "the deconstructive practice of maintaining a vigilant skepticism about the legitimacy or truth-contents of any linguistic proposition" to a critique of ideology. See, for instance, Thomas Docherty, "Introduction," in *Postmodernism: A Reader* (New York: Columbia, 1993), 8.

12. Tongue in cheek, Altieri writes that "where most philosophies have to invent skeptical demons in order to test their claims, those interested in recent Continental thought and literary theory find perhaps a richer demon ready-to-hand" in the work of Derrida. *Act and Quality,* 25.

13. "The Original Discussion of 'Différance'," trans. David Wood, Sarah Richmond, and Malcolm Bernard, in *Derrida and "Différance",* ed. David Wood and Robert Bernasconi (Evanston: Northwestern UP, 1988), 92.

14. *Derrida and "Différance",* 92-93.

15. Richard Rorty, "Philosophy as a Kind of Writing: An Essay on Derrida," in *Consequences of Pragmatism* (Minneapolis: U of Minnesota P, 1982), 91–95.

16. Christopher Butler, *Interpretation, Deconstruction and Ideology,* 86.

17. Michael Fischer, for instance, remains rather unconvinced by the "exaggerated hedonism" of deconstruction. *Stanley Cavell and Literary Skepticism,* 19–20. Sometimes the pleasure in the text is seen as an expression of skepticism in itself—a kind of pyrrhonic happiness stemming from the suspension of rational judgement. S. J. Wilmore, "Skepticism and Deconstruction," 437.

18. Butler, 86.

19. S. J. Wilmore, "Skepticism and Deconstruction," 437–38.

20. Michael Fischer, *Stanley Cavell and Literary Skepticism,* 10. Although I also argue that it is important to bring Cavell's work into the discussions in literary theory, I disagree strongly with Fischer's claim that Cavell would enable one to set up parallels between epistemological skepticism and poststructuralist criticism.

21. For Fischer, deconstructive expectations of certainty or textual coherence are pitched too high and therefore cannot be fulfilled. Against this misunderstanding of Derrida, Rodolphe Gasché argues that "these concepts (aporia and contradiction) [are not] borrowed from the conceptual arsenal of the skeptical tradition of philosophy, a tradition that throws doubt upon philo-

sophical knowledge only from the perspective of a higher mode of truth." *The Tain of the Mirror: Derrida and the Philosophy of Reflection* (Cambridge: Harvard UP, 1986) 128

22. A. J. Cascardi, "Skepticism and Deconstruction," 3.

23. Rorty, "Philosophy as a Kind of Writing," 99.

24. Rorty, "Philosophy as a Kind of Writing," 93. For a succinct discussion of the relation between Derrida and pragmatism, see Norris, *Derrida*, 150–155.

25. See, for instance, the Habermasian argument that whereas the Hegelian dialectic sets up the possibility of the internal critique of modernity, Derrida abandons the project of modernity altogether. *The Philosophical Discourse of Modernity*, 302–306.

26. Rorty, 100.

27. Jay Cantor, "On Stanley Cavell," 50–51.

28. A. J. Cascardi, "Skepticism and Deconstruction," 3.

29. Simon Critchley contests this misreading of textuality in a decisive way in his *The Ethics of Deconstruction: Derrida and Levinas* (Oxford: Blackwell, 1992), 31–41.

30. William V. Spanos, "De-struction and the Critique of Ideology: A Polemic Meditation on the Margin," in *Criticism Without Boundaries: Directions and Crosscurrents in Postmodern Critical Theory*, ed. Joseph A. Buttigieg, (Notre Dame: U of Notre Dame P, 1987), 58.

31. Derrida protests here that deconstructive critique of reference does not amount to the "idealism of the text," but at the same time argues against a simple alternative of "the materialist text": "It is not always in *the* materialist text (is there such a thing, *the* materialist text?) nor in *every* materialist text that the concept of matter has been defined as absolute exterior or radical heterogeneity." *Positions*, trans. Alan Bass, (Chicago: U of Chicago P, 1972), 64.

32. Jacques Derrida, "Deconstruction and the Other," Interview with Richard Kearney, in *Dialogues with Contemporary Continental Thinkers*, ed. Richard Kearney, (Manchester: Manchester UP, 1984), 123–124.

33. Norris, *Derrida*, 144.

34. *Derrida and "Différance"*, 93.

35. "Deconstruction and the Other," 108.

36. Barry Stroud, *The Significance of Philosophical Skepticism* (Oxford: Claredon P, 1984), 38.

37. Drucilla Cornell, *The Philosophy of the Limit* (New York: Routledge, 1992), 70–71.

38. Emmanuel Levinas, *Otherwise than Being or Beyond Essence*, trans. Alphonso Lingis (The Hague: Martinus Nijhoff Publishers, 1981), 165. Subsequent references to this text will be marked parenthetically in the text, preceded by OB.

39. For an excellent discussion of the significance of skepticism in Levinas's approach to language, see Robert Bernasconi, "Skepticism in the Face of Philosophy," 150–161; and Andriaan Peperzak, "Presentation,"

51–67; both essays are in *Re-Reading Levinas*, ed. Robert Bernasconi and Simon Critchley (Bloomington: Indiana UP, 1991). See also, Critchley, *The Ethics of Deconstruction*.

40. Bernasconi, "Skepticism in the Face of Philosophy," 151.

41. Emmanuel Levinas, *Totality and Infinity: An Essay on Exteriority*, trans. Alphonso Lingis (Pittsburgh: Duquesne UP, 1969), 27.

42. Emmanuel Levinas, "Ethics as First Philosophy," trans. Seán Hand and Michael Temple, in *The Levinas Reader*, ed. Seán Hand (Oxford: Basil Blackwell, 1989), 79.

43. It has been the subject of a significant controversy whether this insistence on the exteriority of the other does not lead to empiricism. In response to this question, John Llewelyn argues that Levinas and Derrida can maintain the paradoxical exteriority of the other with respect to being by deconstructing "the ontic metaphors of priority and transgression." "Levinas, Derrida and Others Vis-à-vis," in *The Provocation of Levinas: Rethinking the Other*, ed. Robert Bernasconi and David Wood (New York: Routledge, 1988), 145–154.

44. Emmanuel Levinas, "Wholly Otherwise," trans. Simon Critchley, *Re-Reading Levinas*, 5.

45. Bernasconi, "Skepticism in the Face of Philosophy," 151.

46. Emmanuel Levinas, "Wholly Otherwise," 5–6.

47. Emmanuel Levinas, "The Trace of the Other," trans. A. Lingis, in *Deconstruction in Context*, ed. Mark Taylor (Chicago: U of Chicago P, 1986), 348.

48. Levinas, "The Trace of the Other," 350.

49. For a detailed discussion of the "semantics" of alterity, see Krzysztof Ziarek, "Semantics of Proximity: Language and the Other in the Philosophy of Emmanuel Levinas," in *Research in Phenomenology* 19 (1989): 213–247.

50. Jill Robbins, *Prodigal Son/Elder Brother: Interpretation and Alterity in Augustine, Petrarch, Kafka, Levinas* (Chicago: U of Chicago P, 1991), 107. Presenting the most sustained articulation of Levinas's ethics in the context of the alterity of Judaism, Robbins argues that there is a profound connection between Levinasian re-reading of the forgotten ethical question in the context of the phenomenological tradition and his unreading of the negative interpretation of the Judaic in the Greco-Christian tradition.

51. This thesis is advanced for instance by George Chatalian, *Epistemology and Skepticism: An Enquiry into the Nature of Epistemology, Journal of the History of Philosophy* Monograph Series (Carbondale and Edwardsville: Southern Illinois UP, 1991), 1–12. He argues that since the turn of the century the analytic philosophy has given rise to the new conception of epistemology, "the conception that epistemology is to be defined and otherwise explained in terms of philosophical skepticism," 1.

52. D. W. Hamlyn, "Epistemology, History of," in *The Encyclopedia of Philosophy*, ed. Paul Edwards (New York: Macmillan, 1967), 3:8–9, emphasis added. Also quoted in Chatalian, *Epistemology and Skepticism*, 2–3.

53. For an example of this widespread view, see S. J. Wilmore, "Skepticism and Deconstruction," 437–455.

54. I cannot here do justice to Derrida's elaborate reading of Rousseau's text. For more detailed interpretations, see, for instance, Irene E. Harvey, "Doubling the Space of Existence: Exemplarity in Derrida—The Case of Rousseau," in *Deconstruction and Philosophy: The Texts of Jacques Derrida*, ed. John Sallis (Chicago: U of Chicago P, 1987), 60–70; and Christopher Norris, "Rousseau: Writing as Necessary Evil," *Derrida* , 97–141. For an excellent discussion of supplementarity as an "infrastructure," see Rodolphe Gasché, *The Tain of the Mirror*, 142–154, 205–212.

55. Many of Derrida's commentators point to these contradictory significations attached to the word *pharmakon*. For instance Christopher Norris notes that *pharmakon* "belongs to that same paradoxical system that can take a single word . . . and invest it with meaning so sharply opposed as to render its senses undecidable in any given context." *Derrida*, 42.

56. For an admirably lucid discussion of Derrida's treatment of these topics, see Walter Brogan, "Plato's *Pharmakon*: Between Two Repetitions," *Continental Philosophy II: Derrida and Deconstruction*, ed. Hugh J. Silverman (New York: Routledge, 1989), 7–23.

57. Jürgen Habermas, *The Philosophical Discourse of Modernity*, 295–296.

58. This discussion has been focused somewhat too narrowly on the issue of citationality and on the distinction between the serious and non-serious, i.e., parasitical, forms of speech acts. In his critique of Derrida, John Searl contends that Derrida confuses the difference. See his "Reiterating the Differences: A Reply to Derrida," in *Glyph* 1 (1977): 198–208. For Derrida's response, see "Limited, Inc." in *Glyph* 2 (1977): 162–254. For an illuminating reading of Austin-Derrida-Searl exchange, see Jonathan Culler, *On Deconstruction: Theory and Criticism after Structuralism* (Ithaca: Cornell UP, 1982), 110–134.

59. As Stanley Cavell suggests, Austin's discussion of ordinary language is also motivated by a refutation of skepticism, (especially in his famous paper "Other Minds"). "Austin and Examples," in *The Claim of Reason: Wittgenstein, Skepticism, Morality, and Tragedy* (Oxford: Oxford UP, 1979), 49–65.

60. As Jonathan Culler suggests, this structure of iteration can be described as "the combination of context-bound meaning and boundless context." Jonathan Culler, *On Deconstruction: Theory and Criticism after Structuralism*, 133.

61. Derrida makes this point in "Ulysses Gramophone," 63. I will discuss the notion of the performative force elaborated in this essay in the last part of this chapter.

62. See in particular her "The 'Postmodern' Challenge to the Ideal of Community," in *The Philosophy of the Limit*, 39–61.

63. As Jean-Luc Nancy argues, this nostalgia for the lost community is constitutive of the philosophical discourse on community: "at every moment of its history, the Occident has given itself over to the nostalgia for a more archaic community that has disappeared, and to deploring a loss of familiarity, fraternity and conviviality." *The Inoperative Community*, ed. Peter Connor,

trans. Peter Connor, Lisa Garbus, Michael Holland, and Simona Sawhney (Minneapolis: U of Minnesota P, 1991), 10.

64. Charles Altieri, *Act and Quality*, 38.

65. Christopher Butler, *Interpretation, Deconstruction, and Ideology*, 21.

66. Butler, 22.

67. Habermas, *The Philosophical Discourse of Modernity*, 190.

68. See, for example, Fredric Jameson, "The Ideology of the Text," in *Salmagundi* 31/32 (1975/76): 204–46.

69. Habermas's critique of deconstruction represents, for instance, just the opposite view to Jochen Schulte-Sasse's reading of Derrida's theory of language as one of the most powerful articulations of literary modernism and, at the same time, as a symptom of modern art's separation from social linguistic practice. Schulte-Sasse argues that Derrida's "epistemological project of pointing out metaphysical closures in any discourse" "fails to relate art to social praxis." Jochen Schulte-Sasse, "Foreword," in Peter Bürger, *Theory of the Avant-Garde*, trans. Michael Shaw (Minneapolis: U of Minnesota P, 1984), xxiii.

70. John Llewelyn, "Responsibility with Undecidability," in *Derrida: A Critical Reader*, ed. David Wood (Oxford: Blackwell, 1992), 92

71. Rodolphe Gasché, "Quasi-Metaphoricity and the Question of Being," in *Hermeneutics and Deconstruction*, ed. Hugh Silverman and Don Ihde (Albany: SUNY P, 1985), 167.

72. According to the classical definition in Aristotle's *Poetics*, "metaphor is the application of an alien name by transference either from genus to species, or from species to genus, or from species to species, or by analogy, that is proportion." *Aristotle's Poetics* (xxi, 4–5), trans. S. H. Butcher (New York: Hill and Wang, 1961).

73. For the connection between the figure and mimesis in the philosophical tradition see also, Andrew Benjamin, *Art, Mimesis and the Avant-Garde: Aspects of a Philosophy of Difference* (London and New York: Routledge, 1991), 13-30.

74. This point has been persuasively argued by Gasché in his "Quasi-Metaphoricity and the Question of Being," 177-184.

75. The ethico-political consequences of difference have been most powerfully addressed and developed by Gayatri Chakravorty Spivak's work. See for instance her *In Other Worlds: Essays in Cultural Politics* (New York: Routledge, 1988), 103–117.

76. For Derrida's reading of Joyce, see also his "Two Words for Joyce," in *Post-Structuralist Joyce: Essays from the French*, ed. Derek Attridge and Daniel Ferrer (Cambridge: Cambridge UP, 1984), 145–59. Probably the most famous of Derrida's essays dealing with the question of literary language in the more general context of the relation between philosophy and literature is his work on Mallarmé, "The Double Session," in *Dissemination*, 173–286.

77. Derrida in interview with Kearney, *Dialogues with Contemporary Continental Thinkers*, 100.

78. The distinction between the performative and constative dimension of language is derived from J. L. Austin *How to Do Things with Words* (Cambridge: Harvard UP, 1975), 2–22. Unlike Derrida, however, Austin restricts the discussion of the performative aspect of language to the first person utterances and therefore makes it dependent on the intention of the speaker. For an excellent account of Derrida's engagement with Austin and the speech-act theory, see Jonathan Culler, *On Deconstruction,* 110–134.

79. For Levinas's analysis of welcome, see in particular the section "Habitation and the Feminine" and "The Freedom of Representation and Gift," in *Totality and Infinity: An Essay on Exteriority,* 154–156, 168–173.

80. Although I continue to draw parallels between Levinas's and Derrida's discussion of otherness, I would like to mention their different stand with respect to figurative language. If Derrida elaborates the interconnection between literary language and the affirmation of otherness, Levinas, especially in his early writings, keeps the two opposed to each other. See, for instance, his controversial essay "Reality and Its Shadow," in *The Levinas Reader,* 129–144. I owe this reference to Levinas's early discussion of figurative language in "Reality and Its Shadow" to Jill Robbins.

81. It is not by accident that Derrida refers to *Ulysses,* and especially to the famous passage "Jewgreek is Greekjew. Extremes meet," in the context of Levinas's ethical paradigms represented by the figures of Abraham and Ulysses: "Are we Greeks? Are we Jews? But who, we? . . . And does the strange dialogue between the Jew and the Greek, peace itself, have the form of the absolute, speculative logic of Hegel . . . ? Or, on the contrary, does this peace have the form of infinite separation and of the unthinkable, unsayable transcendence of the other?" "Violence and Metaphysics," in *Writing and Difference,* 153.

82. For the relation between figurality and translation, see Andrew Benjamin, "The Literal and the Figural Translated," in *Translation and the Nature of Philosophy: A New Theory of Words* (London: Routledge, 1989), 9–38.

83. Derrida further discusses the effects of the Babelization and the essential incompleteness of discourse, in his essay "Des Tours de Babel," trans. Joseph F. Graham, in *Difference in Translation,* ed. Joseph F. Graham (Ithaca: Cornell UP, 1985), 165–207.

84. What is usually quoted at this point is the following famous passage:

There are thus two interpretations of interpretation, of structure, of sign, of play. The one seeks to decipher, dreams of deciphering a truth or an origin which escapes play and the order of the sign, and which lives the necessity of interpretation as an exile. The other which is no longer turned toward origin, affirms play and tries to pass beyond man . . . the name of man being the name of that being who . . . throughout his entire history . . . has dreamed of full presence, the reassuring foundation, the origin and the end of play [SSP, 292].

4

"The Beauty of Failure": Kafka and Benjamin on the Task of Transmission and Translation

"On Parables": Exemplarity, Transmissibility, Figuration

Kafka's short pieces have been frequently characterized as parables[1] and, just as frequently, this term has been contested, modified, or rejected as inappropriate. What is at stake in this terminological discussion is a relation between literary language and the exemplary function of the parable, between rhetoric and the revelation of truth. This relationship has been most frequently defined in negative terms, as if one of the main effects of the rhetorical surplus of language were the impossibility of truth. Yet, if Kafka's parables do not just renounce their exemplary function, if they do not leave us only with negative knowledge, then we need to account for a certain negative rhetoric deployed so frequently both in Kafka's texts and in Kafka criticism. Although the production of exemplary sense is undercut in Kafka's parables by their ostensible rhetoric of failure, Kafka's texts, as Walter Benjamin reminds us, do not merely dramatize the inaccessibility of truth but redefine the very function of rhetoric in terms of a paradoxical task, or an impossible obligation of transmission. This rethinking of rhetoric is intertwined with a critique of the often opposite tendencies of modern aesthetics: the autonomy of the work of art and the nostalgia for the lost community. By preserving the sense of obligation, the rhetoric of Kafka's parables contests not only the autonomy of the work of art— what Benjamin calls "a negative theology" of pure art deprived of any social function—but also a reductive understanding of the social function of aesthetics, in particular, a nostalgic longing for the common being.

Before we try to account for the effects of Kafka's peculiar mimicry of parabolic form, we should discuss briefly the exemplary function of the traditional parable. The parable is usually situated between the exemplary tale or the transparent allegory intended to illustrate the general truth of the doctrine on the one hand, and the enigmatic riddle on the other.[2] In the Judeo-Christian tradition, the parable is a traditional tool of exegesis of the Scriptures, or a means to reveal a moral or spiritual truth.[3] Midrash, for example, offers several parables on parables illustrating this hermeneutical function: a parable is like a man cutting a path through a thicket of reeds; it is like a handle with which an unwieldy chest or a jug of boiling water can be carried; it functions as rope with which cold and sweet water can be brought from a well.[4] As all these passages imply, the parable carves a way to the understanding of truth, it functions as a "tool" without which some spiritual or moral insight would not be brought to light.

In biblical hermeneutics, the issue of exemplarity has been a perennial problem, posing difficulties about the proper interpretation of parables. Because the exemplary character of the parable is by no means evident, it can be grasped only through an elaborate process of interpretation. According to the peculiar "theory" of parables in Mark, chapter 4, for example, teaching in parables illuminates but at the same time delays understanding: "Unto you it is given to know the mystery of the kingdom of God: but unto them that are without, all these things are done in parables: That seeing they may see, and not perceive; and hearing they may hear, and not understand" [Mark 4:11–12]. On religious grounds, such a deferral of understanding can be recuperated by some form of eschatology, whereas in the secular text the delay becomes interminable.[5] When a biblical parable dramatizes a delay in understanding, it nonetheless orients the text toward a general truth, toward a promised revelation, even if this revelation remains hidden or postponed. In Mark 4, for instance, the temporal postponement of revelation is eventually neutralized by the spatial split of audience: parables perpetuate the division between those who comprehend and those who fail to do so, between those who can read the spiritual sense and those who stumble on the parable's intentional unreadability.[6] As Jean Starobinski remarks in his interpretation of Mark 4, the teaching in parables preserves a "nonreception of the message," by creating "a cleavage between those who understand" and those who are kept outside understanding.[7]

The relation between the temporality of rhetoric and enigmatic revelation is of particular importance in Kafka's parables. Although placing Kafka in the context of parable is a familiar critical gesture (see Benjamin, Frank Kermode, and J. Hillis Miller among others), Kafka's interpreters feel obliged to provide certain negative qualifications because of the transcendental/theological weight that the traditional term implies. Theodor Adorno, for instance, argues that Kafka's parables signify not "through expression but its repudiation;"[8] Wilhelm Emrich claims that they empty out the classical notion of the universal;[9] and Heinz Politzer suggests that they are organized around a paradox.[10] Certainly, Emrich's and Politzer's approaches complicate or even deflate the content of the "transcendental," or the "universal," in Kafka's works, but their analyses leave the binary structure (example/general truth) intact.

According to Politzer's influential and well-established interpretation, for instance, Kafka's parables reveal the impossibility of translating the transcendental into ordinary language. This impossibility, this negative revelation of truth, constitutes a paradox at the core of the parable:

> Such a paradox will be generated wherever *the natural* and *the supernatural* meet, that is, when a message which is inaccessible to ordinary verbalization is to be *translated* into the vernacular of reasonable and generally intelligible communication . . . . Circling around this nucleus, they maintain a suspense originating in the never defined *relation their actual plots maintain with their backgrounds* (emphasis added).[11]

What is symptomatic about this reading is that the crisis of exemplarity—or what Politzer calls a paradox—is articulated in terms of an aborted transmission. The loss or inaccessibility of truth in Kafka's parables is expressed in the figure of a failed translation. Yet Politzer's emphasis on the *failure* of translation in Kafka's texts still preserves the notion of truth that is not only inaccessible to but also independent of "ordinary" language. This truth cannot be known but it leaves an imprint on the text by fragmenting and splintering its language. Although Politzer is very perceptive of "clefts, cracks, and crevices" in Kafka's parables, these incongruities of rhetoric merely imply a negative relation to the transcendental.[12] Therefore, instead of illustrating the transcendental, the parable bears the evidence of the "incompatible meeting," of the antithetical relation between the quotidian language and the esoteric truth. In Politzer's reading, skepticism about ordinary language remains in complicity with the affirmation of time-less truth "inaccessible to ordinary verbalization." With the emphasis on the inaccessible transcendental or on the emptiness of traditional exemplary forms, this strain of Kafka criticism in fact perpetuates both the notion of linguistic skepticism and the concept of truth distinct and separate from the process of signification.

It is all the more remarkable that Benjamin, one of the first Kafka critics, accounts for Kafka's resistance toward the transcendental with-out either resorting to a negative revelation of truth or simply accept-ing the idea of the "immanence of the text."[13] In his 1934 essay, "Franz Kafka: On the Tenth Anniversary of His Death," and four years later in his programmatic letter to Gershom Scholem (included in the English edition of *Illuminations* as "Some Reflections on Kafka"),[14] Benjamin likewise situates Kafka's prose in the tradition of Hasidic parables, and points to its deficiency in illustrating moral or spiritual teaching. Although Benjamin too admits that the negative characteri-zation of Kafka's parables is probably more rewarding, at the same time he warns us that this negativity of Kafka's texts can be easily mis-read.[15] In his 1934 essay, Benjamin diagnoses this misreading in terms of either a "supernatural" or a "natural" interpretation: "There are two ways to miss the point of Kafka's works. One is to interpret them nat-urally, the other is the supernatural interpretation. Both the psychoan-alytic and the theological interpretations equally miss the essential points" [*I*, 127]. Four years later, Benjamin finds even his own reading of Kafka too apologetic. This time Benjamin sees the deficiency of Kafka's parables explicitly as their failure to transmit truth and argues that in order to "do justice to the figure of Kafka," it is essential to con-front the significance of this failure without apologies.

As Benjamin points out, Kafka, of course, is not the first modern writer to face the loss of truth and the disintegration of tradition. Skepticism about truth and language can be said to describe the con-dition of modernity in general. Yet, whereas other writers "cling" to the loss of truth (by expressing this loss in the form of paradox, empty universal, or linguistic skepticism, we might add), Kafka entirely rede-fines the significance of this loss:

> It is this consistency of truth that has been lost. Kafka was far from being the first to face this situation . . . . Kafka's real genius was that he tried something entirely new: he sacrificed truth for the sake of clinging to its transmissibility, its haggadic element [I, 143–144].

In this brief but remarkable insight, Benjamin stakes his understanding of Kafka's writings and of Kafka's modernity (the sense in which Kafka "tried something entirely new") on his reinterpretation of the very old concept of failure.[16] Reading "failure" in Kafka's parables in a way directly opposite to Politzer (and to the majority of Kafka criticism), Benjamin argues that Kafka's focus on the temporality of linguistic transport of meaning eventually aims to destroy the metaphysical concept of timeless truth separate from the mechanism of signification. Consequently, what Kafka's "failure" exposes is not the inaccessibility of truth but the fact that the very idea of truth is one of the effects produced by language. In this shift from the lost truth to temporal transmission, from the failed illustration to transformation, Benjamin attempts to redefine the effects of rhetoric beyond negative epistemology.

As Benjamin suggests, rhetoric understood as transmissibility is not a counterpart of illustration or a faithful preservation of truth but a linguistic movement that actively trans-forms and de-forms the meaning of the text. Since transmissibility is a process of deformation, it leaves Kafka's interpreters in a position of "pupils who have lost the Holy Writ." Instead of providing the law for the journey of interpretation, Kafka wants the journey itself to find its own law. This is at least the way Benjamin reads Kafka's "law of the journey [*das Gesetz der Fahrt*]": a route of unexpected reversals and distortions that derange causal connections between origins and destinations, wishes and fulfillments, annunciation of messages and their reception [*I*, 139].[17] Without a guiding law or a destination, this temporal movement of Kafka's parables is, however, still tied to a sense of obligation. It requires "attentive listening" to the "indistinct sounds" even though these sounds can no longer be recuperated into knowledge or meaning. Because of this attentiveness—which is perhaps only an openness to the past that can no longer be recuperated or to the future that cannot yet be seen—Benjamin stakes transmissibility against the recuperation of truth and its oblivion.

According to Benjamin, Kafka's "law of the journey" is best expressed in a short parable, entitled "The Truth about Sancho Panza" (*Die Wahrheit über Sancho Panza*). After reading chivalric romances, Sancho separates himself from and then sends ahead his tormenting demon, which becomes forever diverted from its "preordained object." Sancho, a philosophic fool who manages to transform the tradition of the chivalric romances, and in the meantime to get rid of "the burden from his back," follows his demon "perhaps out of sense of responsibility" but derives nonetheless a healthy entertainment from such unconstrained wandering. As the story emphasizes, it is an experience of reading that unexpectedly transforms the relationship between the demon and Sancho Panza. Instead of truth, reading imposes a sense of responsibility and offers a sense of relief—and both of these seemingly incompatible senses are the effects generated by a loss of a "preordained object."

Quite a different figuration of detachment from the origin of truth can be found in a very short text entitled "Couriers" (*Kuriere*). Yet here, too, such detachment not only functions as the condition of transmissibility but also imposes strange obligation. In this text, couriers, representative of the whole class of Kafka messengers, endlessly repeat messages that seem to become meaningless because no one wants to play the king dispatching information. The king functions here as a figure of authority and origin, the one who commands the messenger to repeat his message to the people. The authority of this figure is a guarantee of the consistency of both the message and its transmission. This disregard for the absolute source of meaning may cause the messages to become meaningless, but it does not remove the couriers' obligation of transmission: "They (the couriers) would like to put an end to this miserable life of theirs but they dare not because of their oath of service."[18] Paradoxically, the work and obligation of transmission resumes at the very moment when the origin of meaning is emptied out.

With the king missing in the game from the outset, the couriers—the figures of transmissibility *par excellence*—not only repeat but also produce the messages they carry. Furthermore, they themselves invent the role of the missing king in the first place—it is a part of their game. Since the text evokes the opposition between the king and the couriers, between the origin of truth and its transmission, only to destroy it, the inaccessible origin does not bespeak the failure of transmission but is, in fact, one of its effects. We can read this shift from the figure of the king to the figure of couriers as a peculiar reversal of priority between origin and address, source and destination. No longer tied to the repetition of truth, the couriers' obligation (which they cannot relinquish) is figured therefore as a performative address occurring prior to any revelation or any intention to signify. This predicament of Kafka's couriers may exemplify just what "transmissibility in the absence of truth," in Benjamin's sense, signifies. One additional point should be stressed here: if the couriers' obligation evokes a sense of anxiety, Sancho's story is an example of a joyful playfulness. These two parables are, therefore, symptomatic of ambivalent responses in Kafka's texts to the "sacrifice of truth for the sake of transmissibility."

Benjamin's focus on transmission in Kafka's parables is by no means accidental—it is one of the main concerns in his own writing.[19] Whether it is art collecting, translation, reproduction, or the citationality of history, Benjamin offers a minute analysis of the effects of transmission. In order to understand more precisely the effects of transmissibility, it is essential to refer to Benjamin's two famous essays "The Task of the Translator" (*Die Aufgabe des Übersetzers*, 1923) and "The Work of Art in the Age of Mechanical Reproduction" (*Das Kunstwerk im Zeitalter seiner technischen Reproduzierbarkeit*, 1936). Although these essays analyze two different kinds of "transmissibility" and deploy diametrically opposed rhetoric— the discussion of translation apparently calls for a rhetoric of organicism and kinship between languages, whereas reproduction of the work of art deploys a rhetoric of mechanization—the process of transmission makes these distinctions hard to maintain. Despite the difference in their approaches, both texts focus upon a certain kind of iterability that drastically changes the meaning of the original, its structure, and its relation to history.[20]

"The sacrifice of truth for the sake of transmissibility" in fact quite accurately describes what happens with the meaning of the original in the process of translation. Not surprisingly, one of the main questions Paul de Man asks about "The Task of the Translator" concerns the function of failure in Benjamin's essay: "the question then becomes why this failure with regard to an original text, to an original poet, is for Benjamin *exemplary.*"[21] Inadvertently echoing Benjamin's reading of Kafka, de Man likewise suggests that in order "to do justice to the figure" of Benjamin and his relationship to modernity, one needs to do justice to his peculiar understanding of failure. In both readings (in Benjamin's reading of Kafka and in de Man's of Benjamin), the question of failure, insofar as it is one of the main effects of transmissibility, is intertwined with a redefinition of both language and modernity. As de Man suggests, this strategic use of failure allows for a departure from the notion of modernity as a critical overcoming of the past.[22] In place of either overcoming or preserving the past, Benjamin, we might say, defines the task of modernity by repeating Kafka's posture of "attentive listening" to the dispersed rumors of tradition without assembling them into a fullness of meaning.

From the outset, Benjamin insists that translation aims to restore neither the meaning nor the "poetry" of the original, neither its semantic nor its aesthetic quality. In fact what the process of translation reveals is that meaning or message is not essential even in the original: "Its essential quality is not statement or the imparting of information [*Ihr Wesentliches ist nicht Mitteilung, nicht Aussage*]" [*I*, 69]. Therefore, "any translation which intends to perform a transmitting function cannot transmit anything but information—hence, *something inessential*" [*I*, 69, emphasis added]. If translatability manifests the special significance of the original, how are we to understand this manifestation, which renders the original's meaning as "something inessential"? Such a striking conclusion is possible because Benjamin departs from the traditional theory of translation based on the likeness between languages and replaces it with a notion of their kinship based on complementarity: "translation thus ultimately serves the purpose of expressing the central reciprocal relationship between languages" [I, 72]. Like the obligation of Kafka's couriers, the task of translation, then, is not to reproduce the meaning of the original but to complement its intentions and, thus, to mark the temporality of its historical existence.

In the context of his theory of translation, Benjamin articulates transmissibility not as a reproduction or preservation of truth but rather as a temporal and disruptive process of supplementation, which radically transforms the relation between language and meaning. If in the original, language and signification appear to be as closely related as are the fruit and its skin, in translation meaning is only "loosely" attached to its language, which in its excess resembles "ample folds" of the royal robe. This destruction of the "natural" bond between meaning and language, which eventually proves language "unsuited to its content, overpowering and alien," is the main effect of translatability.[23] As the contrast between the figures of the fruit and the royal robe implies, the supplementary work of transmission not only reveals the excess of language but also changes the entire conception of language: no longer natural, language assumes the character of the social artifice.

Such a linguistic transformation has far-reaching consequences for modern aesthetics. Resembling the effects of the Baroque allegory, translation utterly destroys the conception of the organicist unity of the work of art—in the anticipation of Benjamin's argument in "The Work of Art in the Age of Mechanical Reproduction," we can say that translation destroys the *aura* of the original. In translation the work does not even remotely resemble the organic unity of the fruit and the skin, but instead appears as a fragment of pure language, as a broken part of the vessel.[24] However, since translatability, according to Benjamin, is always already an essential quality of the original, translation cannot disrupt the original unity of meaning or the organic wholeness of the original merely from the outside; instead it supplements or intensifies the "intentions" already inherent in the original work of art.

The effects of "failure" or "sacrifice of truth" performed by translation cannot be confined, however, only to the realm of aesthetics. The process of translation not only disrupts the unity of the original, not only shatters the natural bond between language and meaning, but also destroys a certain nostalgic notion of the linguistic community. Thus, even in this early essay, Benjamin's focus on the excess of language does not lead to aestheticism but examines, if only tacitly, its social implications. Benjamin argues that translation can manifest the kinship between the languages only when it inscribes their foreignness and incompleteness within its own language. A good translation, therefore, allows its own native tongue to turn into a foreign one.[25] That is why the task of the poet and that of the translator are very different: whereas the poet is still concerned with the "immediacy" of meaning, the translator transforms his native language in its totality, and therefore shifts the weight from the subjective to the collective conditions of enunciation. Repeating in an uncanny way the terms of Benjamin's interpretation of Kafka, de Man reads this transformation of the native tongue as the "errancy of language": "this movement of the original is a wandering, an *errance*, a kind of permanent exile if you wish, but it is not really an exile, for there is no homeland."[26] De Man does not pursue this topic further, yet his focus on the condition of "permanent exile" calls attention to the crucial issue raised in Benjamin's essay: the effects of translation on the linguistic community. Although Benjamin insists that translation should not concern itself directly with questions of communication, audience, or readers, the act of translation, by inscribing difference into the native language, questions the very ethos of the common and the shared, and eventually destroys the immanence of the common being. With its emphasis on the differential, fragmentary, and inorganic character of languages, Benjamin's theory of translation can be seen as the antithesis of the community based on the natural and intimate common bonds. As an antidote to the modernist nostalgia for the being in common, translation becomes a safeguard of sorts against the complicity of this nostalgia with fascism.[27] Consequently, translation not only questions the organicist concept of the work of art but also the organicist notion of a unified linguistic community—community of speech without difference or artifice. If, as Benjamin suggests, translation can be seen as a form of criticism, then this criticism intervenes into the aestheticization of linguistic community—or what Benjamin calls, in "The Work of Art in the Age of Mechanical Reproduction," the aestheticization of politics.

Benjamin argues that translation interrupts the linguistic immanence of a given community because it liberates the effects of pure language from the "weight" of the particular meaning: "It is the task of the translator . . . to liberate the language *imprisoned in a work in his re-creation of that work*" [*I*, 80, emphasis added].[28] Again the essay resorts to a metaphor to describe the effects of such liberation. As a circle touched by a tangent, translation "touches the original lightly and only at the infinitely small point of the sense," in order to pursue "its own course according to the laws of fidelity in the freedom of linguistic flux [*so berührt die Übersetzung flüchtig und nur in dem unendlich kleinen Punkte des Sinnes das Original, um nach dem Gesetze der Treue in der Freiheit der Sprachbewegung ihre eigene Bahn zu verfolgen*]" [*I*, 80].[29] This last metaphor is also the most startling depiction of what Benjamin means by "the sacrifice of truth for the sake of transmissibility." As it is with his analysis of Kafka's parables, here too Benjamin stresses the "law of the journey," that is, the trajectory, the path (*Bahn*) and the temporal movement of language, and not the origin or destination, not *Punkte des Sinnes*. Yet it is precisely this transformation of linguistic norms and conventions in the direction of pure language that consti-tutes both the task and the threat of translation—silence and the loss of meaning in the "bottomless depth of language":

> Hölderlin's translations in particular are subject to the enormous danger inherent in all translations (and transmissibility as such, we might add): the gates of a language thus *expanded and modified* may slam shut and enclose the translator with silence [*I*, 81, emphasis added].

The beauty of Kafka's parables, like the beauty of Hölderlin's transla-tions, both of which Benjamin so admires, lies in a similar estrange-ment and extension of language beyond the shared linguistic norms and the commonality of linguistic criteria.

A similar dissolution of the context and disintegration of meaning is performed by the other kind of transmissibility—what Benjamin calls mechanical reproduction. Like translation, mechanical reproduc-tion detaches an object from its original place and time within the tra-dition and substitutes for its unique existence a plurality of copies that can circulate in a multiplicity of new historical situations. Although this transposition of contexts reactivates the reproduced object, retain-ing thus the minimum of its identity, at the same time it shatters the "authenticity," or the *aura*, of the work of art as well as the consisten-cy of tradition [*I*, 221]. Like translation, reproduction does not affect the stability of the work of art merely from the outside, especially in the case of new art, for example film and photography, that is already "designed for reproducibility." Consequently, the process of reproduction not only does not preserve the integrity of the original but entails a radical revision of the traditional aesthetic categories such as authenticity, the organic concept of the *work* of art, and the disinterested contemplation of art.

Although transmissibility questions the very concepts of origin, authenticity, and truth, this does not mean that the significance of the work of art collapses either into linguistic skepticism or into aestheticism. On the contrary, as Benjamin makes clear, the disintegration of the aura destroys the aesthetic distance, that is, the separateness or the autonomy of the work of art, and therefore opens up a possibility for the politicization of art. And yet, because of the radical fragmentation and heterogeneity of the reproduced art, its meaning cannot be absorbed or contemplated in the process of reception. Because reproducibility causes dispersion of meaning, Benjamin relates reception of the work of art to the shock effect. Consequently, even though reproduction destroys separateness or the distance of the work of art, this does not entail an assimilation of art into social praxis but rather a disintegration of the cultural and social context in which the work of art is received.[30] It is this disruption of the social and linguistic immanence that opens a possibility of critical revision of both aesthetics and social praxis.

Both kinds of transmissibility—translation or mechanical reproduction—have a similar shattering effect on the consistency of tradition and truth: they perform a fragmentation of meaning by displacing the work of art from its linguistic or historical context. Whereas the relation of exemplification implies the stability of the context or system in which an example is imbedded (the dependence of an example on a general truth or idea), transmissibility dissolves such stability by revealing an irreducible temporal interval between example and truth. By insisting on a disjunction between transmissibility and truth, Benjamin, in spite of the rhetoric of kinship, puts into question both the primacy of origin and the continuity of derivation.[31] This loss of the consistency of truth, and the subsequent loss of the unity and integrity of meaning, is linked, for Benjamin, both to the sense of obligation and to the possibility of critical intervention.

Benjamin's theory of translation not only illuminates but perhaps is in turn informed by Kafka's parables. Can we say that Kafka's works already include their own intralinear translation? (In his "The Task of the Translator," Benjamin suggests that most of the great works of art do so.) Such a statement of course cannot mean that Kafka's parables lay special claim to completeness but rather that they initiate the process of violent transformation, which brackets the norms of the common language and questions the mastery of the native speakers. Benjamin's emphasis on the estrangement of the familiar language, on the shattering of the myth of the mother tongue and of the nostalgia for a community, describes in fact not only Benjamin's own complicated relationship to German culture but also Kafka's. As Kafka writes in a well-known letter to Max Brod, his multilingual predicament—a Jewish writer writing in German and living in Prague—results in "three impossibilities":

> They existed among three impossibilities, which I just happen to call linguistic impossibilities . . . These are: The impossibility of not writing, the impossibility of writing German, the impossibility of writing differently. One might also add a fourth impossibility, the impossibility of writing . . . Thus what resulted was a literature impossible in all respects, a gypsy literature which had stolen the German child out of its cradle. . . .[32]

A stranger in every language, Kafka literally writes under the exigency of translation, which makes the traditional concept of literature "impossible in all respects."

Such "gypsy" writing, which violates linguistic norms of propriety and property, allows us to rethink the notion of literary language and its relationship to truth and to linguistic community. The characteristic movement of Kafka's parables and their problematic destination is perhaps most explicitly addressed in two very famous texts, "On Parables" (*Von den Gleichnissen*) and "My Destination" (*Das Ziel*). The first text, "On Parables,"[33] is structured around the opposition between the wise, who can speak their wisdom only in parables, and the "many," who complain that such words of wisdom are without use in everyday life. The dispute concerns two different concepts of language: The many insist that language should have a clear referential status, and that it should remain "closely" embedded in community and social praxis. The words of the wise, on the other hand, disrupt this closeness and familiarity by performing the act of crossing over to "something unknown to us," to "some fabulous yonder." Parables may be the words of wisdom, but useless and deadly wisdom because they do not bring the truth closer [*näher*] to us, to our life. On the contrary, parables separate language from the immediacy of the here and now, from life, and from the expression of the singular or collective subject. Contrary to the expectations of the anonymous listeners, the parabolic language questions the unproblematic relation between literary language, everyday practice, and the familiarity of the communal bonds. Consequently, parables do not intend to "translate" truth into an ordinary language, but rather estrange the familiar language so that the stability of linguistic and communal norms can no longer be taken for granted:

> When the sage says: "Go over" *[Gehe hinüber]*, he does not mean that we should cross to some actual place *[die andere Seite]*, . . . ; he means some fabulous yonder *[sagenhaftes Drüben]*, something unknown to us, something too that he cannot designate more precisely *[das auch von ihm nicht näher zu bezeichnen ist*—literally, more closely] and therefore cannot help us *here* in the very least *[PP*, 10–11, emphasis mine].

This complaint of the "many" might arise from an unexpected difference between the parables and the traditional examples, which precisely are supposed to make the truth immediately intuitable, to make it appear in the proximity of our understanding. As Kant writes in the preface to the *Critique of Practical Reason*, examples do not introduce anything new to our knowledge, but they have the important pedagogical role of manifesting the truth in the immediacy of the here and now. By dissociating the obligation of transmission from the pedagogical tasks, Kafka's parables take us away from knowing, from progressing to a precise destination, or from any sense of destination at all. Disrupting the familiarity of linguistic norms, the act of crossing performed by parables merely displaces us from what is familiar and does not promise in return any specific location where the movement of the parable would come to rest. Instead of the proximity of truth, it increases the temporal distance between the words and their meaning—even the sage cannot indicate the direction of the parable "more closely." Since this movement severs language from "the life we have," the adverb *hinüber*, indicates the direction of death, which—like the silence in Hölderlin's translations or the emblem of the skull in baroque allegory—is the ultimate loss of signification. The movement of the parable, its perpetual "going over," undermines proper meaning, the stability of linguistic norms, and the possession of truth in everyday life. Not only are the parables unable to "help" us here in our daily life, but this loss of referential meaning is not compensated by any promise of transcendental wisdom.

This relentless crossing that the parable performs does not leave the initial distinction between the parable and reality (*Wirklichkeit*) intact. The reality in Kafka's text is associated with the set of values based on life, property, pragmatic knowledge, practical results, and the immediacy of the here and now. In the context of such values, parables appear to disclose only negative wisdom: they "merely say that the incomprehensible is incomprehensible," and therefore seem to be deprived of any social relevance. Although it is tempting to read Kafka's figuration of the parabolic language as a manifestation of the complete dissociation of the work of art from the social praxis, such a reading would in fact contain the effects of disruption and limit them to the level of aesthetics. However, the transgressive power of the parables does not allow them either to rest in the negative knowledge of skepticism or to confine that negativity to aesthetics alone. As the ending of the text shows, any clear sense of distinction between reality and the parable, between the aesthetics and social praxis, disappears. The desire to separate the disturbing effects of the parable from reality becomes a matter of gambling, which may bring a gain for the sake of reality, but always a loss in the parable.

So what happens when we follow the parables? The interpreters themselves become "incomprehensible" parables, propelled away from their own self-presence and self-understanding. Consequently, the parable questions not only social but also subjective knowledge:

> If you only followed the parables you yourselves would become parables and with that rid of all your daily cares.

> *Würdet ihr den Gleichnissen folgen, dann wäret ihr selbst Gleichnisse geworden und damit schon der täglichen Mühe frei.* [PP, 10–11]

This problematic destination (*das Ziel*) of Kafka's parables and their enigmatic promise of freedom is elucidated in a very short text, "My Destination" (*Das Ziel*), whose main character can be read as the one who follows the parables. It is a story of a master who prepares for a "truly long journey." However, the only destination that he wants to reach is to be out-of-reach, always Away-From-Here: "'*Weg-von-hier,' das ist mein Ziel*" [PP, 188]. In a very peculiar twist of the familiar causal relations, destination is described only in terms of a displacement from the present site, or a disruption of immanence. Ironically, the parable undermines any teleological fulfillment, such as destination, aim, or possession, within the very rhetoric of teleology that sets its narrative in motion.

This division between those who are concerned with life and those who follow the parables operates in other Kafka stories. In contrast with the characters who want to be admitted and reach their destination, the figures of the drifters—the absent-minded window gazers, meditators without an object to meditate on—constantly risk losing the ground under their feet:

> I stand on the end platform of the tram and am completely unsure of my footing in this world, in this town, in my family. Not even casually could I indicate any claims that I might rightly advance in any direction. I have not even any defence to offer for standing on this platform, . . . , letting myself be carried along by this tram. . . .[34]

"Unsure of their footing in the world," these figures are frequently called writers. Dramatizing a lack of fulfillment and an absence of specific destination, the examples of art in Kafka's parables undermine the ground "under our feet." Although Kafkan artists—like the trapeze artist, or the hunger artist, striving for a perpetual suspension rather than a permanent grounding of meaning—seem to represent extreme aestheticism, these figures disrupt and question the very boundary between performance and ordinary life, between literary and common language.

The movement of transmissibility, which parables perform when they do not say what they mean, when they disrupt socio-linguistic norms and the sense of proper meaning, is associated with the temporality of figurative language. Benjamin himself considers transmissibility to be an irreducible rhetorical feature of poetic language: Kafka "did fail in his grandiose attempt to convert poetry into doctrine, to turn it into a parable and restore to it that stability . . . which, in the face of *reason*, seemed to him to be the only appropriate thing for it" [I, 129, emphasis added]. Precisely because of this failure, or at least what appears as failure in the face of reason, Kafka's texts accomplish something opposite: they turn the language of reason and doctrine into the figurative language of poetry.

Although the crossing of the parable has been compared to the metaphorical transfer,[35] let us point to the important difference between Kafka's parables and classical definition of metaphor based on resemblance. Indeed, the word "parable" in German, (*Gleichnis*)—coming from *gleich*, "similar, like," but also "equal"—would suggest that such metaphorical transfer operates on the basis of analogy, similitude, or proportionality. This etymology emphasizes resemblance and correspondence, which allows for the metaphoric substitution of properties. However, what Kafka describes as *Gleichnis* does not operate on the basis of resemblance; "going across" fails to bridge two poles of metaphorical exchange just as it fails to connect the point of departure with the point of destination. It is an impossible crossing that disrupts the links of similarity or claims to continuity. In an endless departure from any stable site, the movement of *Gleichnis* cannot rest in a crystallization of a complete figure. In Kafka's writing, there is always an extra turn that disrupts the likeness that is the basis of metaphorical crossing. As the frequently recurring figures of crossing in Kafka's parables (entrances, doors, bridges, gates, joints, and graves) suggest, the stability of metaphorical transfer is disrupted by a turning of the figure upon itself. Not surprisingly, metaphors in Kafka's parables extend or violate the boundaries of linguistic norms, which secure the social exchange and communication in discursive community. The story "The Bridge" (*Die Brücke*) presents but one of the many examples of such a fateful metaphoric turn, interrupting the usual traffic of social exchange:

> A bridge to turn around! I had not yet turned quite around when I already began to fall, I fell and in a moment I was torn and transpierced by the sharp rocks which had always gazed up at me so peacefully from the rushing water. [*CS*, 412]

"The Pit of Babel": Translation as the Limit of Formalism and of Linguistic Community

It is not surprising that Kafka should reach to the most exemplary story on language, transmission, and translation—the biblical text of the Tower of Babel. In the wake of the Babelian confusion of tongues, Kafka's parables investigate the effects of rhetoric in the formation of linguistic community and the place of aesthetics in social praxis. Kafka's numerous revisions of the biblical story explore the ways in which a structural or architectonic aspect of language can both presuppose the unity of the common speech and secure an expression of the communal essence. As the monument of construction and signification, the Tower of Babel already assumes, or at least anticipates, the unity of the native tongue and the unity of community. The complicity between construction and communal ethos questions both the fiction of pure formalism separated from social ends and the myth of pure linguistic community free from all conventionality and artifice.

The failure of such a monumental task of exemplary construction leaves in its wake the obligation of translation. Intensifying differences, dispersion, and heterogeneity already at work in the native language, translation in Kafka's texts functions as the limit of both formalism and communal unity.

But we should first consider the "original" biblical text whose twists and tropes inform both Kafka's parables and Benjamin's "The Task of the Translator." From the very beginning the biblical narrative makes explicit the exemplary social function of the tower, which is supposed not only to reach the sky but also to express the name of the builders.[36] The undertaking of this gigantic architectural project is possible in the first place because of the unity of the communal speech: "the whole earth was of one language, and of one speech" [Genesis 11:1]. This reciprocal unity of language and community, a precondition for the coherence of the architectural structure, is very forcefully expressed in a Hebrew idiom: "speaking with the same lip" [Hirsch, 204]. "Speaking with the same lip" suggests not only the phonetic sameness of speech but also transparency of language, which, by precluding all misunderstanding, secures social wholeness. To return to Benjamin's aphorism at this point, "speaking with the same lip" would give us both the access to truth and the guarantee of its transmissibility. The divine intervention confirms this terrifying power of human language: "Behold, the people is one, and they have all one language; and this they begin to do: and now nothing will be restrained from them, which they have imagined to do" [Genesis 11: 6].

However, what is already suspicious about the primordial and seemingly unmediated unity of language and community is the people's anxiety about making a name for themselves and their fear of dispersion, both in a geographical and in a linguistic sense. The unity of language makes the construction of the tower possible, but at the same time it calls for its protection against dispersion. The tower then not merely demonstrates the power of human language ("nothing will be restrained from them") but already functions as a compensation for its original weakness. A certain defect in the "speech with the same lip" calls for the mediation of the architectural project in order to express the name of the people and secure its transmission through the links of genealogical continuity. The unity of "speech with the same lip" is therefore not unmediated but relies on construction/figuration as a means of both expression and preservation. This state of language reflects the double bind of the exemplary narrative itself, in which the moral relies on the mediation of both the redundant narrative and incomplete figural language.

The advent of translation, a result of divine intervention, dissolves the desired unity of the community into the multiplicity of tongues, after which neither the completion of the tower nor the exemplary expression of the name for the generations to come is possible. In his essay "*Des Tours de Babel*," Derrida suggests that this biblical "origin" of translation not only points to the multiplicity of tongues but also to the limits of the structural stability of language:

> The "tower of Babel" does not merely figure the irreducible multiplicity of tongues; it exhibits an incompletion, the impossibility of finishing, of totalizing, of saturating, of completing something on the order of edification, architectural construction, system and architectonics. What the multiplicity of idioms actually limits is not only a "true" translation, a transparent and adequate inter-expression, it is also a structural order, a coherence of construct. There is then (let us translate) something like an internal limit to formalization, an incompleteness of the constructure.[37]

This incompleteness—this interminable postponement of closure that Derrida underscores in his reading—has to be interpreted not only in the formalist but also in the social sense. With an ironic twist of the builders' intentions, God's punishment does not erase the possibility of expression altogether but merely perpetuates the inglorious name for the tower and the builders. Confusion, scattering, reversal are part of this naming act, which is already a retranslation of the name that the builders intended for themselves:

> Therefore is the name of it called Babel; because the Lord did there confound the language of all the earth: and from thence did the Lord scatter them abroad upon the face of all the earth [Genesis 11:9].

This double aspect of God's act (destruction and reinscription of the intended meaning) raises the question about the significance and the consequences of the divine punishment. In his *A Commentary on the Book of Genesis*, Umberto Cassuto gives the literal translation of the phrase: "they shall not understand" as "they shall not hear" [Cassuto, 247]. Thus, God not only confuses people's tongues and lips but also their ears. The destruction of "speaking with the same lip" also destroys a possibility of hearing with the same "ear"—that is, a faithful reception, repetition, translation of the message. Consequently, this dispersion of linguistic unity in turn undercuts the unmediated unity of the discursive community. To use Stanley Cavell's terminology, the figure of the Tower of Babel precisely destroys the primordial *attunement* of the speakers, their agreement in judgments, their capacity to share the same language.

This confusion of hearing might provide some explanation of the problematic ending of the biblical text. Although the story elucidates the meaning by giving an etymological explication of the name "Babel," the fulfillment of this aetiological task is based on mishearing and mistranslation, on the confusion of two different words through phonic similarity. Almost all biblical commentators warn us not to take this etymology literally: "This explanation of...Babel...is of course etymologically irrelevant; it was popularly invented, for Babel means 'gate of God'" [Rad,145]. The biblical text, we are told, derives its etymology from the Hebrew "balal," whereas the derivation "proper" comes from the Mesopotamian word "Bab-ili"—gate of God [Cassuto, 229]. Thus the whole aetiological purpose of the narrative is based on a linguistic confusion, a turn of translation that allows for the obliteration of a primary sense and the reinscription of a derogatory meaning. And it is not one act of mistranslation among others, but the most devastating one, since it confuses the transcendental foundation of meaning—the gate of God, which the tower hopes to reach—with scattering and confusion. Marking the incompleteness of figuration and the dispersion of communal unity, the advent of translation replaces the intended signification and in effect "guarantees" the improper etymology of the proper name. Thus the linguistic and architectonic structure is incomplete on both sides: it cannot provide the safe transmission of the transcendental message, but it does not reach the state of total obliteration either. It remains an emblem of translation, threatening with confusion and unexpected reversals of meaning.

As in the biblical text, the architectonic edifices in Kafka's parables are intertwined with the transmission of obscure messages and precarious ideas "in their magnitude"[*PP*, 37–39].[38] In his many versions of the biblical story, Kafka explicitly emphasizes the parallel between the unfinished construction and dispersed community. Opening an interval between the gate of God and babbling, the Tower of Babel is perhaps emblematic of all architectural metaphors—castles, temples, and burrows—in Kafka's fiction. In this section, however, I will focus on the effects of this figure in several short texts like "The Tower of Babel," "The Pit of Babel," "The City's Coat of Arms," and "The Wall and the Tower of Babel."

Kafka develops the figure of the tower in terms of the basic oppositions implied in the biblical story: ascent/descent, exemplification of truth/confusion, tower/pit, building/digging, communal unity/ dispersion. The shortest, almost aphoristic piece, "The Tower of Babel," juxtaposes the spirituality of ascent with the materiality of building: "if it had been possible to build the Tower of Babel without ascending it, the work would have been permitted" [PP, 35]. In the most laconic form, this commentary points out that the project of construction predicated upon ideas of unity, completeness, and internal harmony is inevitably subordinated to some metaphysical aim. What is at stake is not the actual skills of building but the desire of ascent attached to them. Whatever we mean by this "fabulous yonder" [*PP*, 11], ascending to the top also echoes a familiar hermeneutical task of reaching the peak of understanding and truth. Although constructions like the Tower of Babel tempt us with a disclosure of the ultimate truth, in Kafka's parables they dramatize the interminable deferral of such revelation.

Is there any way of escaping from the construction/ascension pattern, from the structure promising the disclosure of truth and the unity of the community? Although many of Kafka's texts elaborate such "routes of escape," we will focus on his two parables, "The Pit of Babel" and "City's Coat of Arms."[39] Announcing "that some progress must be made," the anonymous worker in the first of these texts proposes digging a subterranean passage, the pit, instead of building the Tower:

> What are you building?—I want to dig a subterranean passage [*Gang*]. Some progress must be made. My station [*Standort*] up there is much too high.

> We are digging the pit of Babel [*PP, 35*].

The pattern is no longer an ascent but a descent, an immersion in the formlessness of earth, which suggests a complete resignation from any revelation of truth. In this transmission of the biblical text, the central metaphor of construction is deliberately confused with digging and endless lateral extension: the word "building" (*bauen*) in the question is replaced by "digging" (*graben*) in the answer. This improper substitution is already a result of a wrong hearing, an unpredictable turn of figuration. Digging as a form of "progress" implies then a radical departure from the ideas of structural unity and coherence associated with architectural metaphors, and especially from the promise of "ascent," or disclosure of truth, that invariably accompanies them. By contrast, Kafka's anonymous digger is not motivated by any desire of ascent but complains that his standpoint "up there is much too high." No longer bound to express a name or to signify, his work is an attempt to escape from "up there." In search of alternatives to "exemplary" constructions, the pits and burrows in Kafka's parables suggest a deliberate "progression" of the text into darkness and obscurity. The substitution of the word "digging" for "building," and of "pit" / "passage" for "the tower" conveys the idea of the formation of a different text, no longer submitted to the ideal of unity, coherent organization, and exemplary expression. As Henry Sussman suggests in his reading of "The Burrow":

> the construction consists in hollowing, not protrusion, in the addition of complication, not assertion, in the expansion of darkness, not illumination. The construction is already deconstruction to the same extent that it has been constructed.[40]

In the context of the explicit reference to the biblical narrative, such a text intensifies the effects of translation. It not only reverses the author's intentions, and thereby destroys the legibility of the text, but also removes the ground of social and linguistic unification. With its shift from singular to collective enunciation, the summative comment of the conversation—"we are digging the pit of Babel" [*PP*, 35]—implies a total collapse of the exemplary structure and the impending communal dispersion. Instead of crystallizing one governing figure, the text deepens an abyss that prevents the saturation of exemplary meaning.

This incompatibility between the "art of building" and the "primacy of idea," between the temporality of construction and timeless truth, is explicitly thematized in "City's Coat of Arms" (*Das Stadtwappen*). The parable accounts for the constant deferral of the building of the Tower of Babel as the result of the workers' deep mistrust in their present skills, which might not be sufficient for materializing "the idea of . . . the tower that will reach to heaven." What paralyzes the generation of builders is then a sense of an unbridgeable gap between the unmediated idea and the discontinuous temporality of mediation. This sense of a gap produces fear that the next generation might "find the work of their predecessors bad, and tear down what has been built so as to begin anew" [*PP*, 37–39]. Thus, the temporality of building, even when it is called progress, is ironically interconnected with destruction: tearing down, ruining, indeed hollowing out the previous construction. The very progress in the skills of building is what threatens both the continuity of construction and the genealogical continuity between the generations of workers.

Workers' reasoning, which tries to find a compromise between the stability of the idea and the incompleteness of the construction, between the timeless truth and the temporal deferral of revelation, results in yet another paralyzing impasse. The apparent flaw lies in the workers' assumption that the essential thing is the very idea of building and that everything else is secondary: "The idea, once seized in its magnitude, can never vanish again" [*PP*, 37]. This general opinion asserts the primacy of thought, truth, and the immediate contemplation of an exemplary idea. However, the defect in what seems to be merely secondary—the limitation of both the material and linguistic resources—not only reverses this hierarchy but eventually destroys the irresistible idea itself: "To this must be added that the second or third generation had already recognized the senselessness of building a heaven-reaching tower [*Die Sinnlosigkeit des Himmelsturmbaus*]" [*PP*, 38–39]. In this way, the divine punishment in the biblical text does not even need to occur because all its consequences are already contained in the temporal character of construction itself.

In the course of the parable, construction becomes a figure for rhetoric—for example, "art of building" requires "roads" of communication, "digging" means also "engraving," workers are at the same time interpreters—which "tears apart" the totalizing exemplary purpose of the text. It seems that even the workers are aware of this rhetorical danger, because in their effort to minimize confusion and multiplicity of tongues, they give much thought to "guides" and "interpreters" who should secure the reliable "roads of communication" [*PP*, 37]. What is at stake, then, in the linguistic impasse brought about by the failure of the exemplary task? In the biblical text, when the roads of communication are destroyed by the advent of translation, the construction of the tower is abandoned. In Kafka's text, however, mere reflection on the temporality of transmissibility already undermines the stability of the transcendental idea and thus leads to the impossibility of even starting the construction—"such thoughts paralyzed people's powers" [*PP*, 39].

This paralysis thematized in Kafka's text raises again a question whether it is possible to build, write, interpret when we already know "that the incomprehensible is incomprehensible" [*PP*, 11]. Walter Benjamin argues, however, that this failure of the transcendental purpose is not an impasse but a liberating force in Kafka's prose:

> To do justice to the figure of Kafka in its purity and its peculiar beauty one must never lose sight of one thing: it is the purity and beauty of a failure. (. . .) One is tempted to say: once he was cer-

tain of eventual failure, everything worked out for him *en route* as in a dream [*I*, 144–145].

Thus, the failure that Benjamin discusses is not a sign of linguistic skepticism in Kafka's texts but rather a strange condition of creativity and social exchange. Kafka's parable not only narrates the failure of the tower but also shows how this failure unpredictably gives rise to a "bastard child": a city whose inhabitants produce new sages and new songs. As in "The Pit of Babel," the impasse of the exemplary construction unexpectedly breeds an alternative route, a mere detour at first, which then takes the place of the original project. By the time the builders have recognized the senselessness of the tower, they find themselves already deeply involved in the unplanned city. The city is a completely different type of construction and presupposes a different understanding of the community: decentered, heterogeneous, built without any governing idea. It arises out of endless confusion, disputes and wars between various nationalities, already caught in the predicament of translation. It does not possess any fixed boundaries or structure, but its monstrous growth is fueled precisely by the development of the skills of construction and destruction occasioned by the conflict between generations and nationalities. It spreads by accommodating the multiplicity of tongues and the war of desires. Such monstrous growth is a further "proof" for the leaders that in the absence of communal unity the construction of the tower should be deferred.

Mirroring the predicament of the builders of the city, Kafka's own interpretation of the biblical text reflects the possibilities and risks of textual transmission. As "The City's Coat of Arms" implies, each generation of workers/interpreters, driven by the "irresistible desire" to complete the structure, will eventually "tear apart" what has already been built. When completion or supplementation of the previous text is indistinguishable from its destruction, then the process of transmissibility implied in Kafka's parables subverts the stability of transcendental ideas both in their own discourse and in the texts that serve them as antecedents.

"The Ground under Our Feet": "The Great Wall of China"

Exceeding the bounds of linguistic norms, the rhetorical effects of Kafka's language prevent the crystallization of a unified meaning. Such a transgressive movement of language questions the possibility of the common ground, of some underlying although frequently hidden foundation that would anchor the text in order to preserve the integrity and stability of its meaning. All the more interesting in this connection are stories like "The Great Wall of China" (*Beim Bau der Chinesischen Mauer*), in which the metaphor of the foundation, of the common ground, is very prominent. Kafka's parables explore the figure of the ground in a double sense: in the epistemological sense as the foundation of truth (*Wahrheitsgrund*) and in the social sense as the unity of the community sustained by its common ways of speaking (the ground under *our* feet). The attempt to restore the lost "true Word" to the community in "Investigations of a Dog" (*Forschungen eines Hundes*), for example, turns around the double notion of a ground (the ground of science on the one hand and the "foundation of universal dog nature" and existence on the other), though both kinds of investigations bring about violence and monstrosity. As Cavell argues, these two ways of grounding the meaning of the text reflect also two different senses of the exemplary task: in the first case, this task can be understood as a revelation of truth, in the second, as a restoration of social representative speech.[41] By looking more closely at parables like "Prometheus" and "The Great Wall of China," we are going to ask the question whether the dissolution of the epistemological foundation can be compensated for by the unity of the community. In other words, can transmissibility be regulated by the community "speaking with the same lip"? Can the linguistic unity of the community restore a possibility of exemplary stories?

Kafka's "Prometheus" focuses on the temporal effects of transmissibility with respect to the epistemological rather then the social ground of truth. It raises the question about the ground of its own linguistic performance, which is especially evident in the recurrence of the word "ground" (*Grund*) in the German compounds such as *grundlos* and *Wahrheitsgrund* [*PP*, 82]. This story, like every Kafka parable, tries to explain "the inexplicable," but instead of providing an exemplary message, it wearily multiplies the versions of itself. Thus, not only does Kafka retell here the myth handed down by tradition, but the narration itself proceeds by progressively turning away from each successive variation. This movement of supplementation empties out previous crystallizations of myth and points out that the wearisomeness of such repetition eventually collapses the legend into the inexplicable.

Kafka's retelling of the myth of Prometheus brings into focus two kinds of transmission. As a messenger who steals, Prometheus is a figure of an improper and discontinuous transmission. In contrast, the outcome of the Greek myth thematizes what a proper repetition might be in the figure of the endlessly renewable punishment. Yet it is precisely the possibility of perpetual repetition (repetition that does not affect the integrity of meaning) that the turns of Kafka's parable undermine:

> *Nach der vierten wurde man des grundlos Gewordenen müde. Die Götter wurden müde, die Adler wurden müde, die Wunde schloss sich müde.*

> According to the fourth, every one grew weary of the meaning-less affair. The Gods grew weary, the eagles grew weary, the wound closed wearily [*PP*, 82–83, emphasis mine].

The movement of becoming—the temporal unfolding of the parable—performs the ungrounding of truth, the dissolution of the common site sustaining all the variations of myth. The parable turns into *grundlos Gewordenen*—a groundless affair (literally—groundless outcome). The parable may derive from a substratum of truth (*Wahrheitsgrund*) but in its progressive turns it has "in turn to end in the inexplicable." The German *grundlos* can mean both "boundless" and "groundless, unfounded." Both of these connotations—lack of determining boundaries and lack of foundation—point to the two aspects of transmission: it is because of the permeability of linguistic bounds that we can no longer find the secure foundation of truth in Kafka's text.

Yet, as the parable "The Great Wall of China" shows, this dissolution of the epistemological ground of truth sustains a desire for the other kind of grounding and for a different kind of myth—for the unity of the community reflected in the common ways of speaking. From the outset, we are told that the wall cannot fulfill its function either as the foundation of a new Tower of Babel or as the secure boundary of the empire, because the continuous construction is replaced by a piecemeal work, which leaves many gaps open for penetration from the outside. Piecemeal construction (*Teilbau*) is characterized by the heterogeneous collage of fragments, unexpected transfers and shifts in the composition, problematic junctions, and necessary gaps, all of which forever postpone totalization and closure of the work. The story is an investigation into the necessity of such a construction, which for all practical purposes is only "a makeshift, and therefore inexpedient" [*CS*, 240].

The sequence of the parables investigates the disturbing social uses of such an "inexpedient" construction. It also reveals how the common ways of talking are created and sustained in the first place. If the Biblical story dramatizes the destruction of the communal unity by the artifice of language, Kafka's text, in an ironic reversal, diagnoses the temptation of appealing to the communal body in order to compensate for the discontinuity of language. Rather than serving as a protection against "the wild hordes" of the enemies, the wall with its discontinuous structure perpetuates the threat of external invasion. And it is this imaginary threat of penetration from the outside that provides the most expedient means to neutralize alterity inside the community: to exclude everything that is foreign, contaminating, or unsettling to its linguistic unity. The porous wall consolidates the community of speech in more pervasive ways than the work of any closure would be able to accomplish: it binds the people together by making them define themselves against the threat of the other—the foreigners, who are in turn marked as locusts or wild beasts, that is, as those who are deprived of community, speech, and humanity. Thus, the unification of the sociolinguistic space simultaneously demarcates its outside as dangerous, inarticulate, and monstrous. Because the wall by itself does not provide a rigid distinction between the native and the foreign, it points out that only the united people—those who have overcome "the confines of the narrow circulation of one body" for the sake of the collective body of the nation—can preserve this difference: "Unity! Unity! Shoulder to shoulder, a ring of brothers, a current of blood no longer confined within the narrow circulation of one body, but sweetly rolling and yet ever returning throughout the endless leagues of China" [*CS*, 238]. The metaphor of the collective body conveys the sense of a uniform social space that rests on the unmediated common ways of "speaking with the same lip" rather than on social institutions or conventions. The transmission of messages within such a community is like the continuous and uninterrupted flow of blood within the body—it only furnishes a further proof of its organic unity. It is as if these common ways of speaking or standing are supposed to give the community the very ground on which its feet can rest.

Although the wall, with its piecemeal construction, cannot secure this sociolinguistic unity against external contamination, the very weakness in its construction (the discontinuities, the gaps, and the shifts in the direction of building) proves "to be one of the greatest unifying influences among our people; indeed, if one may dare to use the expression, the very ground on which we live." And the fact that this "fundamental" (the one that becomes the fundament) weakness is not available to further interpretation implies that the unity of the community would have to be presupposed—or, to use Stanley Cavell's word, acknowledged—rather than proved.[42] What is at stake in those utopian dreams of the community is not only the understanding of truth but also the possibility of dwelling, or rather, *footing*, in the world:

> All the more remarkable is it that this very weakness should seem to be one of the greatest unifying influences among our people; indeed, if one may dare to use the expression, the very ground on which we live. To set about establishing a fundamental defect here would mean undermining not only our consciences, but, what is far worse, our feet [*CS*, 247–248].

The great wall can provide such stable "footing" by locating difference and alterity on the outside and also by sustaining a perpetual threat of their violent penetration into the inside. What the course of the parable insists on, however, is that the fatal alterity infects the body of the community always already from within. The "stupendous" work of closure reveals that the inside of the empire is so heterogenous and unsurveyable that it cannot be subsumed under one body. The sheer vastness of the empire cannot be embraced or traversed: "So vast is our land that no fable could do justice to its vastness, the heavens can scarcely span it." With the eclipse of the uniform sociolinguistic space, the circulation of messages between the emperor and the distant subjects no longer flows "like blood within the body," but is characterized by interruptions and spatiotemporal reversals, which undermine the stable poles of the sender, message, and receiver. As one of the parables proclaims, the emperor sends his message on his deathbed, but his message cannot traverse freely even within the imperial palace because of the collapse of the communal unity:

> But the multitudes are so vast; their numbers have no end . . . . But instead how vainly does he wear out his strength; still he is only making his way through the chambers of the innermost palace; never will he get to the end of them; . . . and if he succeeded in that nothing would be gained; the courts would still have to be crossed; and after the courts, the second outer palace; and once more stairs and courts; and once more another palace; and so on for thousands of years [*CS*, 244].

What this passage implies is that the figure of the living social body is both composed of and disrupted by the dregs and the formless sediments of the city. By exposing a fatal alterity inhabiting the common body, this paralysis of circulation disarticulates the vision of the unified social space. Furthermore, the unsettling power of transmission endlessly postpones the moment when the people could embrace the "palpable living reality to their breasts," for it confuses the living with the dead, the luminous presence with the ghost. Taking the risk of undermining "our feet," the parable suggests that the very idea of the community as one living body is only a "figure fortuitously exalted from an urn already crumbled to dust" [CS, 245]. In place of the living social body, this figure of "the crumbled urn" confronts us with a spectral community, or as Derrida writes, with "the haunted community of the single body."[43] As translation shatters the aura of the work of art, so here too Kafka's parables deprive ordinary communal speech of its life by fragmenting the organic unity of the common body. Returning the social body to its grave, Kafka's text once again leaves us with a disturbing sense of failure. This failure not only destroys the possibility of grounding the exemplary meaning of the text in the common ways of speaking but also exposes the violence inherent in that kind of grounding. Thus, for Kafka as for Benjamin, it is the ghostly beauty of failure that disrupts the aestheticization of politics and enables a turn toward the politicization of aesthetics.

* * *

Intending to articulate what is "entirely new" in Kafka's parables, Benjamin theorizes transmissibility in the context of the possibilities and limitations of modernity. Kafka's relation to modernity cannot be grasped, however, when his texts are interpreted in terms of skepticism, the lost truth, or the inaccessible transcendental; as Benjamin notes, many writers before Kafka have faced and accommodated themselves to such metaphysical predicaments. Benjamin's insight into the temporality of transmission in Kafka's texts offers a way out of this impasse. For Benjamin, what is transmitted is not the "consistency of truth" but the essential possibility of its refiguration. As he writes, "Kafka's writings are by their nature parables. But it is their misery and their beauty that they had to become *more* than parables" [I, 144]. As if accepting Kafka's bet presented in "On Parables," Benjamin thus interprets the deficiency of Kafka's parables—their apparent testimony to the loss of truth as a "predicament" of the modern age—as a gain, and links this surplus to a peculiar obligation. Although it destroys the consistency of truth and tradition, this obligation of "transmissibility" questions the notion of modernity both as a critical overcoming of the past and as a project to provide criteria for itself out of its own present situation.[44] By disrupting both linguistic and social immanence, the obligation of transmission orients the text to an unreachable past, the truth of which can no longer be recuperated in the present, and thus it opens a future without a calculable destination. No longer tied to the recuperation of truth, or the repetition of the same, this sense of obligation nonetheless enables Kafka to make a critical intervention into aestheticism without succumbing to the modern nostalgia for the lost community.[45] Thus, although Kafka's parables often stress a destructive character of rhetoric—its capacity to "tear apart" the inherited systems and traditions—they also present it as a liberating process, and, Benjamin adds, as hope.

NOTES

1. See for example, among others:
Walter Benjamin, "Franz Kafka: on the Tenth Anniversary of His Death," and "Some Reflections on Kafka," in *Illuminations*, trans. Harry Zohn (New York: Schocken, 1969). Subsequent references to this edition are marked parenthetically in the text, preceded by I.
Frank Kermode, *Genesis of Secrecy: On the Interpretation of Narrative* (Cambridge: Harvard UP, 1979), 26–33.
J. Hillis Miller, "Parable and Performative in the Gospels and in Modern Literature," in *Humanizing America's Iconic Book*, ed. Gene M. Tucker and Douglas A. Knight (Chico, California: Scholars P, 1982), 58–71.
Heinz Politzer, *Franz Kafka: Parable and Paradox* (Ithaca: Cornell UP, 1966), 1–23.
2. Kermode, *Genesis of Secrecy*, 23.
3. There exists rich literature on the parable in the Judeo-Christian tradition. Only several sources important for my argument will be mentioned here:
C. H. Dodd, *The Parables of the Kingdom* (New York: Scribner, 1961).
Robert W. Funk, *Language, Hermeneutic, and the Word of God* (New York: Harper, 1966).
J. Jeremias, *The Parables of Jesus* (New York: Scribner's, 1972).
Jean Starobinski, "The Struggle with Legion: A Literary Analysis of Mark 5:1–20," in *NLH* 4 (1973): 330–356.
David Stern, "Rhetoric and Midrash: The Case of the Mashal," in *Prooftexts* 1 (1981): 262–291.
4. *The Universal Jewish Encyclopedia*, ed. Isaac Landman, v. 7 (New York: The Universal Jewish Encyclopedia Inc., 1942), 395.
5. On the difference between the interpretation of the secular and sacred parables see J. Hillis Miller, "Parable and Performative," 59.
6. For a suggestive reading of this parable, especially of the figure of the outsider, see Kermode, *Genesis of Secrecy*, 28–32.

7. Jean Starobinski, "The Struggle with Legion," 348.

8. Theodor W Adorno, "Notes on Kafka," in *Prisms*, trans. Samuel and Shierry Weber (Cambridge: MIT, 1982), 243–272. For the discussion of the relevance of the term parable in Kafka criticism see Alan Udoff's Introduction to *Kafka and the Contemporary Critical Performance*, ed. Alan Udoff (Bloomington: Indiana UP, 1987), 3.

9. Wilhelm Emrich, *Franz Kafka: A Critical Study of His Writings*, trans. Sheema Zeben Buehne (New York: Ungar, 1968), 1–74.

10. Politzer, *Parable and Paradox*, 1–23.

11. Politzer, 21–22.

12. Politzer, 16.

13. The thesis of immanence is most convincingly propagated in Kafka criticism by Gilles Deleuze and Félix Guattari, *Kafka: Toward a Minor Literature*, trans. Dana Polan, (Minneapolis: U of Minnesota P, 1986). According to them, the three misleading themes in Kafka criticism are "the transcendence of the law, the interiority of guilt, the subjectivity of enunciation [45]," which they juxtapose with the immanence of desire. In their analysis of "the writing machine," Deleuze and Guattari see Kafka's prose as "an unlimited field of immanence instead of an infinite transcendence [51]." Unsatisfied and liberated desire is no longer bound toward the inaccessible transcendent law, but always moves forward, displacing the limits and opening new connectors. For the difference between this approach and Benjamin's, see Réda Bensmaïa "Foreword: The Kafka Effect," ix–xxi.

14. The text of "Some Reflections on Kafka" in *Illuminations* is based upon Benjamin's letter to Gershom Scholem from Paris, June 12, 1938, published also in *Briefe*, II, 756–64.

15. Benjamin's interpretations of Kafka are obviously polemical. In addition to his rejection of the theological and psychoanalytical interpretations, Benjamin questions Scholem's understanding of Kafka in the context of Jewish mysticism as well as Brecht's vision of Kafka as a prophetic writer. For an excellent account of the way in which Benjamin negotiates his reading of Kafka with Adorno, Brecht, and Scholem, see Hans Mayer, "Walter Benjamin and Franz Kafka: Report on a Constellation," trans. Gary Smith and Thomas S. Hansen, in *On Walter Benjamin: Critical Essays and Recollections*, ed. Gary Smith (Cambridge: MIT, 1988), 185–209. For an alternative account of the influence of Scholem, in particular of his idea of "deferral as constitutive for Judaism," on Benjamin's reading of Kafka, see Susan A. Handelman, *Fragments of Redemption: Jewish Thought and Literary Theory in Benjamin, Scholem, and Levinas* (Bloomington: Indiana UP, 1991), 44–52. For an excellent account of the way Benjamin's reading of Kafka anticipates contemporary literary theory, see Henry Sussman, *Franz Kafka: Geometrician of Metaphor* (Madison: Coda P, 1979), 1–41.

16. For an illuminating discussion of Benjamin's own relation to modernity, see Rainer Nägele, *Theater, Theory, Speculation: Walter Benjamin and the Scenes of Modernity* (Baltimore: Johns Hopkins UP, 1991), 54–77, 135–166.

17. Walter Benjamin, "Franz Kafka: Zur zehnten Wiederkehr seines Todestages," *Gesammelte Schriften*, II.2, unter Mitw. von Theodor W. Adorno u. Gershom Scholem hrsg. von Rolf Tiedemann u. Hermann Schweppenhäuser (Frankfurt: Suhrkamp, 1977), 437.

18. Franz Kafka, *Parables and Paradoxes*, in German and English (New York: Schocken, 1975), 175. Subsequent references to this edition are marked parenthetically in the text, preceded by PP.

19. For a less frequently mentioned aspect of transmission in Benjamin's work, see an excellent discussion of rumor or street talk in Avital Ronell, "Street-Talk," in *Benjamin's Ground: New Readings of Walter Benjamin*, ed. Rainer Nägele (Detroit: Wayne State UP, 1988), 119–145.

20. By reading these texts—one from the earlier and the other from the later phase of Benjamin's career—against each other, one can avoid reductive interpretations that Benjamin accounts for the changes in modern art solely on the basis of the changes in reproduction techniques. For such a reading, see for instance, Peter Bürger, *Theory of the Avant-Garde*, trans. Michael Shaw (Minneapolis: U of Minnesota P, 1984), 27–34.

21. Paul de Man, "'Conclusions: Walter Benjamin's 'The Task of the Translator,'" in *The Resistance to Theory* (Minneapolis: U of Minnesota P, 1986), 80, emphasis added. In reference to the title of Benjamin's essay, "Die Aufgabe des Übersetzers," de Man reminds us that "*Aufgabe*, task, can also mean the one who has to give up," 80.

22. What de Man's reading of failure contests is a dialectical notion of modernity as "the overcoming of a certain naiveté and a rise of consciousness to another level." De Man argues that this notion of modernity as a critical overcoming of the past still informs Gadamer's "The Philosophical Foundations of the Twentieth Century." Paul de Man, "Conclusions," 74–77.

23. For an excellent account of the overcoming of "this still natural unity rooted in mythical linguistic relations," see Rodolphe Gasché, "Saturnine Vision and the Question of Difference: Reflections on Walter Benjamin's Theory of Language," in *Benjamin's Ground: New Readings of Walter Benjamin*, 86–92.

24. The figure of the broken vessel and its relation to the idea of *Tikkun* of the Lurianic Kabbalah is elaborated by Carol Jacobs, "The Monstrosity of Translation," in *MLN* 90 (1975): 762.

25. See Jacobs, "The Monstrosity of Translation," 763–764.

26. De Man, 92.

27. In his essay "The Work of Art in the Age of Mechanical Reproduction," Benjamin confronts directly the complicity between aestheticism, community, and fascism.

28. For an illuminating discussion of pure language as an inexpressible latent ground "something like a trembling or vibration . . . or the rush and trance of Dionysian music," see Rainer Nägele, "Benjamin's Ground," *Benjamin's Ground*, 32–36.

29. Walter Benjamin, "Die Aufgabe des Übersetzers," in *Gesammelte Schriften*, IV.1, 20.

30. Such an assimilation would erase for Benjamin a distinction between aesthetics and commodity.

31. In structural terms, Benjamin's understanding of transmissibility "bears a kinship" to Derrida's analysis of iterability ("Signature Event Context," in *Margins of Philosophy*, trans. Alan Bass (Chicago: U of Chicago P, 1982), 307–330). Derrida defines iterability as repetition that is linked to alterity as a result of the transposition of contexts. He points out that in the traditional notion of communication the ideal content is not affected by repetition, by the linguistic or semantic transport. Iteration, however, indicates the essential limitation of the "original" context: "a written sign carries with it a force of breaking with its context, that is, the set of presences that organize the moment of its inscription," 317. Because iterability is an inherent quality of the text, it can always be lifted out from its original context and inscribed or "grafted" onto a possible number of other contexts, other "semantic chains" which will affect the consistency of its "original" meaning. Therefore, no single formula, context, law or idea can contain the movement of iteration, and by extension, the meaning of the text. Although iterability subverts the stability of exemplification, this "extraction" from the determining context is what constitutes the possibility of citation, and exemplification.

32. Franz Kafka, *Letters to Friends, Family, and Editors*, trans. Richard and Clara Winston (New York: Schocken, 1977), 289. Probably the most extensive analysis of Kafka's writing as situated on the crossroad of languages and the multiple effects of deterritorialization that they perform can be found in Deleuze and Guattari, *Kafka: Toward the Minor Literature*, 19–27.

33. "On Parables" has inspired many interesting readings. For its interpretation in terms of psychopoetic structures—the Erotic sense of the many corresponding to metonymy and the Thanatotic sense of the wise corresponding to the metaphor—see Charles Bernheimer, *Flaubert and Kafka: Studies in Psychopoetic Structure* (New Haven: Yale UP, 1982), 45–55. "On Parables" in the context of the performative function of language, see J. Hillis Miller, "Parables and Performative in the Gospels and in Modern Literature," in *Humanizing America's Iconic Book*, 67–71.

34. Franz Kafka, "On the Tram," in *The Complete Stories*, ed. Nahum N. Glatzer (New York: Schocken, 1971), 388. Subsequent references to this edition are marked parenthetically in the text, preceded by CS.

35. See for example Charles Bernheimer, *Flaubert and Kafka*, 50–51.

36. The following commentaries on this biblical text are important to my argument and when quoted will be marked in the text parenthetically using the author's name followed by page number:

> Umberto Cassuto, *A Commentary on the Book of Genesis*, Part II, trans. Israel Abrahams (Jerusalem: The Magnes Press, 1974), 225–249.
>
> Samson Raphael Hirsch, *The Pentateuch*, vol. I "Genesis," trans. Isaac Levy (Judaica Press, 1976), 204–217.
>
> Benno Jacob, *The First Book of the Bible: Genesis*, trans. Ernest I.

Jacob and Walter Jacob (New York: KTAV, 1974), 77–79.

Gerhard von Rad, *Genesis: A Commentary*, trans. H. Marks (Philadelphia: Westminster Press, 1961), 143–151.

37. Jacques Derrida, "Des Tours de Babel," in *Difference in Translation*, ed. Joseph F. Graham (Ithaca: Cornell UP, 1985), 165–166.

38. In his reflection on "The Burrow" in *Franz Kafka: Geometrician of Metaphor*, Henry Sussman points out that construction functions as "all embracing metaphor" in Kafka's works: "We are appraised from the outset that the project under construction is a literary as well as architectural object, bespeaking the same duplicity, illusoriness, impenetrability and limits characteristic of the literary text," 150.

39. For a discussion of "lines of escape" in Kafka's text see Deleuze and Guattari, *Kafka: Toward a Minor Literature*, 34–42.

40. Henry Sussman, *Geometrician of Metaphor*, 149.

41. For a detailed discussion of the ways in which the claim to the community can assure a stability of meaning in the absence of the epistemological foundation, see Stanley Cavell, *The Claim of Reason* (Oxford: Oxford UP, 1979), 32–78.

42. Cavell claims that there is no further epistemological grounding available for the claim of the linguistic unity of the community. Since the idea of the mutual agreement of speakers is itself groundless, it can be only acknowledged but not proved: it is open "to question whether a philosophical explanation is needed, or wanted, for the fact of agreement in the language human beings use together . . . . For nothing is deeper than the fact, or the extent, of agreement itself." *Claim of Reason*, 32.

43. Jacques Derrida, 133.

44. For an excellent discussion of modernity's consciousness of time and of Benjamin's critique of the modern notion of time in his concept of history, see Jürgen Habermas, *The Philosophical Discourse of Modernity*, trans. Frederick Lawrence (Cambridge: MIT, 1987), 1–22.

45. The connection between transmissibility and critical intervention is emphasized by Benjamin as well. Translation is compared directly to critical epistemology and to literary criticism, and the process of mechanical reproduction situates the audience in the position of the critics.

5

The Paratactic Prose
of Samuel Beckett:
How It Is

This is an author to whom I feel very close, or to whom I would like
to feel very close; but also too close. Precisely because of this
proximity, it is too hard for me, too easy and too hard . . . How
could I write, sign, countersign performatively texts which
"respond" to Beckett?

    Jacques Derrida, "This Strange Institution Called Literature"

A book is interrupted discourse catching up with its own breaks.

    Emmanuel Levinas, *Otherwise than Being or Beyond Essence*

The Remains of Aesthetics:
Failure, Task, Obligation

How should one respond to, Derrida asks, Beckett? What is an
appropriate mode of critical response—whether literary or
philosophical—to Beckett's texts? Recalling Benjamin's cir-
cumspection in front of Kafka's work, Derrida's questions
about the limits of interpretation are obviously not raised for
the first time in Beckett's scholarship. Beckett's "unapproach-
ability" is frequently compared to the difficulty of Kafka, who,
predictably, is evoked as Beckett's precursor.[1] Mounting similar obstacles in their texts, both writers seem to paralyze the
work of interpretation, as Beckett writes in the famous letter to
Alex Kaun, with an "assault against words."[2] The "assault

against words" invariably turns into an assault against the interpreter, who, as Harold Bloom suggests, occupies a precarious position "where one is neither alive nor dead. It is Beckett's peculiar triumph that he disputes with Kafka the dark eminence of being the Dante of that world."[3]

Beckett's work, like Kafka's, occupies an extreme position in modernism, where art exhausts both the aesthetic and the philosophical resources of signification. For Derrida, this closure of interpretative reason is at the core of the aesthetic experience in modernity: such a limit of interpretation questions not only the self-reflective character of modern art—its capacity for critical self-interrogation—but also the possibility of a philosophical reflection on art's significance. Derrida argues, however, that this impasse of interpretation cannot be reduced to the philosophical problem of nihilism or skepticism; rather, it calls for the invention of a different task of aesthetics, beyond the negation of truth and beyond the formalism of aestheticism. By exploring the affinity between Derrida's and Beckett's work, I am especially interested in the peculiar sense of invention emerging from the most decomposed texts and in the obligations such inventiveness can impose upon aesthetics.

In Beckett's case, the impasse of interpretation is inseparably intertwined with the relentlessly negative formulation of the aesthetic project. As Beckett emphatically insists in several conversations with his critics, the task of his texts is to dissolve the fundamental concepts of being, art, and language: "at the end of my work there's nothing but dust . . . . In the last book—*L'Innommable*—there's complete disintegration. No 'I,' no 'have,' no 'being.' No nominative, no accusative, no verb. There's no way to go."[4] Beckett's reflection on art presents modern aesthetics as an austere process of undoing—as a disintegration of the fundamental categories of subject and object, identity and being, representation and property. This task of dissolution is extended even to the most basic grammatical structure of language.[5] As Wolfgang Iser observes, the very core of Beckett's project consists of "a relentless process of negation, which in the novels applies even on the level of the individual sentences themselves, which follow one another as a ceaseless rejection and denial of what has just been said."[6]

Although Beckett associates the work of undoing with an impasse or even an impossibility of aesthetics, ironically, this negative formulation of modernism has proved to be one of the most productive trends in Beckett studies. Before we can trace the enormous work the negative definition of Beckett's aesthetics has performed, let us note two different senses—epistemological and aesthetic—in which the "relentless process of negation" is deployed. As David Watson suggests, the negativity of Beckett's texts is interpreted in terms of either unavoidable or deliberate failure, as if failure itself could be read as a matter of fate (that is, a linguistic predicament that befalls art), or as artistic intention (that is, a task that art aims to achieve): "on the one hand the text is doomed to failure; on the other it sets out with the deliberate intention of failing."[7] Figured in contradictory ways as both aspiration and resignation, this ambiguous sense of failure already announces a peculiar task to be assumed and given up. Before this notion of the task can be pursued further, let us notice that the difference in question also reveals the more familiar contrast between the aesthetic and the conceptual interpretations of art's negativity. In the context of modernist aesthetics, negation can be seen as a process of purification of art from any external significance—from truth, moral obligations, and social relevance. As Clement Greenberg writes, this purification is the essential project of aestheticism: "the essence of Modernism lies, as I see it, in the use of the characteristic methods of a discipline to criticize the discipline itself—not in order to subvert it, but to entrench it more firmly in its area of competence."[8] Yet, in Beckett's texts, negation seems to exceed the proper boundaries of aesthetics and to assume disturbing philosophical or cognitive implications as well. Leaving its "proper" area of competence, modern art questions the very possibility of truth not only within but also outside the sphere of aesthetics. It contests the claims of rationality by testifying to the disappointing limitations of language or by revealing its perverse aberrations. Bearing the fate that befalls language in general—its shortcomings, deviations, and failures—art seems to succumb to mourning for the lost truth.

In practice, these two operations of the negative are not easily distinguishable but, on the contrary, open themselves to endless permutations and parasitical cooperation. One such striking permutation in Beckett studies lies in the complicity between the formal achievements of modern aesthetics—its peculiar beauty and self-conscious experimentation with style—and the frustration of the desire for knowledge. With an unmistakable subtext of modernist aesthetics, evocative of T. S. Eliot's escapist reading of Joyce, Northrop Fry, for instance, reads failure in Beckett's texts as a withdrawal from the facile chatter of quotidian communication: "In a world given over to obsessive utterance...to restore silence is the role of serious writing."[9] For Iser, the negativity of Beckett's work collapses the very distinction between fiction and knowledge: it exposes the fictionality of truth while simultaneously denouncing the bad faith of fiction masquerading as knowledge: "In our everyday lives we are always guided by the conviction that our conceptions can grasp realities . . . . But in Beckett's dramas, we can only provide motives for the continual negation of the dialogue by realizing that our explanatory conceptions are in fact nothing more than fictions."[10] For Linda Ben-Zvi these denunciations of the fictionality of truth reveal a sober fidelity to the unsurpassable limitations of language: for Beckett "words . . . become signs, not of knowledge, but rather of the failure of knowledge. Instead of being about anything, words . . . indicate the very impossibility of moving beyond language."[11]

Bringing these negative formulations of modern aesthetics to their logical conclusions, Ben-Zvi links Beckett's self-conscious experimentation with style to linguistic skepticism, which Beckett could have learned from the philosophy of Fritz Mauthner.[12] The skeptical interpretation of the negativity of literary language is only strengthened in Beckett studies by the fact that Beckett so frequently criticizes the task of representation in the context of Cartesian dualisms.[13] In his first English novels, especially in *Murphy* and *Watt*, Beckett playfully exploits the *non sequiturs* of Cartesian philosophy: the dissociations between mind and body, subject and object, and eventually, between words and things.[14] As Gerald Bruns, among other Beckett interpreters, suggests, the predictable consequence of the Cartesian incommensurability of mind and body is the dissociation of words and objects, suggested for instance in a famous passage in *Molloy*: "there could be no things but nameless things, no names but thingless names . . . . All I know is what the words know, and the dead things, and that makes a handsome little sum . . . . the long sonata of the dead."[15] Explicitly or implicitly, this skeptical interpretation of the negativity of modern aesthetics underwrites most of the readings of Beckett's texts—from existential humanism to formalist concerns with the poetic and aesthetic aspects of style; from the emphasis on the sublime to the analysis of the comic effects of Beckett's language.

Although both interpretations of art's negativity—aesthetic and epistemological—are firmly entrenched in Beckett studies, the excess of Beckett's "art of failure" cannot be contained within either of these paradigms. Rather, this excess points to the remainder—literally, to what is left over when the work has been stripped from its linguistic, philosophic, and aesthetic resources of signification. For Derrida, the residue left by the most stringent process of decomposition reveals the limitation of both the philosophical and the aesthetic interpretations of the negative and calls instead for a redefinition of the task of aesthetics. By juxtaposing Adorno's and Derrida's readings of modernism, I argue that in Beckett's work this task, which is assumed and abandoned at the same time, emerges as a paradoxical sense of obligation associated with the process of writing.

This evocation of deconstruction to contest the negative formulation of Beckett's aesthetics might appear surprising if not contrived. After all, the similarities between Beckett's work and Derrida's philosophy, when elaborated at all, have been most frequently stressed in the context of "a pervasive skepticism about language as an expressive medium."[16] With its emphasis on the indeterminacy of meaning, fragmentation of form, and failure of representation, Beckett's work appears as a "perfect embodiment of deconstructive method,"[17] just as Beckett criticism seems to prefigure the negative rhetoric of deconstruction.[18] And yet, when construed in these negative terms, the engagement between poststructuralist criticism and Beckett's texts seems to be unproductive, as if the very closeness between the aesthetic and philosophical concerns were paralyzing. By assimilating Beckett's writings to negative epistemology, such interpretations simultaneously reduce the role of deconstruction to a merely redundant commentary on Beckett's own undoing of language: "theoretical and narratological interest in Beckett's art . . . has not been sustained (partly no doubt because Beckett deconstructs his own texts so thoroughly that deconstructive analyses, at any rate, often seem merely redundant)."[19] Not surprisingly, Steven Connor, in an otherwise enthusiastic review of "the work which is reading Beckett according to the linguistic antihumanism of Derrida rather than the existential humanism of Sartre," proceeds rightly with a word of caution: "There are times in this work [i.e., poststructuralist approaches to Beckett], to be sure, when the denunciation of presence and logocentric certainty can begin to seem as routine and uninspected as the affirmations of the eternal, self-making spirit of man used to be, and some of the ways in which Beckett has recently been enlisted to the posthumanist cause have indeed seemed both reductive and predictable."[20]

Can the encounter between Derrida and Beckett be less "routine" and predictable—can it still generate surprising reevaluations of modernism and perhaps of deconstruction as well? By looking closely at some of the main concerns of Beckett's texts, I want to retrace the proximity between Beckett and Derrida beyond the familiar negative paradigms of aesthetics. Instead of assimilating Beckett's writings all too quickly to the supposedly negative epistemology of deconstruction—that is, instead of construing this proximity primarily in philosophical terms—I would like to reconsider first the place of modern aesthetics within the deconstructive project. In other words, before reading

Beckett according to Derrida, we could for a moment reread Derrida in the light of Beckett's work. Perhaps the focus on the significance of modernism within deconstruction—that is, on its explicitly literary affiliation—will allow us to bring about the inventive and affirmative rather than simply negative character of the deconstructive enterprise. What is at stake here is not only a reevaluation of modernism but also a future of deconstruction itself—its capacity of invention. As Derrida asks, "in what respect can a movement of deconstruction, far from being limited to the negative or destructuring forms that are often naively attributed to it, be inventive in itself, or be the signal of an inventiveness at work in a sociohistorical field? And finally, how can a deconstruction of the very concept of invention . . . still invent?"[21]

In his few and all too brief remarks on Beckett, Derrida offers us nothing that would resemble a familiar "denunciation of presence and logocentric certainty." On the contrary, emphasizing his strong "identification" with Beckett, Derrida questions whether this very identification can be read primarily philosophically, as a negation of meaning and rationality. And yet the alternative, let us say, more literary, figuration of this affinity is not easily forthcoming: "Precisely because of this proximity, it is too hard for me, too easy and too hard . . . . How could I write, sign, countersign performatively texts which 'respond' to Beckett?"[22] Derrida's silent identification with Beckett presents us therefore with a double bind: on the one hand, it testifies to the unquestionable centrality of aesthetic modernism in the deconstructive project, but, on the other hand, it relinquishes the philosophical reflection on modernism's significance. By risking affiliation with aesthetic modernism, deconstruction renounces the philosophical reflection on aesthetics as such: it not only abandons the coherence of a philosophical project but also brings about the impossibility of the philosophical interpretation of art. Derrida concedes as much and adds an even more disquieting remark that this very impossibility marks what is most "literary" about deconstruction: "In the suggestion that a deconstruction of metaphysics is impossible 'to the precise extent that it is "literary",' I suspect there may be more irony than first appears . . . And I would say that deconstruction loses nothing from admitting that it is impossible . . . . The interest of deconstruction, of such force and desire as it may have, is a certain experience of the impossible" [*PIO*, 36]. If we still want to maintain that Derrida's work is "a theory of modernism," than we have to confront the fact that deconstruction makes such a theory impossible.

Based on "a certain experience of the impossible" (which is not the same as the experience of the negative), the affinity between Beckett's and Derrida's projects traces a peculiar chiasmus—as Jay Bernstein writes, "in Derrida artistic modernism becomes philosophical, and philosophy becomes modernist."[23] Often misread as an unproblematic identification of deconstruction and modernism, or philosophy and rhetoric, this chiasmus appears as an inoperative or dangerous figure, raising doubts as to whether an aesthetic critique of philosophical modernity could possibly succeed. According to Bernstein, for instance, Derrida's paralyzing identification with Beckett only confirms the lethal effects of such a chiasmus: "For in aligning himself directly with artistic modernism he by-passes the one question about it that is intransigently philosophical, namely, what does its critique mean in relation to our dominant habits of knowing? By philosophically repeating modernism Derrida . . . leaves untransformed the forces that make the aesthetic marginal, and leaves untransformed the contemporary regimes of knowing."[24] Philosophy's passing into modern aesthetics appears paralyzing because it risks the ultimate loss of meaning—the erasure of the philosophical question *par excellence* about the significance of aesthetics in relation to knowledge.

In contrast to Adorno's reading of Beckett (and we have to add that Beckett, to whom *Aesthetic Theory* was supposed to be dedicated, is for Adorno a paradigmatic figure of modernism), Derrida's refusal of a philosophical interpretation of modern aesthetics not only contests philosophy's prerogatives but also questions the negative formulation of modernism. It is not too difficult to note a profound correlation between these two gestures in Adorno's aesthetic theory: because art is posited as a determinate negation of instrumental rationality characteristic of modernity, it speaks an incomprehensible truth that only philosophy can decipher. As Adorno writes, "Art works are true in the medium of determinate negation only . . . . Truth content cannot be identified directly. It is mediated in itself and, if it is to be known, *calls for mediation by philosophy* (emphasis added)."[25] Finding art's refusal of interpretation to be irrelevant, Adorno legitimates philosophical reflection as a solution called for by the enigmatic "riddle" of aesthetics.[26] Although for Adorno philosophy can interpret art's truth—its promise of reconciliation without domination—only by interrupting its own coherence and by tempering its own temptation to obliterate the unintelligible, the conceptual mode of knowledge, no matter how transformed, remains nonetheless privileged: "The function of a philosophy of art should not be to explain away the unintelligible, as speculative philosophy has almost invariably been tempted to do. Instead, that function should be to understand the unintelligible as it persists in the work, thus avoiding doing violence to art."[27]

Adorno defines the central task of a philosophy of art in terms of *understanding* "the unintelligible as it persists in the work." By bypassing the issue of the philosophical significance of art, Derrida raises a far more troubling question—namely, whether an outside of "the contemporary regimes of knowing," revealed and sustained by modern aesthetics, poses primarily a philosophical problem of understanding. For Derrida, modernism's refusal of interpretation is not at all an irrelevant gesture that could be disregarded. Rather, this refusal bears an ethical significance—it implicates the attempt to understand the unintelligible, insofar as it still grants privilege to understanding, in the violence of discursive reason.

What Derrida's hesitation in front of Beckett's texts questions, therefore, is whether the implications of Beckett's aesthetics, and by extension, modernist aesthetics, are entirely exhausted by the epistemological, existentialist, or even rhetorical elaborations of art's negativity. Although in Beckett scholarship the negative interpretation of aesthetics has been far more productive than any of its positive expositions, this productivity still misses the most crucial point of Beckett's work.[28] As Derrida suggests in the interview with Derek Attridge, the peculiar signature of Beckett's texts is tied not to the epistemological or aesthetic negation but to the remainder, to the residue, left behind the process of decomposition. By carrying out the process of decomposition to its very limit, Beckett's work interrogates in an exemplary manner the very limitations of the negative formulation of aesthetics:

> A certain nihilism is both interior to metaphysics . . . and, then, already beyond. With Beckett in particular, the two possibilities are in the greatest possible proximity and competition. He is nihilist and he is not nihilist. Above all, this question should not be treated as a philosophical problem outside or above the texts . . . . The composition, the rhetoric, the construction and the rhythm of his works, even the ones that seem the most "decomposed," *that's what "remains"* finally the most "interesting," that's the work, that's the signature, *this remainder which remains when the thematics is exhausted* . . . (emphasis added).[29]

For Derrida, the question of Beckett's aesthetics cannot be reduced to a philosophical problem of nihilism or skepticism. Even "the most decomposed texts" do not just stage the spectacle of mourning for the lost truth—the spectacle, which, as Derrida suggests elsewhere, always provides compensations for the loss. Despite Derrida's opposition of philosophical interpretation to rhetoric, composition, and rhythm, that is, to the literary qualities of the text, we should not conclude too quickly that at stake in this rejection of philosophical response is a turn to the aesthetic interpretation of negativity, which, by relinquishing the conceptual significance of the work, focuses exclusively on the aesthetic uniqueness of style or on the undecidable rhetorical play of language. Rather, the issue of the literary force of the text is intertwined with the enigmatic "remainder," the significance of which resists an assimilation to both the thematics and the rhetoric of the text, to its constative and performative layers. Tracing a certain outside to metaphysics, this remainder persists beyond the most austere negations and most ingenious inventions of the text. Needless to say, the question about "what remains in the most decomposed text" refers not only to the significance of Beckett's aesthetics but is addressed, perhaps even more urgently, to the outcome of deconstruction.

No longer a symptom of an unfortunate separation of language from the unnameable reality or a sign of artistic autonomy, "the remains" exposed by the process of decomposition confront us, Derrida suggests, with the experience of otherness—with the experience of the other as the impossible. Enabled by the rhetorical instability of language, this experience calls nonetheless for a certain rereading of the rhetorical effects, so that they are no longer associated exclusively with the undoing of meaning. Referring to Paul de Man's specific deployment of rhetoric in the critique of metaphysics, Derrida reminds us that for de Man rhetoric is structured as an aporia of the performative and the constative, figure and grammar. The rapid oscillation between the performative and the constative creates a vertigo of linguistic speculum, where the mechanism of reflection produces what it describes. Although deconstruction of metaphysics relies on the aporia of rhetoric in order to unmask truth as an effect of linguistic play, Derrida warns us that this aporia can be all too easily misread as the "distress of a fabulous discourse able only to reflect itself without ever moving out of itself. In this case, the misfortune would be the mirror itself . . . it would consist—so as to ground the infinity of reflection—. . . in the specular play for which language provides" [*PIO*, 37]. If rhetoric is understood only in terms of an endless play of linguistic specularity, the price of the deconstruction of metaphysics is linguistic immanence. According to Derrida, any critique of representation is then inseparable from deconstructing its opposite—the infinite spiral of linguistic self-reflection. Only by disregarding this fact can we confuse Derrida's attention to linguistic form with the aestheticism of modernism.

In order to alleviate this "distress" of discourse reflecting only itself, Derrida reads the rhetorical instability of language as a possibility of an event. The significance of such an event can no longer be derived from the linguistic structure or grammar:

> The infinitely rapid oscillation between the performative and the constative . . . fiction and nonfiction, autoreference and heteroreference, etc., does not just produce an essential instability. This instability constitutes that very event—let us say, the work—whose invention disturbs . . . the norms, the statutes, and the rules [*PIO*, 34–35].

> Deconstruction is inventive or it is nothing at all; it does not settle for methodical procedures, it opens up a passageway . . . Its *process* involves an affirmation, this latter being linked to the coming—the *venire*—in event, advent, invention [*PIO*, 42].

This subtle rereading of rhetorical instability as an unpredictable event interrupts the endless play of linguistic reflection and allows for the experience of alterity, for "the coming of a still unanticipatable alterity and for which no horizon of waiting as yet seems ready, in place, available" [*PIO*, 55]. Derrida reserves for this impossible experience of alterity the old term "invention" while deconstructing its philosophical genealogy, especially its reliance on the subjective initiative and on the techno-theological horizon of truth. What is at stake here is an altogether different sense of invention that no longer produces alterity but allows for its possibility by interrupting the machinery of discourse—by suspending the capacity of grammar to anticipate, calculate, or absorb the unexpected within the range of present possibilities of signification. Derrida deploys the term "invention" in order to stress that the event—the experience of alterity—although not dependent on the subjective initiative, does not nonetheless imply inertia. The possibility of such an event requires intervention, which is directed in an equal measure against the violent subjective constitution of the other as well as against the impersonal specular play of language: "If the other is precisely what is not invented, the initiative or deconstructive inventiveness can consist only in opening, in uncloseting, destabilizing the foreclusionary structures so as to allow for the passage toward the other" [*PIO*, 60]. This strategic use of invention is different, for instance, from Manfred Frank's interpretation of the unpredictability of style, which all too quickly leads to the affirmation of subjective freedom. In contrast, Derrida's stress on the signification of otherness questions not only the generality of linguistic structure but also its opposite, the freedom of subjective expression. Unlike subjective freedom, deconstructive initiative—its capacity of invention—is figured as a strange task, the fulfillment of which coincides with a resignation from all initiative.

The inventiveness understood as a task (and, I would add, as an obligation) to be assumed and given up reveals the proximity between deconstruction and modern aesthetics, and perhaps explains Derrida's silent identification with Beckett. Let us look, therefore, one more time at the famous passage from Beckett's *Three Dialogues* where the inventiveness of art is almost indistinguishable from its "fidelity to failure," and where the task of aesthetics enables the experience of alterity at the very moment when all inventiveness is renounced.[30] In this strikingly self-reflective passage, the process of reflection interrupts the specular play of language itself:

> All that should concern us is the acute and increasing anxiety of the relation itself, as though shadowed more and more darkly by a sense of invalidity, of inadequacy, of existence at the expense of all that it excludes, all that it blinds to. The history of painting . . . is the history of its attempts to escape from this sense of failure, by means of more authentic, more ample, less exclusive relations between representer and representee, in a kind of tropism towards a light . . . . Van Velde is the first to desist from this estheticized automatism, the first to admit that to be an artist is to fail, as no other dare fail, that failure is his world . . . . I know that all that is required now, in order to bring even this horrible matter to an acceptable conclusion, is to make of this submission, this admission, this fidelity to failure, a new occasion . . .[31]

Foregrounding the inadequacy of representation, and, by extension, the lack of correspondence between "nameless things" and "thingless names," art's austere fidelity to failure destroys the remnants of mimetologism and seems to illustrate instead the unhappy predicament of discourse reflecting only itself. Renouncing the tasks of representation, this reflection of art on itself, insofar as it is still a reflection, achieves a total separation of the work of art from its dependence on the empirical world. If posed as the only alternative to representation, the specular play of language would confirm Clement Greenberg's philosophical diagnosis of aestheticism. That is why Beckett warns us ironically that once "this fidelity to failure" is turned into an aesthetic principle or a negative essence of style, it merely invents a new "estheticized automatism" in place of the old regime of representation.

In what way can Beckett's critique of representation escape the "estheticized automatism" of discourse reflecting itself? To disrupt the automatism of self-reflection, Beckett, with a great deal of irony, reveals first a powerful complicity between art's claims to autonomy— its formal unity—and the philosophical task of understanding achieved more directly through an adequate representation. Art's obsessive "tropism toward a light" coordinates even an unmediated aesthetic synthesis of form with the movement toward reason. As Emmanuel Levinas suggests, the price of the formal coherence of discourse is the erasure of otherness: reason "consists in assuring the coexistence of . . . [the] terms, the coherence of the one and the other despite their difference . . . it ensures the agreement of the different terms without breaking up the present in which the theme is held."[32] Similarly, Beckett charges that the tropism toward light is blinding; that its "estheticized automatism" coordinates seemingly autonomous aesthetics with the claims of reason. Implicating aesthetic coherence in an insidious (because far more subtle) obliteration of alterity, Beckett's art of failure renounces the illusion that the formal unity of the work of art is less repressive than a conceptual synthesis in the cognitive judgment. By the same token, he destroys the persistent hope, running from Kant's to Arendt's and Adorno's theories of aesthetics, that the formal unity of the work of art can pre-figure social integration without domination.

In a mode similar to Levinas and Derrida, Beckett's disruption of the formal coherence and the generality of grammar is bound with a critique of the subjective initiative rather than with an affirmation of subjective freedom. The coherence and synchronicity of the one and the other, whether achieved by cognition or by a free play of imagination, is correlative with the act of reason and the primacy of consciousness. Artistic or philosophical, consciousness is characterized by its capacity to reassemble and synthesize the manifold. As Levinas argues, "reason, in which the different terms are present, that is, are contemporaneous in a system, is also the fact that they are present to consciousness inasmuch as consciousness is representation, beginning, freedom."[33] In this sense, representation of the other is coextensive with its constitution, with its violent invention by the subject. Instead of mourning for the lost truth, Beckett's work creates anxiety about violence—violence which implicates both representation and the formal coherence of the work in obliteration of alterity.

If "the tropism toward light" reveals a concealed analogy between aesthetic unity and the claims of truth, Beckett's "fidelity to failure" delineates a rift between aesthetics and reason. Rejecting both the tasks of representation and the autonomy of art, Beckett's texts move toward the other of reason, as if situating themselves below the light. As Beckett writes in *How It Is*, "it's the place without knowledge . . . that is above in the light."[34] This disjunction between aesthetics and knowledge, revealed by the crisis of representation, intensifies the "acute anxiety" of the relation between representation and what it represents. In a movement away from light, Beckett's texts turn against representation, not to purify the medium of art or to demonstrate the impossibility of knowledge, but to uncover "a sense of invalidity, . . . of existence *at the expense of all that it excludes,* all that it blinds to." By increasing a sense of the incommensurability of what is represented and representation itself, "the anxiety of relation" reveals what remains outside of both representation and aesthetic synthesis. This "remainder" marks the precarious signification of the other desisting from the movement toward synthesis, unity, or comprehension.

By enabling an experience of alterity, the most rigorous decomposition of grammar and form can be also seen as a certain act of invention. No longer a manifestation of subjective freedom, this invention turns against the machinery of discourse in order to make the experience of alterity possible. This sense of invention beyond subjective initiative recalls Levinas's suggestion that the experience of the other is intertwined with a process of decomposition—otherness manifests itself in "a difference, a non-coinciding, an arrythmia in time, a diachrony refractory to thematization."[35] Levinas's description of a heteronomous text comes in fact very close to Beckett's own practice of writing. There is no better way to describe the style of Beckett's work than to call it, in Levinas's words, an "interrupted discourse catching up with its own breaks."[36] The interruption of the aesthetic unity of the text and the suspension of the specular play of language reveals the only effects of invention that Beckett's texts claim for themselves.

How is it possible to acknowledge the claims of alterity in the process of interpretation? Jay Bernstein argues that "alterity, the excess, the non-identical" is also what is at stake in Adorno's reading of Beckett. According to Bernstein, interpretation redeems the experience of otherness if it sustains "the *cognitive* significance of works' incomprehensibility, their moment of non-discursive *cognition* [emphasis added]."[37] Locating this task at the center of Adorno's theory of modern aesthetics, Bernstein deplores the absence of a similar philosophical gesture in Derrida's readings of modernism. Derrida's refusal to elaborate a cognitive significance of art's incomprehensibility questions, however, whether the experience of alterity can be redeemed by cognition, even a "non-discursive" one. To authenticate the excess of alterity preserved in the work of art through "the cognitive significance of the work" is to assume that both the claims of alterity and the aesthetic invention can be co-extensive with the discovery of truth. As Derrida points out, however, nothing in Beckett's texts allows us to make such an assumption. Because Beckett's aesthetics maintains the disjunction between alterity and reason, the claims of otherness do not call for a philosophical legitimation but rather impose a powerful sense of obligation. As Beckett writes in "Three Dialogues," the task of aesthetics is to "express" a sense of obligation beyond desire, knowledge, or aesthetic pleasure: "The expression that there is nothing to express, nothing with which to express, nothing from which to express, no power to express, no desire to express, together with the obligation to express."[38] At the limits of representation and at the limits of aesthetic unity, obligation emerges as the only possible response to the claims of alterity preserved by art. Although irreducible to the task of representation, such obligation does not allow art to rest within the inertia of self-referentiality or aesthetic autonomy.

Rejecting the impasses of modern aesthetics where the tasks of representation are pitted against artistic autonomy, or where a participation in social praxis is pitted against the purification of art, Beckett's "fidelity to failure" places "obligation" at the core of his aesthetic project. And yet, the most frequent interpretations of Beckett's aesthetics usually focus on the professed "impotence" of his work while eliding this surprising, and perhaps incomprehensible, sense of obligation. How can impotence bestow responsibility upon the work of art—not to mention the fact that this peculiar rhetoric of responsibility and obligation sounds somewhat embarrassing, moralistic, and out of place in a modern aesthetics dominated by the idea of the independent or formally innovative art? Neither inertia nor initiative, such an obligation in Beckett's work does not bear any specific content but merely preserves fidelity to the outside as the other, as the residue escaping the order of representation and aesthetic synthesis. This "haunting" relation between aesthetics and obligation implies that neither mourning for truth nor the aesthetic appreciation of the uniqueness of style can exhaust art's significance. By manifesting the inadequacies of aesthetic and epistemological interpretations of art's negativity, Beckett's "fidelity to failure" situates aesthetics in the context of the paradoxical ethics in the Levinasian sense. Thus, a disjunction between knowledge and aesthetics reveals an even more disturbing disparity between representation and obligation, between truth and ethics. In this often ignored, and yet so characteristic for Beckett, movement from "failure" to "obligation," the proximity between modern aesthetics and deconstructive philosophy manifests itself with an unexpected force.

Impossible Invention: Aesthetics and the Signification of Alterity

We are not far now from the main concerns of *How It Is*. Beckett published his *Comment C'est* in 1960, after almost a ten-year break from longer fiction. Four years later, the text, translated by the author himself, appeared in English as *How It Is*. This return to fiction, after a period of fruitful work with theater, resulted in Beckett's most penetrating reflection on the impasses threatening aesthetics, and in the astounding invention of the tasks art is still obligated to perform. Although many of Beckett's readers feel that such a major "shift" (one of the many in Beckett's career) in his approach to aesthetics occurs in *How It Is*, few link this change with Beckett's focus on the role aesthetics can play in the context of the social and ethical aspects of language. Paradoxically, the text, which stages almost obsessively a violent clash between the signification of alterity and the rationality inherent in communication, between the shock of otherness and absorption of this shock within a discursive community, has been read almost exclusively within the paradigms of self-expression or self-referential language.[39] Yet, what the text makes clear from the outset is that its central aesthetic and linguistic concerns are inseparable from the signification of alterity and its effects on the speaking subject, on the dynamics of dialogue, and on the claims to community.

The frequently and obsessively repeated phrase, a refrain of sorts with which the text opens and closes, "how it was I quote before Pim with Pim after Pim how it is three parts I say it as I hear it" [*H*, 7], describes in a nutshell the main event of the text. Yet, the significance of this event—"how it was"—is never recovered, as if the encounter with the other could no longer be taken for granted. Confronting the dangers of the obliteration of alterity, Beckett's text assumes the obligation to invent and preserve the very possibility of such an event. Neither initiative nor inertia, the work of invention in *How It Is* is not a matter of representation, memory, or knowledge. Figured as a disruption of the aesthetic unity of the text and the decomposition of grammar, such a minimal invention merely opens a passage toward the other, it lets the unexpected manifest itself in the intervals of discourse. One of the most striking stylistic and rhetorical effects of Beckett's invention is the figure of parataxis—a trope of disconnection and interruption *par excellence*. In this text where disintegration and dissolution are played out to the fullest, all the familiar Beckettian conflicts, tensions, and spiraling self-negations seem to be left undone. No longer do we encounter a familiar narrator mounting paradoxes, denouncing his power and means to speak and yet unable to stop the prolific stream of words, as for instance is the case with the narrator of *The Unnameable*: "What am I to do, what shall I do . . . , in my situation, how proceed? By aporia pure and simple? Or by affirmations and negations invalidated as uttered, or sooner or later? . . . There must be other shifts."[40] The change in Beckett's narrative structure from a solipsistic subject preoccupied with the aporias of self-reflection to a subject situated in relation to the other is reflected at the level of the composition of the text and its language: *How It Is* moves away from an aporetic discourse, sustained and immediately undercut by the narrator's power of contradiction, to the calmness of paratactic prose, as if to underscore the fact that the invention of the other no longer depends on the subject's initiative.

The relation of the "I" and the "other" is the central and most problematic linguistic question in the entire text; this relation provides the narrative with the minimum of content and structure while at the same time undercutting all remnants of structural stability. The minimal content of the narrative is well known and yet insufficient to account for the fragmented style of the text: An interrupted flow of words murmured by a solitary anonymous character crawling in mud, with a sack tied to his neck, toward his companion, Pim, constitutes part I. The second part, structured around "the couple," presents their dialogue as gruesome parody of the master/slave dialectic. In the third part, called "the abandonment," the forsaken tormentor awaits his share of suffering while speculating on the nature of linguistic community. In contrast to this almost schematic and rigid outline of the plot, the figures of the mud, murmur, and panting suggest an erosion of articulation, a dissolution of even minimal order. The dissolution of form, manifest in a glaring disregard for syntax, grammar or narrative linearity, culminates in the intimation that the entire narrative could be told just as easily backwards. The only exception to the endless reversals of every possible arrangement is the encounter with the other. The narrative structure can be turned backwards but only "on condition that by an effort of the imagination the still central episode of the couple be duly adjusted" [*H*, 132]. The possibility of inversion suggests that the central "relation" to the other puts every other mode of synthesis or arrangement into question.[41] Although it seems to preserve at least one semantic connective, suggested by the pronoun "with," the relation to the other in Beckett's text not only destroys the figure of the couple but also destabilizes the semantic and logical function of a copula—the very possibility of connection and synthesis in general.

The most immediate stylistic effect of this erosion of synthesis is visible in the elliptic, dislocated, and fragmented syntax.[42] Written with a complete disregard for sentences, punctuation, and even the connectives between the words themselves, *How It Is* is composed of repeated clusters of phrases brought together without any internal cohesion:

> suddenly like all that was not then is I go not because of the shit and vomit something else not known not said whence preparatives sudden series subject object subject object quick succession and away [*H*, 11]

In spite of the presence of the subordinating conjunctions like "because of" and "whence," the paratactic style of writing disengages words instead of grouping them together. With an increasing uncertainty about logical and semantic connectives, words appear in isolation, in "quick succession," as if the function of their physical proximity on the page were to preserve distance and dehiscence. The omission of major verbs, the unknown referents of pronouns and a fundamental uncertainty about the logical and semantic relations between syntactical elements destroys any sense of correlation between the subject and the predicate. As Marjorie Perloff observes, even if we manage to correct or fill in the absences in this prose, the sentences still refuse to be units of meaning: "But even when we succeed in determining the boundaries of Beckett's fragmented phrases, the condensed text remains an enigma."[43]

These rhetorical effects of parataxis are not, however, only a matter of formal experimentation; rather, they expose a signification of alterity incommensurate with the coherence of discourse, whether this coherence is expressed in the form of philosophical propositions or the grammar of ordinary language. Beckett's explicit focus on the incompatibility between signification of otherness and the rules of grammar prefigures Derrida's attempt to theorize syntax beyond the requirements of semantics.[44] For Derrida, the excess of syntax, overflowing the closure of the sentence as the unity of meaning, preserves not only the heterogeneity and the non-coincidence of elements brought into play but also their non-simultaneity. In place of the syntactic rules supporting the unity of sense, both Derrida and Beckett explore the unstable possibilities of heterogeneous and unexpected constellations. For

Derrida, this emphasis on the heterogeneity of discourse is inter-twined with the strategic importance of "in-betweens," which, instead of spelling out stable logical relations, constitute both the possibility of relation and its interruption, connection, and rupture. Similarly, Beckett's use of parataxis replaces clear semantic connectives with far more ambiguous gaps and intervals. These temporal and spatial inter-vals become the source both of signification and of semantic instabili-ty—in Beckett's words, the source of "anxiety over relation itself."

The rhetorical effects of parataxis allow for the inscription of alter-ity in language and simultaneously prevent its assimilation into the present possibilities of signification. Beckett's peculiar stylistic inven-tion preserves the signification of otherness not in what is said but in a blank between the words—in a retreat of "something else not known not said." This retreat marks the temporal and spatial distance between the subject and the source of language: "how it *was* I quote before Pim with Pim after Pim how it *is*/ three parts I say it as I hear it// voice once without quaqua on all sides then in me when the/ panting stops tell me again finish telling me invocation" [*H*, 7, emphasis added]. The saying is already a repetition of the voice that is both internal and exter-nal, within the subject and dispersed outside "on all sides."

Saying as quoting reveals a strange temporality that is neither pre-sent nor past: it continually slides from "how it is" to "how it was," without ever suggesting that the past can be synchronized with the present. This temporal lapse reveals that the signification of the other belongs to the irretrievable past, which cannot be recuperated within the present moment of speaking. Derrida credits Levinas with articu-lating this specifically temporal aspect of alterity: "A past that has never been present: this formula is the one that Emmanuel Levinas uses . . . to qualify the trace and enigma of absolute alterity: the Other."[45] In Beckett's text, this temporal exteriority of the other is also reflected in the composition of the narrative, which, from the outset, replaces the logical relations, which usually synchronize various parts of a narrative into one whole, with unstable temporal links: "I quote a given moment long past vast stretch of time on from there that moment and following not at all a selection natural order vast tracts of time" [*H*, 7]. In place of the connectives indicating a subjective purpose and direction of the journey— "toward," and "away from"—the text eliminates synchronizing semantic conjunctions and replaces them with the purely temporal markers of before and after, with the traces of the "vast tracts of time".[46]

Beckett's impossible invention places the speaking subject in a secondary position with respect to a speech he does not originate.

From the outset, the monologue of "I" becomes indistinguishable from quoting. The withdrawal of "something not said" from the flow of words not only interrupts the order of syntax but also splits the identity of the speaking subject. As the narrative is sustained by forming and breaking the couples of tormentors and victims, the narrative voice likewise bifurcates into "I" and "other." Not limited to the second part "with Pim," the movement toward the other marks the interval in the subject's relation to itself and to its own speech.[47] The voice, which impels the narrator to speak as if independent of any subjective initiative, inscribes difference between the same and the other within the interiority of self. The vacillating temporal and spatial interval between voice and subject, between the self and the other, enables the experience of alterity by disrupting the circle of self-reflection. As Derrida suggests,

> what is called the speaking subject is no longer the person himself, or the person alone, who speaks. The speaking subject discovers his irreducible secondarity, his origin that is always already eluded . . .[48]

In Beckett's fiction this belatedness of consciousness—revealed in the difference between what is quoted and quoting itself—indicates that each "present version," "present formulation" is incapable of recuperating the saying which belongs to the past. Yet, what precedes the quoted version is nothing, it has no identity on its own. "How it was" withdraws from "how it is"—it cannot be recovered, or be assimilated into the presence of the subject and the presence of speaking. The temporal withdrawal of "how it was" from every speech act announces the signification of alterity, to use Levinas's term, as irreducible diachrony. The insurmountable diachrony of the past—the enigma of "how it was with Pim"—suggests that the signification of the other cannot be recovered even after the entire process of quoting is exhausted: "here then at last part two where I have still to say how it was as I hear it in me . . . vast stretch of time" [*H*, 51]. Rather, the signification of the other is bound to an uncertainty about the receding past: "there's a past perhaps this will work in the past part two with Pim how it was another little difference perhaps compared to what precedes" [*H*, 52]. The quotation marks constantly refer us to this past and at the same time "mark" its retreat from the speaking subject: "nothing is coming back to me" [*H*, 15]. Quoting therefore does not explain the past as the origin of the subject and its speech but reveals a signification that is no longer contemporaneous with the order of consciousness.

The quotation of the unknown voice is by no means identical with the work of memory. Calling it "Proustian parody," Perloff interprets *How It Is* as a "radical deformation" of the modernist text, a parody of the privileged moments of memory.[49] Indeed, the few instances of recollection or dream, such as the scene of the lovers or the mother teaching the child his prayers, contribute more to the loss rather than to the recuperation of the narrator's identity: "what about it my memory we're talking of my memory not much . . . things are coming back to me nothing is coming back to me " [*H*, 15]. As the axis of "dream, memory, moment," pointed out by Perloff, fails to reassemble the coherence of the text, this failure underscores even further the irreducible diachrony and exteriority of the past. It is as if the other belongs to the "immemorial" past the work of memory fails to recover in the presence of the speaking self.

Beckett's refusal to name the source of language in a more precise way than "not-I" bears a striking affinity to Derrida's critique of auto-affection:

> To hear oneself is the most normal and the most impossible experience. One might conclude from this, first, that the source is always other, and that whatever hears itself, not itself hearing itself, always comes from elsewhere, from outside and afar. The lure of the I, of consciousness as hearing-oneself-speak would consist in dreaming of an operation of ideal and idealizing mastery, transforming hetero-affection into auto-affection, heteronomy into autonomy . . . . This possibility of a "normal" double hallucination permits me to give myself to hear what I desire to hear . . .[50]

In destroying all the appearance of auto-affection and autonomy of consciousness, Beckett's fiction situates the speaking subject in the field of listening to the unnameable voice. Focusing on the movement toward the other rather than on the contradictions of self-expression, *How It Is* marks the irreducible heterogeneity of language and its distance from the speaking self.[51]

The repetition implied in quoting which, nonetheless, functions as an original speech act, questions the very possibility of beginning, initiating, or inventing in a conventional sense. As most Beckett commentators notice, the French title *Comment c'est*—"how it is"—is a pun on *commencer*—"to begin." This undecidable difference between the repetition of the same and the origination of the new suggest that invention in Beckett's text is associated with a withdrawal of the other rather than with an initiative of the subject: "how I got here no question not known not said" [*H*, 7]. The invention, which merely allows for the withdrawal of alterity from the present order of discourse, can hardly be equated with the subject's initiative, its power to begin, its freedom to signify or represent. Rather, the narrator's inability to claim language as one's own, or to posit consciousness as the origin of voice, situates every initiative of the self as already a response to the other. The very act of speaking, of inventing and originating, puts into question the freedom and agency of self. As Levinas writes, alterity signifies "before the thematization of signification by a thinking subject, before the assembling of terms in a present, a pre-original reason that does not proceed from any initiative of the subject."[52] In *How It Is*, the subjective power to begin, to say "I," is thwarted by the inability to recover the signification of the other—*commencer* is each time indistinguishable from *comment c'est*. The only trace that the withdrawal of the other leaves—"all that almost blank...a few traces that's all"—is the mark of belatedness attached to the utterance of the first person narrator.

Because of this withdrawal of the origin of voice from consciousness, the awareness of speaking, of "I say it," is bound up with an essential ignorance about "who" speaks. The very question about the source of voice becomes irrelevant, or even of no "interest":

> I hear and don't deny don't believe *don't say any more who is speaking* that's not said any more *it must have ceased to be of interest* but words like now before Pim no no that's not said only mine my words mine alone . . . that's the difference great confusion [*H*, 21, emphasis mine].

> but words like now words not mine before Pim no no that's not said *that's the difference* I hear it between then and now *one of the differences among the similarities* [*H*, 21, emphasis mine]

As the movement of these two passages suggests, a withdrawal of the source of voice from conscious knowledge undermines all sense of possession and control over language: it introduces endless vacillation between statements like "mine words mine alone" and "words not mine." By creating "the great confusion" rather than a clear distinction between the "I" and "other," the "I" and speech, language inscribes the difference between the same and the other in the relation of the subject to itself, interrupting in this way the circle of self-identification.

The indifference to the identity of the speaker manifests itself throughout the text in the slippage from the active to the passive voice, from "I don't say" to "it's not said." Used in utterances in which the subject is semantically empty, the passive mode in Beckett's fiction is extended to memory, dreams, and images, which also recur in the same involuntary, unpredictable, and uncontrollable manner: for instance "that's not how I'm told this time" is parallel to "and yet a dream *I am given* a dream" [*H*, 12–13, emphasis added]. Occurring without the subject's initiative, the impossible invention preserves the signification of alterity as an unexpected event that befalls the subject. By renouncing knowledge based on freedom and initiative, the subject abandons the intention of saying for the sake of repeating the voice that is and is not in his possession. As Gerald Bruns suggests, in Beckett's fiction language "compels itself" into being without the intention of the speaker: "What emerges . . . [is] a problem of the literary utterance compelled into being by language itself, which impinges upon the storyteller, thus to wrench from him an act of speech that is utterly without motive."[53] This passivity of the subject, its renunciation of initiative and the power of representation, does not imply, however, inertia. Rather, as the composition of the text reminds us, this invention beyond all possible initiative can be only described as the movement of the self toward the other, as a certain task undertaken for the sake of the other.

The task undertaken for the other is repeatedly associated in *How It Is* with the act of writing. The text the narrator is called to record is different, however, from the narrative of "life in natural order":

> here then part one how it was before Pim we follow I quote the natural order more or less my life last state last version what remains bits and scraps I hear it my life natural order more or less [*H*, 7].

The fragmentation of language—"what remains bits and scraps"—implies that the movement toward the other escapes the teleology of the narrative because this movement no longer culminates in self-knowledge. Not absorbed into an autobiographical narrative of a self returning to itself, the signification of alterity requires a strange testimony to an event that escapes the order of memory and consciousness.

Incompatible with the model of an autobiography, the movement toward the other is compared instead to a recording of a witness. As the parallels between the movement in the mud and the quoted monologue, between the listening to the alien voice and the movement of the hand, suggest, the invention of the other undoes the opposition between inertia and initiative. This impossible invention puts the self in the position of a witness and a scribe, as if to suggests that speaking

to the other is from its inception caught in the secondariness characteristic of writing. Yet, what listening, quoting, witnessing, and writing all have in common is not only a sense of belated repetition but
also a sense of obligation. The analogy between writing and witnessing suggests that even an "originary" speech act is obligated to preserve the exteriority of otherness and its irreducibility to the intentionality of consciousness.[54]

The first part of *How It Is* stages the invention of the other not in
terms of representation but in terms of an interminable movement
toward the other. Analogous to the process of writing, this movement
is no longer sustained by the subject's desire, initiative, or need,
because, as the text implies, both need and desire would turn the other
into an invention of the self.[55] This absence of desire inscribes the narrator in the dubious position of an "incurious seeker," who, in the
process of writing, abandons all curiosity and aspirations to knowledge.[56] What kind of a motivation could sustain such a peculiar invention which begins only "when the great needs fail the need to move on
the need to shit and vomit and the other great needs all my great categories of being" [*H*, 14], including even the need for words: "no preference no searching not even for a language meet for me meet for here
no more searching" [*H*, 17]? As Beckett's insistence on "no preference
no searching" makes clear, the movement toward the other is not a
quest for self-knowledge or for mutual understanding, but a matter of
obligation. When all "the great categories of being" are displaced, the
irreducible exteriority of the other imposes on Beckett's narrators an
obligation "to express," an obligation to continue speaking. This obligation is consistently associated in *How It Is* with the function of a witness, whose testimony, however, does not represent any specific event
but merely registers what withdraws itself from the order of discourse.
Irreducible to knowledge or need, one could call such obligation, perhaps, a matter of ethics.

Inventions of the Possible: Beckett's Couples and Nightmare of Communicative Reason

The movement toward the other—the impossible invention of the
event, the experience of radical alterity—removes the speaking subject
from the origin of meaning and imposes on him an obligation of being
a witness. In part II of *How It Is*, this impossible invention is contrast-
ed with a more familiar act of subjective creativity, understood as freedom and initiative, as if to suggest that the obligation associated with

writing is inseparable from an undoing of violence implied in a conventional sense of invention. This more conventional sense of invention is displayed in Beckett's text in a rather surprising, if not shocking, context of torture and cruelty. The only scene of a direct communication in the entire text is staged as a monstrous invention, as a violent constitution of the other's identity. Beckett turns a seemingly ordinary communicative situation—a scene of dialogue with the other—into an extraordinary spectacle of cruelty. This relentless emphasis on the nightmarish aspect of communication and on the violence of intersubjective understanding puts Beckett at odds with those approaches to modernity which thematize the renewal of its emancipatory potential in terms of communicative rationality. Whether it is Cavell's belief in the therapeutic effect of the intersubjective agreement, or Habermas's recovery of the emancipatory power of communicative reason, the intersubjective communication is appealed to as the only means to salvage modern culture's endangered rationality. Despite his concern with the signification of alterity, Beckett refuses, however, to enlist aesthetics in the service of emancipation or therapeutic cure associated with communicative rationality. This refusal of "dialogical therapy" cannot simply be blamed on the increasing reification of culture or on the predominance of instrumental, means-ends rationality, which destroys the openness, responsiveness, or empathy usually associated with intersubjective dialogue. Nor is it merely the case, as Adorno would have it, that Beckett's prose confronts modernity with its own negative but true image—with the nightmare that modern culture denies in its rational self-representation. Rather, the failure of communication staged in the second part of *How It Is* reveals a violent clash between the signification of alterity and the ends of communicative reason itself.

The monstrous scene of communication stages a violent, though no doubt "therapeutic," attempt to mend the instabilities of discourse by overcoming the asymmetry between the self and the other. Toward this end, the text explores the way the figure of the couple functions on three related levels: on the level of language, it dramatizes the possibilities of the unification of discourse; on the level of hermeneutics—the possibility of understanding the other; and on the level of communication—the possibility of intersubjective rationality and consensus. In an attempt to reunite or to bridge the fluctuating gap between the I and the other, between saying and quoting, between self and language, the couple episode inscribes the relation to the other within a familiar mode of communication and mutual understanding.

The seemingly innocuous desire to comprehend the other, to achieve reciprocity and mutual understanding between the partners in dialogue, culminates in Beckett's text in the most violent language lesson. We are confronted here with quite a different sense of invention—with the invention of the other as a complement of the self. Coextensive with an obliteration of alterity, this invention is presented in the text as both a condition and an achievement of a dialogue. Beckett's relentless, almost vicious, emphasis on the cruelty of the linguistic exchange dramatizes the fact that what are usually taken as the necessary conditions of intersubjective communication—reciprocity, the symmetrical relationship between the speakers, and their mutual "attunement," or as Beckett says ironically, "our life in common"—is in fact violently produced in the course of linguistic exchange. Communicative reason is not divorced from the power of invention; on the contrary, it violently produces the necessary conditions for its success. Intertwined with the effort to overcome the opacity of the other, the violence of dialogue brings the other into the light of comprehension. In *How It Is*, violence becomes paradoxically a measure of both the success and failure of this linguistic invention: success—because the necessary conditions of communication are inevitably produced and reproduced; failure—because "successful" communication can no longer maintain the pretensions of reciprocity and openness.

In order to demonstrate how the dimension of intersubjectivity is produced, Beckett makes the central linguistic exchange in the text inseparable from the process of instruction. The invention of the possible is in fact one of the effects of the pedagogical operation. It is tempting at this point to read *How It Is* as a gruesome parody of the numerous language lessons in Wittgenstein's *Philosophical Investigations*. Yet if Wittenstein's examples of failed instruction suggest the inevitable breakdown of pedagogical machinery, Beckett's scenes of linguistic torture illustrate its "success" and thus implicate the seemingly spontaneous intersubjective agreements in the operation of pedagogical apparatus. The scene of dialogue starts with a discovery that the encountered companion can speak and sing, although he does so in an incomprehensible, foreign language. The foreign language blocks from the outset all possibilities of comprehension—the other remains outside the horizon of intelligibility despite his tantalizing closeness: "a human voice there within an inch or two . . . even a human mind if I have to learn Italian" [*H*, 56]. Since a foreign language resists univocal translation, the narrator invents his own code of communication in order to establish the "mutuality" of understanding. With every gesture representing a univocal signification—the thumb on the skull meaning stop, for instance—the language lesson turns into a process of training and discipline. When, in the course of the lesson, the narrator carves the entire Roman alphabet and Arabic numerals on Pim's body, these bodily inscriptions emphasize again and again that mutual understanding— call it mutual attunement, or the condition of being in common—does not occur spontaneously but is accomplished at the price of a violent obliteration of alterity. In order to comprehend his partner in a dialogue, the subject violently constitutes the other's identity. This act of invention is, however, identical with the erasure of alterity: instead of finding the source of the voice in the other *self*, the narrator constitutes the other as a passive receptor or a blank page to be covered with his own writing. Yet, even though writing on the body seems to close the gap between the subject and the other, and between the message and the addressee, it only perpetuates their non-coincidence, since the reception is obstructed by the body, and comprehension obliterated by pain. Instead of mutual reciprocity, the narrator merely reproduces in his relation to the other his own subjection to language.

The "significant" part of this monstrous invention consists in naming the other "Pim" "for more commodity more convenience." The violence of this first naming act not only dispels the anonymity of the other, creating thus a semblance of knowledge and familiarity, but also creates reciprocity between the I and the other: "I too Pim." The non-coincidence between the self and the other is now reduced to their inequality, expressed in their roles of tormentor and victim, instructor and student, master and slave. Although still subjected to quoting the unrecognizable voice, the subject becomes an active agent in the attempt to master the passive but nonetheless resistant source of language in Pim. So far passive, separated from itself, and held in suspension by language, the Beckettian subject assures himself of his control over language by literally afflicting the other with the letter. In this way the traditional role of subjective initiative is equated with one of the most drastic forms of "activity"—with torment.

Violence perpetuated on the body of the victim triggers then a release (but not a relief) from the continuous vacillation between the self and the other. In Beckett's text, the gruesome master/slave dialectic is fuelled by desire to comprehend the other, to comprehend oneself, and finally, to master the other within oneself. If quoting places the self in an uncertain relation to speech, both passive and active at the same time, violence reifies those simultaneous aspects of utterance into "stable" roles of tormentor and victim. With its clear distribution of the passive and active roles, the scene of torment locates the origin of invention in the self. The subject is defined now as an active tormentor, the one who "subjects" the other to the violence of the letter. As the passive recipient, the victim, subjected to violent carnal disfiguration, is constituted as an object of discourse.

In contrast to communication between two conscious selves, the dialogue in *How It Is* is constantly obstructed by the exteriority of the body. In a vicious parody of intersubjectivity, oral communication between two subjects is displaced onto the terrain of the body and writing.[57] In this reversal from voice to letter, the instrument of articulation is transferred from mouth to hand. The attempt to comprehend the other is literalized as the groping gesture of the hand, as a possessive grasp. In another morbid linguistic joke, the process of comprehension—of bringing what is concealed into the openness of light—is carried out by instruments like the can opener, with which the tormentor proceeds to "open" his victim. As numerous and not so subtle allusions to devouring, voracity, and "gorging on his fables" suggest, the desire to comprehend the other amounts to the violent incorporation of alterity within the self. The unsuppressed appetite for understanding links the scene of communication to cannibalism.

Reproducing his own subjection to language in the subjection of Pim's body, the narrator does not respect the other as a "subject" but turns him into an "object" measured according to its "utility." And yet, the repeated attempt to appropriate the other's self-understanding, to find an "access to his language," to reach his inner sense, fails because what is exposed to the hold of the subject is merely a formless, asexual and passive body: "Pim never be but for me anything but a dumb limp lump flat for ever in the mud" [*H*, 52]. Despite the violent objectification, the narrator's clutch fails to trace the complete contour of the other's body or to render it intelligible:

> the hand approaches under the mud comes up at a venture the
> index encounters the mouth it's vague it's well judged the thumb
> the cheek somewhere something wrong there dimple malar the
> anatomy all astir lips hairs buccinators [*H*, 56]

Just as the ear of the narrator cannot make out Pim's words, so his hand, despite its "touch of ownership" cannot make out the figure of Pim's body. The enumeration of parts does not produce the figure of the face; the body as a whole cannot be articulated by the touch—"the anatomy all astir" remains incomplete, fragmented, and vague. Although the body becomes an arena of subjection to language, this subjection, no matter how violent, fails nonetheless to assimilate the other into what Levinas calls "the order of the same," because language constantly slides from the interior of consciousness to the exterior of the body, from the inferiority of voice to the exteriority of writing. Despite the violent desire of incorporation, the exteriority of the body and the opacity of the letter preserve the non-coincidence between the other and the same.

This non-coincidence is projected back on the body of the narrator who is now reduced to the involuntary movement of his index finger, the thumb and the nails. As the parts of the body come to occupy the position of the agent, the pronoun "I" frequently disappears in part II as if to suggest that the attempt to master language only further disfigures the subject:

> can't go on we are talking of me not Pim Pim is finished he has finished me now part three not Pim my voice not his saying this these words . . . no Pim no Bom and this voice quaqua of us all never was only one voice my voice never any other [*H*, 86–87]

The disfiguring reflexivity of the touch of the body in relation to the subject is further illustrated in the macabre parable of the eastern sage who "having clenched his fists from the tenderest age . . . till the hour of his death," could see his nails piercing his palms and emerging on the other side of his hand [*H*, 53]. The horror of the sage at the sight of his living body pierced by its most inanimate part, is intensified by the suspicion that the nails would grow even after the death of consciousness. The touch that withdraws from the world and recoils on itself (a parallel to the sage's withdrawal from the world into mental meditations) points to the non-coincidence of the body with itself: the body touching itself literally disarticulates itself.[58]

All the more ironic seems the fact that the scene of torment is nonetheless a "successful" invention, abounding in such expressions as "meaning," "signification," "deduction," "the bloom of relation proper"—all of which are absent or denied in other parts of the text. The language lesson repeatedly insists on implementing the principles of rationality and logic in intersubjective exchange: "what is required of me now what is the meaning of this new torment" [*H*, 67]. This semantic success of invention coincides, however, with the loss of all inventiveness. Based either on yes or no question-and-answer exchanges, or on commands and rules, the language lesson resembles more and more a police-like investigation or an instruction in logic. As this particular collusion of invention, interrogation, and pedagogy suggests, whether it is the level of proposition or the level of ordinary communication, "significant" and proper relations are secured by domination.

The submission of the other's body to a methodical training attempts to turn it into a perfect semantic machine. Beckett's scene of pedagogical instruction does not even remotely create the Barthesian "body of bliss," but converts the inarticulate and polymorphous body into a rational apparatus: "I make it stop suffer it to stop then set it off again" [*H*, 94]. At this point the style of the text becomes more and more mechanical as if the discovery of the objective truth about the other were coextensive with a technological invention, with a production of a techno-mathematical knowledge. As Michael Robinson suggests, this reduction of the other to a perfect rational machine is reminiscent of Descartes' vision of the talking machine in *Discourse on Method*:

> we can certainly conceive of a machine so constructed that it can utter words, can even utter words in relation to bodily actions that cause some change in its organs. Thus, if we touch it in one spot, it may ask us what we want with it . . . [59]

The invention of such a mechanical apparatus allows for a violent conversion of an even most inarticulate cry into rational language, and consequently, on the epistemological level, into a "proof" of the other's life. Only when it is reduced to the most mechanical solicitation of language—"this music as sure as if I pressed a button" [*H*, 64]—can the inscription on the other's body be figured as a "meaningful" and rational act. Stressing the parasitical cooperation between truth and technology, invention and pedagogy, Beckett refuses to separate the hermeneutical task of understanding from the instrumental rationality. Instrumental rationality, as Derrida reminds us, is also intertwined with an invention of a certain sort—the invention of a logical or technological apparatus that would allow for the anticipation and calculation of the unexpected in advance. Always possible, such an invention inscribes the other within the present possibilities, within "the order of the calculable." Its essence lies in a creation of "an order where there is no absolute surprise, the order of what I shall call the invention of the same" [*PIO*, 55]. With tongue in cheek, Beckett suggests that this technological invention is fully consonant with "signification, expression and humanity," and even with justice. Yet, the only "justice" possible in these cruel language games depends on the symmetrical reversal of roles, on the calculated "proportionality" between suffering and torment. Committed to the rational idea of proportionality, the tormentor in turn hopes to become a victim for some other tormentor:

"who for me for whom I what I for Pim Pim for me" [H, 60]. Even violent exchange, in so far as it is a rational exchange, has to preserve its ratio intact: an equal distribution of pain and torment.

Perhaps more strikingly than other Beckett texts, *How It Is* pursues the questions of the intelligibility of the text, of the estrangement of the subject from discourse, and intersubjective communication in the context of violent and gruesome scenes of torment and suffering. As Beckett admits, his texts "act on the nerves" rather than speak to "intellect": "I am not unduly concerned with intelligibility. I hope my piece may work on the nerves of the audience not on its intellect."[60] Beckett's language fluctuates between the pathos of torment that "acts on the nerves" and the indifference of rational language that allows the issues of suffering to be regulated by mathematical justice. Even the most revolting scenes are accompanied by laconic comments of affirmation and satisfaction: "soon unbearable thump on skull...to conclude happy end" [H, 75].[61] This incongruity between subsisting revulsion and the neutrality of rational language creates two paradoxical effects. First, if revulsion to violence continues to work on our "nerves" despite all the appearances of rational justice, then the ideal of communication is contested once again because violence regulating linguistic exchange escapes all forms of intelligibility. A certain synthesis of affect and judgement, revulsion marks a breakdown of all rational regulation. Second, the issues this text so obsessively returns to—violence, cruelty, and suffering—suggest more strongly than ever that Beckett's preoccupation with the failure of communication and the crisis of representation does not situate his writings in the context of formalist aesthetics. What uproots the opposition between formalism and existentialism—an opposition very strongly entrenched in Beckett scholarship—is an invention of an altogether different aesthetics, which bears a sober testimony to the violence of communicative reason.

"The Inevitable Number": Calculation, Community, and the Divine

Although still subjected to quoting hardly comprehensible "rumors," the abandoned narrator in part III continues to invent. Not limited to a violent constitution of the companion, his next invention is even more sweeping and comprehensive—it is a discovery of a common being, or what Beckett sardonically calls, of "our life in common." In contrast to the asymmetry between the I and the other in part I, and their violent inequality in part II, the concluding part of *How It Is* parodies the appeal to discursive community as a predictable way of reclaiming the endangered rationality of language. By exploring what is at stake in this invention of rational community, Beckett pushes the ideal of rationality based on the agreement among speakers to its logical and at the same time grotesque conclusion—the rationality of communicative reason finds its expression in mathematical calculations. On the linguistic level, such a project of "a common being" calls for a replacement of the undecidable syntax, which maintains non-coincidence between the self and the other, with more rigorous operations of mathematical predictions and equations. In its vicious parody of the nostalgia for the common being, Beckett's text stages the invention of a rational community based on the mechanical justice of calculation, indistinguishable from the "fatal monotony" of the "same fate."

In contrast to the obligation to the other pursued in part I, or to the revulsion to violence reenacted in the scene of torment, the invention of a rational community promises to resolve the problems of inequality and difference by neutral operations of adding, subtracting, and multiplying. Although posited as the framework of universality and the justice "of the same," the appeal to rational community does not secure, however, equality; it merely promises a global and proportional distribution of suffering and torment. The inequality of the I and the other calls for an endless repetition of pairing and systematic role reversals of tormentors and victims with obsessive mathematical regularity. Since the couple episode stages the non-coincidence within the subject as the reversible and proportional difference between the same and the other, the pursuit of rational justice generates an infinite series of tormentors and victims:

> there he is then again last figures the inevitable number 777777 at the instant when he buries the opener in the arse of number 777778 . . . . at the same instant and in the same way by number 777776 makes his own private moan which same fate [*H*, 140]

The recourse to calculus is the last and desperate attempt to predict the unexpected, to calculate chance, and to integrate alterity into the homogeneous socio-linguistic order. As the end of this passage suggests, the possibility of being in common is taken here in its most "common" sense, namely, as the universality of "the same fate," which could bridge the gap between the subject and the other by positing both as members of the same community and the inheritors of the same language. Yet, as this passage also makes clear, the universality promised by discursive community is predicated on the economy of the same, in which everything occurs "at the same instance and in the same way." The semblance of universality is secured by impersonal, abstract, and semantically empty mathematical operations, which proceed endlessly and automatically: "each always leaves *the same* always goes towards *the same* always loses *the same* . . . our justice" [*H*, 114, emphasis mine]. In his early essay "Dante . . . Bruno. Vico . . . Joyce," Beckett sardonically describes this rational coherence of the community as the monotony of the circular repetition: "In a word, here is all humanity circling with fatal monotony about the Providential fulcrum."[62] According to Derrida, such a fatal monotony of repetition is a symptom of the homogeneous order, in which all the unexpected occurrences are eliminated or anticipated in advance. Creating a semblance of the inescapable fate, the linguistic repetition without difference marks a collapse of rationality into myth. With stunning sobriety, *How It Is* demonstrates not so much a slackened conviction in the community but the grotesque and violent consequences of the claim that community, communication, being in common, and linguistic exchange should preserve or submit to rational regulations. When appealed to as a paradigm of communicative reason, the discursive community is invariably reduced to the "fatal monotony" of a myth.[63]

The grotesque reduction of communicative reason in *How It Is* to mathematical calculations destroys all illusions about the inherent rationality of the discursive community. The mathematical distribution of tormentors and victims reveals the fact that "inherent" rationality of the community is indistinguishable from the operation of the technological apparatus, from the external and arbitrary regulations of discourse. As Steven Connor rightly points out, this recourse to calculation, evocative of *Watt*'s obsession with numbers and series, provides a sort of metanarrative with its promise of control over the randomness of language and thought: "mathematics can have the function of a metalanguage, which can place and subordinate the more slippery, perishable forms of verbal language. To resort, as Watt does, to diagrams and calculations is to attempt to master the imperfections of the ordinary language in the most visible way."[64] In place of an "incoercible absence" and the unstable relation between the I and the other, between the subject and language, mathematics offers a Pythagorean promise of a perfect regulation of the socio-linguistic exchange by number:

> there he is then again last figures *the inevitable number 777777*
> at the instant when he buries the opener in the *arse of number*

> 777778 and is rewarded by a feeble cry . . . at the same instant
> and in the same way by number 777776 makes his own private
> moan which same fate

> something wrong there [*H*, 140, emphasis mine].

Although there are unavoidable disturbances in these calculations, as is the case with the distribution of sacks, the mathematical metalanguage regulates the exchange of tormentors and victims by obliterating the background noise of "so many words ill-given ill-received ill-rendered to the mud" [*H*, 135].

In supplanting the fundamental instability of the relation between the subject and the other, the recourse to numbers points to the exteriority and arbitrariness of all social and semantic relations. The text collapses the ideal of inner communal unity into the abstract determination of exteriority. As Derrida in his analysis of Hegelian logic points out, the recourse to mathematics is an evidence of the absence of necessary, intrinsic relations.[65] Thought engaged in calculations combines elements devoid of any necessary relationships. According to Hegel, mathematical calculation offers absolute determination of relations but such determination is absolutely indifferent and wholly external to the entities that are thus related. Absolutely indifferent with respect to the subject matter on which it performs its operations, the number, like the body, represents the externalization of consciousness and thought. In this way, the number continues the problematic of exteriority but on the highest level of abstraction and indifference: purified of bodily sensuality, the number functions merely as the "determination of externality itself." No longer acting on our "nerves," the text collapses rationality into indifference and arbitrariness. Deployed as the rational regulation of intersubjective relations, mathematical calculations in *How It Is* intensify the "incoercible absence" of any intrinsic intersubjective relatedness.

In the pursuit of the perfect order and regulation, at once social and linguistic, the text transforms itself from a paratactic narration to a gigantic calculating machine which exchanges and distributes with the same indifference arses, can openers, tormentors and victims. An extension of Beckett's fascination with machines, which, like the tape recorder in *Krapp's Last Tape*, replace failing memory and introspective consciousness with mechanical reproductions, the calculating machine in part III submits intersubjective relations to the mediation of a mechanical apparatus. Refusing to distinguish technical and instrumental rationality from communicative reason, Beckett presents the discovery of the communal unity as a technological invention—as an effect of the semantic and mathematical *tekhné*. This return to communicative reason then not only does not provide an alternative but, on the contrary, extends the domain of instrumental rationality.

Yet, this social apparatus is a malfunctioning machine. There is always something "wrong" with its calculations and mathematical proportions imposed upon the formlessness of linguistic transmission—the mathematical equations are never solved completely. This failure to continue the mathematical series according to a rule recalls Wittgenstein's argument in *Philosophical Investigations* that even mathematical rules cannot function outside social language games.[66] For instance, even in the smallest combination of four members, required for the cycle to run its full course (journey, couple, abandonment), some participants never meet:

> as for number of 3 I do not know him nor consequently he me just as number 2 and the number 4 do not know each other
>
> for each of us then if only four of us one of us for ever unknown or known only by repute there is that possibility [*H*, 118].

Although the logical justice constantly reverses the categories of the other and the same, and reduces them to mathematical functions or ratios of proportionality, there are elements that can never be encountered or known directly. Thus, even in the mathematical reduction of the categories of being to numerical equations, something like the "absolute other" emerges—the other that can be known only "by repute."

Mathematical calculations are then juxtaposed with a different kind of repetition, which is represented in the text either as knowledge "by repute" or as quoting. Quoting—the persistent "I say it as I hear it"—is a substitute for the meetings that do not take place and a link between the members that are not connected to each other:

> number 814327 may speak misnomer the tormentors being mute as we have seen part two may speak of number 814326 to number 814328 who may speak of him to number 814329 who may speak of him to number 814330 and so on . . .
>
> all these words I repeat I quote on victims tormentors confidences repeat quote I and the others all these words too strong I say it again as I hear it again murmur it again . . . [*H*, 119–120]

In this passage, quoting reappears as the passing on of language from the unreachable past to an unreachable futurity, from a creature one never knew to a creature ahead one will never meet. An unavoidable supplement to the rational calculations, quoting reveals that even a rigid mathematical regulation of the couples is still intertwined with a different mode of linguistic repetition—with a barely heard "rumor transmissible ad infinitum in either direction." By pitting these two different notions of repetition—the predictability of rules and the quoting of rumor—against each other, Beckett links the social circulation of language with discontinuity and imperfection.

To counteract these imperfections and mathematical errors, the narrator invents two last hypotheses, two grand attempts to recuperate meaning: the first represents a familiar note of solipsism that posits the solitary consciousness as the origin of meaning; the second imagines a transcendental source of intelligibility outside human consciousness. These two inventions are the reversed mirror images of each other—in both cases, it is an attempt to invent a being absolved or removed from the unstable relations to others. In the hypothesis of the mysterious quasi divine "Him," Beckett parodies theological speculations, which emerge when the calculating machine breaks down. Since the unpredictable relations to others escape even mathematical or logical ordering, the last escape from relatedness seems to lie in the invention of the Divine transcending all relations. Such an invention imagines a solitary monadological being who listens only to himself, to his own story. In this image of a being closed upon himself, we are offered for a moment a guarantee of the absolute intelligibility—an assurance of the monological reason raised to the status of the Absolute. Once the Divine is imagined as a speaking being, however, then even the Absolute cannot escape linguistic vacillations between hearing and quoting, between the same and the other:

> there he is then at last that not one of us . . . at last who listens to himself and who when he lends his ear to our murmur does *no more than lend it to a story of his own devising ill-inspired ill-told and so ancient so forgotten at each telling* that ours may seem faithful [*H*, 139, emphasis added]

If the supposition of the absolute intelligibility does not fix the instability between saying and quoting then the invention of the solitary self as the mirror image of God, as the origin of the entire story, equally fails: "a formulation that would eliminate him completely . . . while rendering me in the same breath sole responsible for this unqualifiable murmur of which consequently here the last scraps" [*H*, 144].

The impossibility of *eliminating otherness completely* prevents the final return to solipsism. At the moment when the self seems to fold back upon itself and to pose itself again as the *active* subject, syntax returns to the *passive mood*: "in the familiar form of questions *I am said to ask myself* and answers *I am said to give myself* however unlikely that may appear" [*H*, 144, emphasis mine]. The ideal circle of auto-affection—I ask myself, I hear myself—is interrupted by a displacement of the "I" from the nominative to the accusative position. In the grammatical construction chosen by Beckett, the "I" occupies only the illusory position of the subject in order to mark a radical impossibility of becoming an autonomous source of meaning.[67]

With a collapse of two symmetrically opposed hypotheses—a solitary subject cut off from all relations to others and a community founded upon the source of transcendental intelligibility—the text ends with an address to the other that remains without an answer:

> I may choke no answer . . . sully the mud no more no answer the dark no answer trouble the peace no more no answer the silence no answer die no answer DIE screams I MAY DIE screams I SHALL DIE screams good [*H*, 147].

In contrast to the exact repetition secured by rational rules, quoting suggests an alternative notion of discursive community, opened by "a voice ill-spoken ill-heard murmur ill." The last pages of *How It Is* abandon both mathematical and theological speculations, and, with the emphasis on quoting, return to the signification of alterity that withdraws itself from the immanence of the common being. This withdrawal of alterity creates an almost complete dissolution of meaning: "how it was that's lacking before Pim with Pim all lost almost all nothing left almost nothing . . . leaving only silence" [*H*, 104]. Impossible to interpret or read, "all that almost blank nothing to get out of it almost nothing nothing to put in" [*H*, 104], the signification of the other reveals a minimal community founded on "almost nothing." With the emphasis on the withdrawal of otherness from linguistic coherence and social totality, the text suggests that both the signification of the other and the fate of the community rest on this "almost." As Derrida suggests, such an invention of the impossible community does not correspond to the fictive identity of a "we": "what is promised here is not, is no longer or not yet, the identifiable "we" of a community of human subjects . . . . It is another "we" that is offered to this inventiveness . . .

a "we" that does not find *itself* anywhere, does not invent itself: it can be invented only by the other who says 'come'" [*PIO*, 61].

By opposing the signification of the other to mathematical calculations, *How It Is* exposes a crucial difference between two notions of community: one being an embodiment of rational totality, the other founded upon the withdrawal of alterity from social and linguistic immanence. The couple, the meeting, the spectacle of the two, the master/slave dialectic, and the mechanical language lessons constitute the rational community of the same, whereas the discontinuity, indeterminate temporal and spatial distancing, and the "anxiety" of relation suggest a notion of sociality inaugurated by a perpetual retreat of the other from the common being. If the first appeal to being in common integrates otherness within the social and pedagogical apparatus, the second one allows for a more emphatic notion of difference that is not resolved in the production of *sensus communis*. Although it refuses nostalgia or even rational demands for the communal unity, Beckett's aesthetics is engaged nonetheless in an invention of different ways of being in common—of being with others beyond the common essence:

> it's no I'm sorry no one here knows anyone either personally or otherwise it's the no that turns up I murmur it

> and no again I'm sorry again no one here knows himself it's the place without knowledge whence no doubt its peerlessness [*H*, 123].

NOTES

1. For a comparison of Kafka's and Beckett's approaches to language, see for instance, Charles Bernheimer, "Watt's in The Castle: The Aporetic Quest in Kafka and Beckett," in *Newsletter of the Kafka Society of America* 6 (1982): 19–24.

2. Samuel Beckett, "German Letter of 1937," trans. Martin Esslin, in *Disjecta: Miscellaneous Writings and a Dramatic Fragment by Samuel Beckett*, ed. Ruby Cohn (New York: Grove, 1984), 173.

3. Harold Bloom, "Introduction," in *Samuel Beckett: Modern Critical Views*, ed. Harold Bloom (New York: Chelsea House, 1985), 5.

4. Samuel Beckett, An Interview with Israel Shenker, in *Samuel Beckett: The Critical Heritage*; ed. Lawrence Graver and Raymond Federman (London: Routledge, 1979), 148. Beckett further suggests that this process of disintegra-

tion results from an attempt to "accommodate chaos into the artistic form": "one cannot speak anymore of being, one must speak only of the mess." "Beckett by the Madeleine," An Interview with Tom Driver, in *Columbia University Forum* 4 (1961): 128.

5. S. E. Gontarski suggests, for instance, that the most characteristic effort of Beckett's aesthetics is "to undo the realistic sources of the text, to undo the coherence of the character and to undo the author's presence." Yet he links this process of effacement to the movement "toward simplicity, toward the essential, toward the universal." *The Intent of "Undoing" in Samuel Beckett's Dramatic Texts* (Bloomington: Indiana UP, 1985), 3–4.

6. Wolfgang Iser, "The Pattern of Negativity in Beckett's Prose," in *Samuel Beckett*, ed. Harold Bloom, 126.

7. David Watson, *Paradox and Desire in Samuel Beckett's Fiction* (New York: St. Martin's P, 1991), 9.

8. Clement Greenberg, "Modernist Painting," in *The New Art: A Critical Anthology*, ed. Gregory Battock (New York: E.P. Dutton, 1966), 101.

9. Northrop Fry, "Life in Death," in *Samuel Beckett*, ed. Harold Bloom, 25.

10. Iser, "The Pattern of Negativity in Beckett's Prose," 128.

11. Linda Ben-Zvi, "Samuel Beckett, Fritz Mauthner, and The Limits of Language," in *PMLA* 95 (1980): 188.

12. By placing the "fidelity to failure" at the center of his work, Beckett, according to Ben-Zvi promotes the "recognition of the basic condition of human experience—'unknown and unknowable.'" Linda Ben-Zvi, "Samuel Beckett, Fritz Mauthner and the Limits of Language," 187.

13. The parody of Cartesianism in Beckett's fiction has been discussed, for instance, by Hugh Kenner, *Samuel Beckett: A Critical Study* (Berkeley: U of California P, 1968), 117–132; and Michael Robinson, *The Long Sonata of the Dead* (London: Rupert Hart-Davis, 1969), 86–91.

14. One of the most "celebrated" emblems of such incommensurability is the famous kick which Murphy experiences in the "correlated modes of consciousness and extension, the kick in intellectu and the kick *in re*." Samuel Beckett, *Murphy* (New York: Grove, 1957), 109. Despite its new aesthetic departures, *The Trilogy* is likewise dominated by the impasses and limitations of first person narration—a solitary man immobilized in a room, telling himself stories as if cut off from any reference to the external world.

15. Samuel Beckett, *Molloy*, in *Three Novels* (New York: Grove P, 1965), 31–32. Interpreted as Cartesian skepticism, Beckett's emphasis on failure would suggest a continuity between the solipsistic mental landscape and language separated from "the fiasco of reality." Like skepticism, the aporias of solipsism have been one of the main preoccupations in Beckett criticism; for a fine analysis of the philosophical sources of Beckett's solipsism, see Ileana Marculescu, "Beckett and the Temptation of Solipsism," in *Journal of Beckett Studies* 11–12 (1989): 53–64.

16. P. J. Murphy, *Reconstructing Beckett: Language for Being in Samuel Beckett's Fiction* (Toronto: U of Toronto P, 1990), xiv.

17. P. J. Murphy, xii–xv.

18. It is somewhat paradoxical that despite all these worries about the reductive affinities between poststructuralism and Beckett's work, Beckett has not occupied the center of the theoretical debates the way Kafka has. Even with the new and comparatively late strain of theoretically invested scholarship, we still do not have, to my knowledge, the phenomenon that could be called "the poststructuralist Beckett" on the scale comparable to the "poststructuralist Kafka." There are, of course, important exceptions. One can mention here, for instance, Paul A. Bové's Heideggerian and deconstructive reading of *Molloy*, in which he sees Beckett's deconstruction of aesthetic form and teleological narrative as an exposure of "the transitional moment between habits" revealing both "a direct perception of an object stripped of preconceptions" and the moments of despair. "Beckett's Dreadful Postmodern: The Deconstruction of Form in *Molloy*," in *De-Structing the Novel: Essays in Applied Postmodern Hermeneutics*, ed. Leonard Orr (Troy: The Whitston Publishing Company, 1982), 185–221. See also Steven Connor's study of repetition in Beckett's texts in the context of Derrida's and Deleuze's theories of language and textuality, in his *Samuel Beckett: Repetition, Theory and Text* (Oxford: Basil Blackwell, 1988); and the essays in the excellent collection *Rethinking Beckett: A Collection of Critical Essays*, ed. John Butler and Robert Davis (London: Macmillan 1990). For a political reading of the logic of consumption and commodification in Beckett's plays, see Stephen Watt, "Beckett by Way of Baudrillard: Toward a Political Reading of Samuel Beckett's Drama," in *Myth and Ritual in the Plays of Samuel Beckett*, ed. Katherine H. Burkman (Toronto: Associated UPs, 1987), 103–123. A Foucauldian analysis of narrative and power in Beckett texts is at the center of David Watson's *Paradox and Desire in Samuel Beckett's Fiction*.

19. S. E. Gontarski, "Crritics and Crriticism: 'Getting Known,'" in *On Beckett: Essays and Criticism*, ed. S. E. Gontarski (New York: Grove P, 1986), 6. More often than not, the relation between Beckett and poststructuralism is summed up in one-sentence comments like the following: "But while Beckett's characters and texts would seem to be—and indeed have been treated as if they were—perfect embodiments of deconstructive method, they do not revel in it . . ." P. J. Murphy, *Reconstructing Beckett: Language for Being in Samuel Beckett's Fiction*, xiv–xv.

20. Steven Connor, Review Essay, *Journal of Beckett Studies* 2 (1992): 121.

21. Jacques Derrida, "Psyche: Inventions of the Other," trans. Catherine Porter, in *Reading De Man Reading*, ed., Lindsay Waters and Wlad Godzich (Minneapolis: U of Minnesota P, 1989), 42. Subsequent references to this essay will be marked parenthetically in the text, preceded by PIO.

22. "This Strange Institution Called Literature," An Interview with Jacques Derrida, in *Acts of Literature*, ed. Derek Attridge (New York: Routlege, 1992), 61.

23. Jay M. Bernstein, *The Fate of Art: Aesthetic Alienation from Kant to Derrida and Adorno* (University Park: The Pennsylvania State UP, 1992), 159.

24. Jay M. Bernstein, T*he Fate of Art: Aesthetic Alienation from Kant to Derrida and Adorno,* 159.

25. Theodor W. Adorno, *Aesthetic Theory,* trans. C. Lenhardt, ed. Gretel Adorno and Rolf Tiedemann (London: Routledge, 1984), 187.

26. *Aesthetic Theory,* 186.

27. *Aesthetic Theory,* 476.

28. In addition to sources directly discussed below, see, for instance, Michael Robinson for a most consistent elaboration of Beckett's "poetics of failure," in *The Long Sonata of the Dead: A Study of Samuel Beckett,* 33–61; and Steven Rossen, who places Beckett's skepticism and pessimism in "a long philosophical tradition stemming from Socrates, who also claimed to know that he knew nothing" in *Samuel Beckett and the Pessimistic Tradition* (New Brunswick: Rutgers UP, 1976), 11.

29. Derrida, "This Strange Institution Called Literature," 61.

30. Beckett's emphasis on a crisis of representation explains why this text, as Ruby Cohn points out, has been so overused in Beckett studies. Ruby Cohn, "Foreword," in *Disjecta,* 14–15.

31. Samuel Beckett and Georges Duthuit, "Three Dialogues," in *Disjecta,* 145.

32. Emmanuel Levinas, *Otherwise than Being or Beyond Essence,* trans. Alphonso Lingis (The Hague: Martinus Nijhoff, 1981), 165.

33. Emmanuel Levinas, *Otherwise than Being of Beyond Essence,* 165.

34. Samuel Beckett, *How It Is* (New York: Grove P, 1964), 123. Subsequent references to this edition will be marked parenthetically in the text, preceded by H.

35. Levinas, 166.

36. Levinas, 171.

37. The first quotation comes from Bernstein, "Philosophy's Refuge: Adorno in Beckett," in *Philosophers' Poets,* ed. David Wood (London: Routledge, 1990), 183. The second one is from *The Fate of Art,* 250.

38. "Three Dialogues," 139.

39. J. E. Dearlove, for instance, describes this change as a celebration of the artificiality of language without "lamenting its dissociation from material reality." *Accommodating the Chaos: Samuel Beckett's Nonrelational Art* (Durham: Duke UP, 1982), 87. In a similar mode, Frederik N. Smith argues that *How It Is* is about "the composing process itself" "Fiction as Composing Process," in *Samuel Beckett: Humanistic Perspectives,* ed. Morris Beja, S. E. Gontarski, Pierre Astier (Columbus: Ohio State UP, 1983), 107–121. In an argument almost directly opposite to Dearlove's, P. J. Murphy suggests that this "contiguity disorder" created by Beckett's syntax "results in a counter-movement toward similarity and metaphor" enabling the narrator to identify and eventually to possess his voice. Murphy sees this act of possession as a condition of authentification which allows the narrator to break away from formalism. Although I am sympathetic with this anti-formalist reading, Murphy's emphasis on

authentification as possession, in a way similar to the interpretations he opposes, completely disregards the problematic of otherness in this text. See his "Rituals of Syntax in *How It Is*," in *Reconstructing Beckett*, 74–75.

40. Samuel Beckett, *The Unnameable, Three Novels* (New York: Grove Press, 1965), 293.

41. Such an invitation to a "backward reading" has been tried by Beckett before—it evokes the efforts of Watt to invert every possible order in his narrative about the sojourn in Mr Knott's house: "Then he took it into his head to invert . . . now simultaneously that [the order] of the letters in the word and that of the sentences in the period, and now simultaneously that of the letters in the word and that of the words in the sentence and that of the sentences in the period." Samuel Beckett, *Watt* (New York: Grove P, 1959), 168. If in *Watt* linguistic inversions mark a certain liberation of language from cognition, in *How It Is*, this dissolution of every possible narrative and syntactic arrangement is the main effect of the relation to the other.

42. A number of critics have remarked on the importance of syntax in this text. Hugh Kenner, for instance, argues that Beckett equates syntax with logic in order to create a sense of symmetry and then "traps us with the consequences" of the semantically empty order. "Shades of Syntax," in *Samuel Beckett: A Collection of Criticism*, ed. Ruby Cohn (New York: McGraw-Hill, 1975), 29.

43. Marjorie Perloff, *The Poetics of Indeterminacy: Rimbaud to Cage* (Evanston: Northwestern UP, 1983), 232.

44. For Derrida's theory of syntax see "The Double Session," in *Dissemination*, trans. Barbara Johnson (Chicago: U of Chicago P, 1981), 212–285.

45. Jacques Derrida, "Différance," in *Margins of Philosophy*, trans. Alan Bass (Chicago: U of Chicago P, 1982), 21.

46. Nonetheless the journey in *How it is* has been frequently interpreted in terms of desire, however frustrated, for a human encounter and for the knowledge resulting from such a encounter. See for instance Ruby Cohn, *Back to Beckett* (Princeton: Princeton UP, 1973), 239–240.

47. In a different context, J. E. Dearlove stresses the "paradoxical" nature of voice as both internal and external, universal and individual. See "The Voice and its Words: 'How It Is'" in S. E. Gontarski ed., *On Beckett: Essays and Criticism*, 157.

48. Jacques Derrida, "La parole soufflée," in *Writing and Difference*, trans. Alan Bass (Chicago: U of Chicago P, 1978), 178.

49. *The Poetics of Indeterminacy*, 229–234.

50. Jacques Derrida, "Qual Quelle: Valéry's Sources" in *Margins of Philosophy*, 297.

51. Many of Beckett's commentators have stressed the "insecurity" of his characters' identity in psychological or existential terms, but usually neglecting the role of language in such a crisis. See for instance John Fletcher, *The Novels of Samuel Beckett* (New York: Barnes & Noble, 1964), 213–218.

52. Emmanuel Levinas, *Otherwise than Being or Beyond Essence*, 166.

53. Gerald L. Bruns, *Modern Poetry and the Idea of Language: A Critical and Historical Study* (New Haven: Yale UP, 1974), 166.

54. Linda Ben-Zvi argues that Beckett's interest in the incommensurability between language and self might have been inspired by Fritz Mauthner's philosophy of language. "Samuel Beckett, Fritz Mauthner, and the Limits of Language," 193–4.

55. In his study of the dynamics of narrative in terms of desire, Peter Brooks admits that Beckett's works impose a limit to this type of analysis. *Reading for the Plot: Design and Intention in Narrative*, (New York: Random House, 1984), 313–314.

56. For the discussion of the process of dissolution in *How It Is* see Raymond Federman, "The Fiction of Mud," in *Journey to Chaos: Samuel Beckett's Early Fiction* (Berkeley: U of California P, 1965), 3–27.

57. William Hutchings, for instance, discusses the function of the body solely in terms of the scatological. *How It Is*, then, becomes merely "a journey through the cosmic digestive tract." "'Shat into Grace' or, a Tale of a Turd: Why It Is How It Is in Samuel Beckett's *How It Is*," in *Papers on Language and Literature* 21 (1985): 65–87.

58. The story of the sage with clenched fists reads like a painful exaggeration of Merleau-Ponty's theory of body reflexivity as the non-coincidence of the touching and the touched. Maurice Merleau-Ponty, *The Visible and the Invisible*, Northwestern University Studies in Phenomenology and Existential Philosophy, ed. John Wild (Evanston: Northwestern UP, 1968), 130–155. For the excellent account of the postmodern economies of the body see Jeffner Allen, "The Economy of the Body in a Post-Nietzschean Era" in *The Collegium Phaenomenologicum: The First Ten Years*, ed. John C. Sallis, Giuseppina Moneta and Jacques Taminiaux (Dordrecht: Kluwer Academic Publishers, 1988), 289–308.

59. I owe this quotation to Robinson, *The Long Sonata of the Dead*, 219–220.

60. From the letter to Jessica Tandy, quoted in Enoch Brater, "Dada, Surrealism and the Genesis of *Not I*," in *Modern Drama* 18 (1975): 53.

61. This conflict between indifference and pathos resembles what Neil Hertz calls "the pathos of uncertain agency." See Neil Hertz, "Lurid Figures," in *Reading De Man Reading*, 82–104.

62. Samuel Beckett, "Dante . . . Bruno. Vico . . . Joyce," in *Disjecta*, 23.

63. This collapse of rational community into myth in *How It Is* explains why Beckett occupies such a central place in Adorno's aesthetic theory and in his critique of Enlightenment.

64. Steven Connor, *Samuel Beckett: Repetition, Theory and Text*, 173.

65. Jacques Derrida, "The Pit and the Pyramid: Introduction to Hegel's Semiology," in *Margins of Philosophy*, 107–108.

66. For an interesting discussion of the status of voice in Beckett's fiction in the context of Wittgenstein's theory of language, see Allen Thiher,

"Wittgenstein, Heidegger, the Unnameable, and Some Thoughts on the Status of Voice in Fiction," in *Samuel Beckett: Humanistic Perspectives*, 80–90.

67. One of the few Beckett critics attuned to the effects of this disappearance is Maurice Blanchot. The following comment is a very apt description of what happens with the narrative voice in Beckett's prose: "the narrative voice that is inside only insofar as it is outside, at a distance without any distance, cannot be embodied: . . . it is always different from what utters it, it is the indifferent-difference that alters the personal voice." Maurice Blanchot, *The Gaze of Orpheus and Other Literary Essays*, trans. Lydia Davis (Barrytown: Station Hill P, 1981), 142. See also Blanchot's essay "Where Now? Who Now?" reprinted in *On Beckett*, ed. Gontarski, 141–149.

6

Witold Gombrowicz:
Forms of Life as Disfigurement

> To conclude that such issues are undecidable would be to
> decide that the conclusion of skepticism is true, that we never know
> so certainly but that we can doubt.
>
> **Stanley Cavell, *In Quest of the Ordinary***

In place of a conclusion bringing together all the different
strands of my argument, I would like to revisit and defamil-
iarize some of the main points of departure of this book, especially to return to the role modern aesthetics plays in the poststructuralist critiques of reason and the subject. In what way is
the aesthetics of modernism implicated in the search for "the
other of reason" and the "other of language"? Although not
always acknowledged as such, the question of aesthetics is at
the core of Stanley Cavell's resolution of the linguistic difficulties in the philosophy of later Wittgenstein. Referring to
Wittgenstein's famous formulation that "to imagine a language means to imagine a form of life," Cavell reduces the act
of imagination to the "acceptance" of the "given forms of
life."[1] This harnessing of aesthetics allows Cavell to harmonize
the claim of reason with those social and ethical aspects of signification which exceed the subject-centered rationality.
Preserving the possibility of a spontaneous synthesis without
recourse to the rules of reason, aesthetics in Cavell's project
mediates between the ends of reason and the claims of alterity, between community and otherness. As Cavell himself

admits, however, the aesthetics of modernism undercuts the possibility of such a synthesis, and therefore only deepens the rift between reason and its other. In modern art, the aesthetic form no longer reflects the linguistic and social unity but disrupts the sense of immanence, and thus preserves the experience of the heterogenous and the incommensurable.

I would like to reexamine this vexed relation between the aesthetics of modernism and social forms of life from yet another literary perspective opened by the writings of a Polish avant-garde writer, Witold Gombrowicz. There is, admittedly, a certain risk involved in this intervention: it is not only the case that a philosophical difficulty is re-read here in the context of modern literary texts but also that the literature in question belongs to the very margins of European tradition. And yet, I would like to close *The Rhetoric of Failure* with Witold Gombrowicz because his experimentation with aesthetic forms is so centrally motivated by a recovery of alterity in intersubjective praxis. By looking closely at the main premises of Gombrowicz's aesthetics, we are going to ask about how the encounter with the other signifies within the grammar of the forms of life. Undoing the *sensus communis* based on the aesthetic synthesis, Gombrowicz's texts offer us an instance of the modernist project actively engaged in the redefinition of the intersubjective character of language. By suggesting that Gombrowicz's ongoing reflection on form allows us to intervene into Cavell's aesthetization of "forms of life," I am particularly interested in the implications of this intervention for the aesthetic critique of modernity.

Rethinking the Parameters of Modern Aesthetics: Form, "Immaturity," "The Interhuman"

Gombrowicz belongs with those modernist writers who elaborate both the philosophical and the aesthetic significance of their literary production. In the numerous commentaries on his literary texts, Gombrowicz develops his own critical and theoretical discourse with its specific terminology, interpretative categories, concepts, and metaphors. With some of these expressions infiltrating the colloquial Polish, this Gombrowiczan lexicon is by now quite familiar to his readers, especially his playful use of the most unlikely "aesthetic" terms, such as immaturity, inferiority, *pupa* (fanny), *gęba* (mug), or "the interhuman." Despite this familiarity, however, the main concerns of Gombrowicz's aesthetics are not easily understood. In fact, Gombrowicz still remains his own best critic, and any interpretation of his texts has to begin with his efforts to theorize the main tasks of modern aesthetics. In his literary texts, diaries, and direct reflections on literature, Gombrowicz leaves little doubt that the central concern of his work is, what he calls, the imperative of Form.[2] Developed in the thirties, the problematic of form was already one of the dominant concerns of Gombrowicz's pre-war writings published in Poland (in *Iwona, Princess of Burgundia*, 1935, and especially in his most famous novel, *Ferdydurke*, 1937), and it continued to shape his literary career in exile. During the twenty-three years spent in Argentina (1939–63), Gombrowicz further developed his theory of form in his main literary texts of this period—*Marriage* (Ślub), *Trans-Atlantic, Pornografia*—and in his diaries, written for *Kultura*, the most important Polish emigre review in Paris. The final articulation of the significance of form is expressed in his last novel, *Cosmos* (*Kosmos*), written in France in 1966, in the collection of interviews entitled *A Kind of Testament*, and in the series of "lectures" in the history of modern philosophy given to his friends shortly before his death.

In a manner symptomatic of the developments of modernist experimental literature, Gombrowicz turns *Form* (often capitalized) not only into a privileged content of the work of art but also into a privileged category of literary interpretation. Yet, we will not be able to understand the stakes of Gombrowicz's aesthetics if we confuse his persistent preoccupation with form—or, rather, his obsessive dissolution of form—with the aestheticism of high modernism. As Peter Bürger reminds us, the conventional interpretation of aestheticism perceives the self-conscious preoccupation with literary medium and form as a symptom of art's separation from social life: "In Aestheticism, finally, where bourgeois art reaches the stage of self-reflection, . . . apartness from the praxis of life, which had always . . . characterized the way art functioned in bourgeois society, now becomes its content."[3] Yet, although Gombrowicz turns form into a privileged content of his texts, he at the same time all the more rigorously opposes aesthetic formalism. He has never tired of parodying the stance of high modernism with its "aseptic-aristocratic" view of the artist, "according to which the artist-priest cannot 'lower himself,' and has to pretend to be inaccessible to other people's judgement"[4] [*KT*, 113]. Later in his career, Gombrowicz launched a similar critique against what he saw as the revival of modernist formalism in structuralism and in the literary practice of the *nouveau roman*:[5]

The analyses which certain critics have made of my work according to the rules of structuralism have never fully convinced me . . . . It seems to me typical of over-refined cultures, like the Parisian culture, to tend to reduce the gigantic problem of Form to the elaboration of ever new models of the *nouveau roman,* to literature, and worse still, to literature about literature. I know that it's their way of searching for a writer's reality, but I don't think it gets us very far [*KT,* 72].

Gombrowicz's criticism here is directed against the reduction of "the gigantic problem" of *Form* to an aesthetic category, that is, to the medium of the work of art. As if foreseeing the future scholarship on his own works, Gombrowicz frequently complains that his "view of Form has often been interpreted somewhat too narrowly."[6] Typical of certain misreadings of modernism as a whole, the emphasis on literary form as the condition of the autonomy of the work of art "does not get us very far," even though it might illuminate the process of writing.

If the reductive association of form with aestheticism leads us to a dead end, perhaps it would be more productive to place Gombrowicz's ongoing reflection and experimentation with form in the context of Wittgenstein's "forms of life." As if supplementing Wittgenstein's argument that "to imagine a language is to imagine a form of life," Gombrowicz focuses on the function of aesthetics implied in such an act of imagination. By divorcing aesthetics from the passive reproduction of the given forms of life, Gombrowicz argues that the act of imagination not only displays but further intensifies the antinomy inherent in the very formulation "forms of life":

Here's another antinomy: he alone will know what Form is who never moves a step away from the full intensity of the whirlwind of life [*KT,* 72–73].

As the necessary but conflicting relationship between signifying forms and "life" implies, Gombrowicz does not appeal to an aesthetic synthesis of form and life in order to stabilize or reconcile the diverse effects of language games. On the contrary, "form" and "life" are caught in a contradiction—the antinomy Gombrowicz places at the very core of modern aesthetics: "there was undoubtedly a contradiction at the very root of my artistic efforts . . . But contradiction, which is the philosopher's death, is the artist's life. Let us repeat this: one can never emphasize it sufficiently: art is born out of contradiction" [*KT,* 78].[7] Shattering the illusion of the organicist unity of either the work of art or linguistic community, the aporetic structure of the aesthetic form underscores the irreducible heterogeneity and incongruity of social *forms of life.*

A sober testimony to the unsurpassable incommensurability of language games, Gombrowicz's emphasis on the incoherence of aesthetic form might remind us of Lyotard's linguistic reformulation of the aesthetics of the sublime.[8] Although Lyotard retrieves the old name of the sublime for the aesthetic effects of the irreconcilable, he at the same time submits Kantian aesthetics, still articulated within the parameters of subjectivity, to a language critique initiated by later Wittgenstein and continued by certain varieties of poststructuralism. In the aftermath of this linguistic turn, the incongruity between the presentable and the conceivable no longer expresses the conflict of subjective faculties, but thematizes the incommensurability of the divergent language games, renouncing thus all nostalgia for their reconciliation. Although initially inspired by the relation between form and antinomy in Kant's philosophy, Gombrowicz is more interested in the disjunctions in the topography of intersubjective linguistic praxis than in the incongruities of consciousness. Reflecting the heterogeneity of intersubjective language games, the destruction of the aesthetic coherence in Gombrowicz's texts is therefore inseparable from his attempt to redefine the intersubjective character of language. Neither simply reproducing nor repudiating common forms of life, the dissolution of form in Gombrowicz's work registers the breakdown of the intersubjective grammar in a "direct" encounter with the other.

Given these parameters of his project, it is not surprising that Gombrowicz's redefinition of aesthetics aims to undercut the centrality of the subject both in modern philosophy and literature.[9] In his numerous polemics with Western culture, Gombrowicz argues that "in spite of everything, the West lives with a vision of isolated man and absolute values."[10] This primacy of the subject, Gombrowicz remarks, conveys an illusion of the solitary being in the desert, preoccupied first of all with self-reflection and representation of the world, and only secondarily concerned with others. If philosophical concepts of will, identity and knowledge are some of the "positive" manifestations of this tenacious illusion, skepticism and solipsism belong to its negative, obverse side. Such a fiction of the solitary self in the desert, precisely insofar as it is fiction, determines not only the development of modern philosophy but also the value of aesthetics and its formulations of beauty, form, and taste. As the popularity of existentialist humanism demonstrates all too clearly, even the value of modern literature is, for Gombrowicz, deeply enmeshed in the problematic of subjectivity:

the problem of individual conscience is beginning to melt in our hands while it is still fattening half of French literature, and [to us] Lady Macbeth and Dostoyevski become unbelievable. At least half the texts written by the various Mauriacs seem to have been written on the moon. We sense certain indigestible luxuries in the voices of Camus, Sartre, Gide, Valéry, Eliot, and Huxley, remnants of times which are over for us. These differences become so sharp in practice that I...am incapable of talking about art with artists because the West has remained faithful to absolute values and still believes in art . . . [*D* I, 21].

As this passage suggests, the problem of individual expression is not only interconnected with but determines the aesthetic value of litera-ture. Gombrowicz argues, however, that despite their amazing cur-rency, both the value of subjectivity and the value of aesthetics are "indigestible luxuries" of the Western culture. More specifically, they belong to the persistent remnants of philosophical modernity—"times which are over for us".[11] In his series of lectures, called ironically "Guide to Philosophy in Six Hours and Fifteen Minutes," Gombrowicz discusses extensively the development of the modern philosophy of the subject from Kant to Sartre in terms of the history of successive reductions and limitations of thinking.[12] If modern literature is to accomplish a decisive break with the tradition of philosophical moder-nity, this cut has to be performed precisely at the spot where aesthet-ics is linked to subjectivity. Directed against the remnants of moderni-ty, Gombrowicz's specific understanding of forms of life hopes to perform such a break.

In contrast to subjective intention as the source of meaning, Gombrowicz's fictional and autobiographical works relentlessly explore the impact of signifying forms on the speaking subject: "Form penetrates us to the marrow. We only have to change our tone of voice for certain things within ourselves to become inexpressible—we can no longer think them, or even feel them . . . . To this we must add the colossal pressure of pre-established Form elaborated by culture" [*KT*, 74].[13] Despite, or perhaps because of, their constitutive role, the signi-fying forms underscore the limit of the subject-centered understand-ing of language. Gombrowicz dramatizes this limit by comparing the effect of the linguistic forms on the subject to nothing short of the amputation—to a cut destroying the illusory fullness of being.[14] To destroy this lingering illusion would be the most radical act performed by writing:

'I must perform a still more radical operation! I must amputate myself from myself!'

I suppose that Nietzsche might have formulated my dilemma in these terms. I proceeded to amputate. The following was the scalpel: accept, understand that you are not yourself, that no-one is ever himself with anyone, in any situation, that to be a man is to be artificial [*KT*, 58].

Paradoxically, and here we reach yet another antinomy in Gombrowicz's work, the signifying forms constitute both the very possibility of the speaking subject and its impossibility, its cohesion and dismemberment, its formation and deformation.[15]

This paradoxical and contradictory effect of form stems from the fact that Gombrowicz's subject, even in its most intimate interiority, is constituted from the outside, continually formed and deformed by linguistic, cultural, and intersubjective relations. As Gombrowicz writes in the preface to the French edition of *Pornografia*, "Created by form, he is created from outside, in other words unauthentic and deformed. To be a man means never to be oneself."[16] In light of this linguistic constitution of the subject, the traditional notions of authenticity and identity bespeak merely a nostalgia and delusion of humanistic understanding. Perhaps more intensely than elsewhere, Gombrowicz struggles against the generic expectations of the authenticity of subjective expression in the context of his diaries. Despite some deeply ingrained expectations produced by the conventions of realistic or psychological fiction, Gombrowicz argues that even the intimacy of autobiographical and confessional writing is disrupted by the detour of language: "In literature sincerity leads nowhere. There is another of the dynamic antinomies of art: the more artificial we are, the closer we come to frankness. Artificiality allows the artist to approach shameful truths" [*KT*, 115].

Artificiality does not mean, however, that linguistic form remains separate from life. Despite this relentless emphasis on the exteriority and artifice of linguistic expression, Gombrowicz refrains from thinking about form merely in terms of a mask obstructing authentic expression, because the figure of the mask still implies the nostalgia for an authentic, naked, true "inner" self. Rather, form is often synonymous with the vulgarized word for face [*gęba*]. Although most of Gombrowicz's characters are passionately engaged in the struggle to "unmask" themselves and others, they realize that to unmask would mean to de-face, to lose one's constitution: "Not that man should get rid of his own mug—for beyond it he has no face—here one can only demand that he be conscious of his artificiality and confess it" [*D* II, 4].

To divorce form from the expression of the subject is already one of the main preoccupations of Gombrowicz's first novel *Ferdydurke*, published in Warsaw in 1937. This is why, even at the outset of his career, Gombrowicz's concept of art and the speaking subject is pro-grammatically anti-romantic[17] and belongs more appropriately, as Gilles Deleuze suggests, to the neo-Baroque strain of modernism.[18] In the chapter functioning as a critical interpretation of *Ferdydurke* as a whole, Gombrowicz underscores the crisis of subjectivity brought about by the incongruities of linguistic forms:

> We shall soon begin to be afraid of ourselves and our personali-ties, because we shall discover that they do not completely belong to us. And instead of bellowing and shouting: I believe this, I feel that, I am this, I stand for that, we shall say more humbly: In me there is a belief, a feeling, a thought, I am the vehi-cle for such-and-such an action, production, or whatever it may be . . . [*KT*, 60].

What is undercut in this reversal from the active to passive voice is precisely the spontaneity, the self-determination, and the initiative of the speaking self. Rather than being a spontaneous agent, the speaking subject becomes a "vehicle" of action, production, and thought. Or perhaps it is more precise to say that, like Derrida in his articulation of the middle voice, Gombrowicz stresses an intermediary position of the speaking being—a precarious position between the "agency" and the "vehicle," between invention and a passive reception of forms.

This limit of subjectivity is expressed perhaps most forcefully in Gombrowicz's writing through the frequently recurring figures of "immaturity" and "inferiority." To oppose the remnants of the "absolute" values, still inherent in the aesthetics of the sublime, Gombrowicz's works explore strategically the lacunae of the cultural peripheries and linguistic underdevelopment. Deployed in the dual context of language and the speaking subject, the rhetoric of "under-development" and "immaturity" in Gombrowicz's texts not only exposes but also undercuts the interconnection between the value of aesthetics and subjectivity. In the context of aesthetics, the rhetoric of underdevelopment is intertwined with the endless bifurcations and disjunctions of form, which no longer can be reduced to structural coherence or organic unity. Rather than a static structure, the aesthetic form for Gombrowicz emerges from a dialectic of perfection and "degradation," of completion and "underdevelopment."

The rhetoric of immaturity in Gombrowicz's writing underscores those aspects of language that Cavell associates with the manifestation of skepticism in Wittgenstein's philosophy, that is—the limitations of intersubjective linguistic criteria, discontinuity of meaning, and instability of conventions. Similarly to Gombrowicz, Cavell claims that skepticism is an obverse side of the excessive desire for absolute knowledge—a human desire to "have God's knowledge; hence, doubtless, to be God"—that is, a desire which repudiates the level of the ordinary language and experience.[19] By contrast, Cavell finds that the emphasis in poststructuralism or modernism on the "undecidability" of language "trivializes the claim of the skeptic, whose power lies not in some decision but in his apparent discovery of the ineluctable fact that we cannot know. Perhaps our most practical courses against the impositions of philosophy are indeed to trivialize or to theatricalize them."[20] Yet, to "trivialize," "theatricalize," or parody the failure of knowledge and linguistic criteria is, for Gombrowicz, perhaps the only way art can escape the impositions of subject-centered rationality— and dissociate itself from the "remnants" of philosophical modernity.[21] By undoing the pathos of skepticism and the profundity of the sublime, the rhetoric of immaturity liberates aesthetics from the nostalgia for the "absolute values":

> "Being youth it is below the level of all values." These last words ("below all values") explained why I have been unable to take root in any contemporary existentialism. Existentialism tries to re-establish value, while for me the 'undervalue,' the 'insufficiency', the 'underdevelopment' are closer to man than any value. I believe the formula 'Man wants to be God' expresses very well the nostalgia of existentialism, while I set up another immeasurable formula against it: 'Man wants to be young.'[22]

By relentlessly reversing the hierarchies of high and low, profound and trivial, Gombrowicz resists turning the negativity of literary language—or the dissolution of form—into a new aesthetic value.

Situated between the rigidity of conventions and the fluidity of forms, between inherited linguistic norms and their undecidability,[23] the speaking subject in Gombrowicz's texts is likewise torn between two contradictory desires. On the one hand a rational desire for order, truth, and knowledge propels Gombrowicz's characters toward mastery and self-determination. But on the other hand, an equally strong, if somewhat shameful and illegitimate, desire for the unfinished pulls them back into a state of compromising immaturity and inferiority:

> Man, as we know, aims at the absolute. At fulfillment. At truth, at God, at total maturity . . . . To seize everything, to realize himself entirely—this is his imperative.

> Now, in *Pornografia* it seems to me that another of man's aims appears, a more secret one, undoubtedly, one which is in some way illegal: his need for the unfinished . . . for imperfection . . . for inferiority . . . for youth.[24]

In a reversal of the Enlightenment's constitutive connection between rationality and maturation, what Gombrowicz opposes to the desire for truth is not skepticism but, indeed, something much more trivial—the secret immaturity of the subject. By preserving, as Bartoszyński argues, a certain unreflective, formless, and not yet crystallized way of being, immaturity escapes the very opposition between rationality and skepticism, and opens in this way a mode of being with others that is irreducible to either knowledge or its failure.[25]

As many critics have remarked, the desire for immaturity expresses a state of being similar to Freud's polymorphous perversity of childhood.[26] Yet, even more strikingly, the secret immaturity of Gombrowicz's characters resembles the fate of Wittgenstein's uncomprehending students who unpredictably break down the rules, misunderstand instructions, or fail to play language games according to their normative criteria. This is certainly the predicament of the main protagonist of *Ferdydurke*, a thirty year old writer, who, unmasked in his immaturity, is sent back to school by the old pedagogue, Professor Pimko. The scandal of immaturity signals not only the breakdown of rationality but also the collapse of the normative character of language and culture. In a radical reversal of the *Bildungsroman*, the rhetoric of immaturity in Gombrowicz's texts stages the collapse of pedagogy—the "crisis" of initiation into the shared "forms of life." As a mode of being "below all values," the incurable immaturity of Gombrowicz's characters threatens the reproduction of the "forms of life" with unexpected transformations and disruptions. In this sense, the rhetoric of immaturity for Gombrowicz not only reveals the fluidity of signifying forms but also problematizes their *common* normative character.

In the cultural context, the rhetoric of immaturity and inferiority not only refers to the always already lost state of youth but points to the forgotten layers of subculture and the lacunae of the undercivilized. Identified with the refuse and remnants of civilization, immaturity uncovers the so-called compromising provincialism of culture. Gombrowicz often resorts to his professed eastern-European "provincialism," and its "second rate" cultural productions in order to oppose, or at least to frustrate, the self-assurance and revolutionary pretenses of the Western avant-garde artists. Although Gombrowicz's understanding of language, subjectivity, and modern aesthetics puts him, no doubt, in the ranks of the European avant-garde movements, and even though Gombrowicz himself on many occasions professes his allegiance to the Avant-Garde, he is at the same time deeply skeptical about its self-proclaimed and often self-congratulatory claims of revolutionary subversion and resistance:

> How could I, a Pole, believe in theories? That would be grotesque. Against the Polish sky, against the sky of a paling, waning Europe, one can see why so much paper coming from the West falls to the ground, into the mud, onto the sand, so that little boys grazing their cows can make the usual use of it. But these theories, which drift across the sky, become ridiculous, blind, ignoble, bloody, vain. Gentle ideas are pregnant with mountains of corpses. What can one do? Everyone sees the world from where he stands [*KT*, 55–56].

> Think of my diary as the intrusion into European culture of a villager, of a Polish country gentleman, with all the mistrust, the common-sense and the realism of a peasant . . . . Despite so many years of exile and urban life, I still remain a Polish yokel. Somewhere in my diary I have already noted that when I was young I pretended to be a land-owner in order to annoy the intellectuals, and, in order to annoy my family and the neighbors, I pretended to be an artist, a gypsy, an intellectual . . . . I am a little like an aspirin relieving congestion [*KT*, 118].

Embracing his self-professed eastern-European provincialism with a vengeance, Gombrowicz explores the cultural levels of "undervalue," in order to achieve the effects similar to what Deleuze and Guattari describe as deterritorialization of "minor literature."[27] What the provincial immaturity reveals here are the most marginal and overlooked aspects of cultural production.[28]

    If Gombrowicz's ongoing reflection on the incongruities of the signifying forms in general, and literary language in particular, brings about both the crisis of cultural values and, to use Habermas's term, the exhaustion of the subject, this exhaustion does not occur only because consciousness fails to control the play of external and artificial forms of signification. Nor is this exhaustion of subjectivity merely a function of the social or inherited character of language, always in excess of subjective intentions. What is much more fundamentally at stake in Gombrowicz's aesthetics is a redefinition of the intersubjective character of signification—the inscription of alterity within the "inter-human" linguistic topography. I would like to suggest that for Gombrowicz, this signification of alterity is one of the consequences of the displacement of the incommensurable from the conflict of the subjective faculties to what he calls the "interhuman" forms of life. If we follow through the consequences of this linguistic displacement, then the incongruity between the presentable and the conceivable points not just to the privation of the subject or the failure of representation but to the excess of alterity in the collective conditions of enunciation. The aporetic structure of the aesthetic form, implied in the rhetoric of immaturity and underdevelopment, not only exposes the limits of subject-centered notions of language but also preserves the signification of alterity in intersubjective praxis. That is why for Gombrowicz, the irreducible alterity functions not as the obstruction of knowledge or as the limitation of subjective freedom but rather as "a creative principle."

However, Gombrowicz's focus on the intersubjective character of language becomes yet another source of misunderstanding of his concept of form, which is often reduced either to social determinism or cultural conventionalism:

> [critics] say—and correctly—that in *Ferdydurke* man is created by people. But they understand this primarily as man's being dependent on a social group, which imposes custom, convention, and style upon him . . . [*D* II, 3].

Because Gombrowicz's aporetic form displays incommensurability in intersubjective relations, his texts are engaged in a critique not only of the subject but also of the philosophies of community and "collectivism." Gombrowicz objects here against the subordination of otherness to social totality, or to "such abstractions as social class, state, nation, and race." Although class, nation, or race constitute powerful cultural forms and although Gombrowicz repeatedly underscores their institutional impact on literature, the alternative conception of language he proposes transcends the very opposition between the 'solitary man in the desert' and social totality: "It will be on the corpses of these worldviews that the third vision of man will be born:

man in relation to another man, a concrete man, I in relation to you . . . "[*D* I, 20]. As this passage implies, Gombrowicz attempts to develop the signification of alterity through his rereading of Sartre's concept of the other and Buber's "Thou."[29] However, what he finds limiting in both of these philosophies is that Sartre discerns exclusively negative implications of alterity as the limitation of the subjective freedom, whereas Buber confines the positive signification of the other to inter-subjective dialogue.[30]

It is an established critical gesture to read Gombrowicz's articulation of "the interhuman," the way Czeslaw Miłosz, for instance, does, as the formation and deformation of personality under the pressure of others, as a struggle for domination or preservation of one's own identity—in short, as an endless repetition of the master-slave dialectic.[31] There are certainly numerous examples in Gombrowicz's texts to support such a reading, most notably, the demonic figure of Fryderyk in *Pornografia*. Yet, these instances of dialectical struggle between youth and maturity, between servants and masters, believers and atheists—always sober reminders of the domination in intersubjective relations—do not exhaust Gombrowicz's understanding of the "interhuman." Opposing the trappings of both individualism and collectivism, or the private and communal language, Gombrowicz's "interhuman" forms of life are irreducibly linked to the singular and unmediated encounters with others:

> I do not deny that the individual is dependent on his milieu—but for me it is far more important, *artistically far more creative*, psychologically far more profound, and *philosophically far more disturbing* that man is also created by an individual man, by another person. In chance encounters. Every minute of the day. . . . Therefore it is not a matter of my milieu's imposing a convention . . . but that the depiction of man's encounter with man with all of its fortuitousness, directness, wildness, results in showing how Form, and often the most unpredictable, absurd form is born of these accidental encounters [*D* II, 3–4, emphasis added].

In this well-known passage from his diaries, Gombrowicz captures particularly well the central tension, or antinomy, informing his understanding of the "interhuman" forms of life. Rather than unifying discourse, forms of life exhibit the endless discord between irreducible alterity and linguistic community—or what Gombrowicz sometimes refers to as "social milieu." More specifically, it is the conflict between the unpredictable encounters with others and the pre-existing, norma-tive criteria, or intersubjective grammar. Without denying the element of social conventions and their regulatory, normative power, Gombrowicz suggests, however, that by reducing forms of life solely to normative conventions, we forget that the encounter with the other is primarily an event. When recovered as an event—in all "its direct-ness, unpredictability and wildness"—such an encounter entails a breakdown of intersubjective norms. Exceeding the normative, or what Wittgenstein calls grammatical, character of forms of life, the dis-junction of form preserves the singularity and directness of these "accidental" events.

If form expresses the limits of subjectivity, it is not only because it coincides with the impersonal social conventions but also because its fluidity enables the subject's always unpredictable exposure to the other. These encounters appear "philosophically disturbing" (they even might be misread as a symptom of linguistic skepticism) because they destroy the grammatical stability of forms of life and open a dizzying prospect of deviation, disorder, and contingency:

> Can't you see this Form is something far more powerful than a simple social convention? And that it is an uncontrollable ele-ment? As long as you understand *Ferdydurke* as a battle with con-vention, it will trot calmly down the well-beaten path; but if you understand that man creates himself with another man in the sense of the wildest debauchery, *Ferdydurke* will . . . leap forward as if you had jabbed it with a spur, carrying you off into the realm of the Unpredictable [*D* II, 4].

The encounter with the other necessitates an extension of language beyond the stability of pre-established intersubjective norms. However, as the above passage warns us, to think the implications of such encounters is not an easy or comfortable task, because the signi-fication of alterity resists any attempt to totalize or stabilize meaning. Thus, the shift from the conventional grammar regulating discourse to form arising from the momentary exposure to the other is described as a threatening possibility of losing one's orientation in the world, of stepping outside the "well-beaten" tract and wandering into the "realm of the Unpredictable." As we shall see, Gombrowicz's *Cosmos* unfolds all the consequences of such a risk.

This gap between two different notions of "interhuman" form—between intersubjective linguistic norms on the one hand and the event of alterity on the other—reveals the fact that the singular encounters exceed the very grammar of language games. This sense of excess is often dramatized in Gombrowicz's texts through the rhetoric of unconstrained elements: *"Ferdydurke* is more a form-element than a form-convention" [*D* II, 4]. As such rhetoric implies, the "dynamism" of the event disrupts the grammaticality of language:

> I have just given . . . only the first letters of an alphabet which knows no end. What a powerful and unfathomable dynamism! Man submitted to the interhuman is like a twig on a rough sea: he bobs up and down, plunges into the raging waters, slides gently along the surface of the luminous waves, he is engulfed by rhymes and vertiginous rhythms, and loses himself in unforeseen perspectives . . . . Unsuspected paths appear and he sometimes no longer knows what is happening to him . . . . This interhuman creation, *unknown and unseizable,* determines his possibilities [*KT,* 75, emphasis added].

The image of the subject "submitted to the interhuman like a twig on a rough sea" suggests some of the startling consequences of Gombrowicz's revision of the forms of life. In contrast to the conventional picture of intersubjective communication, Gombrowicz's interhuman form, born in the momentary encounters with others, opens the most vertiginous and dizzying aspects of language. What Gombrowicz stresses here is that the signification of the other, which the interhuman form reveals, cannot be submitted to and regulated by the grammar of language games. On the contrary, by opening "unforeseen perspectives," alterity reveals the limits of regulation and the limits of the grammatical precision of language. One almost hesitates to say whether this disruptive signification can be still called a form in the traditional sense, and whether this relation to the other can still be called "interhuman".

The grammatical or normative crisis brought about by the signification of alterity cannot be resolved by some deeper aesthetic synthesis—by the spontaneous harmony occurring without the mediation of rules—which is implied in Cavell's idea of intersubjective *attunement.* As a precarious "alphabet which knows no end," Gombrowicz's conception of the "interhuman" resists such aestheticization by underscoring the "vertiginous rhythms and rhymes" of form—or perhaps what we might call, to play on the familiar opposition, the rhetoric of forms of life. No longer bridged by aesthetics, the disjunctions between structure and event, norm and contingency, grammar and rhetoric, do not, however, merely display the negative epistemological consequences of form or its "philosophically disturbing" implications. Although the interhuman form, "unknown and unseizable," questions the stability of both subjective and intersubjective knowledge, it at the same time preserves the signification of alterity, which Gombrowicz associates with "artistically creative" possibilities of language. By situating his aesthetics in the context of forms of life, Gombrowicz allows us to recast the familiar opposition between the grammar and rhetoric as the discrepancy between the "artistically creative" and "philosophically disturbing" signification of alterity.

Commenting in his diaries on *Ferdydurke* many years after its publication, Gombrowicz attempts to give us a somewhat more restrained formulation of the interhuman form—to lay out its basic grammatical structure. In this ironic manifesto of sorts, Gombrowicz assembles all the crucial relationships between form, language, subjectivity and intersubjectivity into one central constellation that has become, since then, a familiar hallmark of his aesthetics:

(1) Human being created by form, in the profoundest, most general sense.

(2) Human being as the creator, the indefatigable producer of form.

(3) Human being degraded by form (always being an "under-" or an "im-"—undereducated, immature).

(4) Human being in love with immaturity.

(5) Human being constituted by Inferiority and Youngerness.

(6) Human being subjected to the 'interhuman'—a superior creative force, our only accessible divinity.

(7) Human being for another human being, knowing no higher authority.

(8) Human being made dynamic, elevated and magnified by other people . . .

Do you want to reduce all of this to one single revolt against the social forms of being? [*D* II, 6, trans. modified].

If, for the strategic purpose of the polemics with his interpreters, Gombrowicz neatly assembles all the crucial oppositions informing his thinking about form—human/interhuman, created/creator, immaturity/divinity, degradation/elevation, inferiority/superiority—into an admirably precise diagram, there is nothing to assure us that this grammatical coherence will not be submerged again in the twirl of "unexpected perspectives" of rhetoric, leaving Gombrowicz's readers "engulfed by rhymes and vertiginous rhythms" of his prose.

Between Philosophy and Art: The Double Articulation of Form in *Cosmos*

It is tempting to read *Cosmos*—Gombrowicz's last novel, published in Paris in 1965—as a literary testament of sorts, providing the most mature synthesis of his artistic achievement. If the novel nonetheless frustrates this interpretative desire it is because *Cosmos* not only does not resolve but, on the contrary, further deepens the disparity between the "philosophically disturbing" and "aesthetically productive" implications of form. The disjunction between the philosophical and aesthetic implications of Gombrowicz's writing is perhaps more intense here than in his other texts, because *Cosmos* explicitly focuses on the difficulty of interpretation posed by the interhuman character of form. By pitting literature against philosophy, Gombrowicz suggests that the disjunction between grammar and rhetoric reveals the ethical significance of the interhuman form.

Predictably enough, Gombrowicz's critics, however, have stressed "philosophically disturbing" implications of form over its "creative" possibilities. According to its critical reception, *Cosmos* is an overwhelmingly pessimistic "testament," in which Gombrowicz, coming to terms with his life-long preoccupations with form, language and subjectivity, finally acknowledges their most negative consequences—a devastating threat of skepticism. In one of the few book length studies on Gombrowicz in English language, Ewa Thomson writes that *Cosmos* "whose action takes place in a conventional middle class setting presents the same unintelligible world which the heroes of Kafka and Beckett confront."[32] *Cosmos* indeed presents a certain kind of incomprehensibility that for Western readers provokes associations with Kafka and Beckett or, for those who are familiar with Polish literature, with such grotesque writers as Witkacy and Bruno Schulz. Gombrowicz's own description of *Cosmos* confirms the feeling that there is something incomprehensible and "frightening" about this text—an obscurity that overpowers even the usual playfulness of his style:[33]

For me *Cosmos* is black, primarily black, something like a black
stream, turbulent, full of whirlpools, obstacles and flooded areas,
carrying a mass of refuse, and in this stream a besotted man, at
the mercy of the waters, trying to decipher and to understand so
that he can assemble what he sees into some whole. Blackness,
terror and night [*KT*, 133–134].

Not surprisingly, then, the similarity between *Cosmos* and Western
modern writers like Beckett and Kafka is usually pursued in the context of the deep, skeptical "crisis of European culture." Gombrowicz
himself suggests that his protagonist succumbs to his interpretative
endeavors "not without a certain skepticism." Following this suggestion, Wojciech Karpiński describes *Cosmos* as one of the most "brave
attempts to reflect the crisis caused by the persistent presence of skepticism in European culture."[34] According to this argument,
Gombrowicz's model of artistic sensitivity stems from the uncompro-
misingly atheistic, critical, and skeptical position. Taking skeptical
doubts to their extreme conclusions, *Cosmos* would then be a devastating testimony that "being in the world is split into two parts, the inaccessible world and the imprisoned consciousness."[35] What is symptomatic of these readings is precisely their emphasis on the negative
epistemological consequences of the text and the corresponding exclusion of "creative" possibilities of form. If we recall, however, that for
Gombrowicz it is the "other" that is raised to a creative principle, then
this critical emphasis on the devastating consequences of the disinte-
grated form does not only entail privileging the philosophical over the
aesthetic but also the epistemological over the ethical.

The seemingly grave epistemological consequences of *Cosmos* are
not confined to the problem of the interpretative rigor transcending
everyday comprehension, but are precisely extended to most ordinary
quotidian language and mundane attempts to make sense of reality.
Despite his characteristically melodramatic (and deliberate) exaggeration of the obscurity of *Cosmos*, Gombrowicz at the same time insists
that the novel is in fact a very "simple story of a simple student," a
kind of story that can happen to anyone, and therefore a story that
needs to be told in the most "straightforward narrative form" [*KT*,
137]. The two "straightforward narrative forms" Gombrowicz appro-
priates and destroys in the process are the genre of a detective and a
gothic novel. The text opens with two young protagonists—Witold, a
university student, and his former class mate, Fuchs, a rather unsuccessful and pathetic bank apprentice—arriving in the country to take a
break from some vexing personal problems. In these tired, apathetic,

and bored characters of *Cosmos*, always at odds with institutional authority, one can recognize a certain deliberate parody of modern alienation—perhaps its more provincial version. Searching for an inexpensive lodging place, Witold and Fuchs, two alter egos, spot a hanging sparrow—an insignificant event yet bizzare enough to provoke their frenetic interpretative desire. Attempting to solve the case of the hanged bird, the young detectives stay in the provincial household of the retired bank official, where they uncover other, equally trivial, anomalies: a hanging piece of wood, a distorted mouth of a maid contrasting so much with a beautiful mouth of the owner's daughter, a strange crack in the ceiling which might be just an ordinary fissure or an arrow intentionally pointing to some hidden clue. Drawn to these anomalies, Witold and Fuchs become obsessed interpreters, compulsive readers, and fanatic detectives of sense. Yet, their repeatedly futile attempts to convert these anomalies into meaningful clues, and eventually into an intelligible picture of the world, or at least a coherent aesthetic form, only increase obscurity. In a parody of a detective novel, *Cosmos* crowns all these interpretative and aesthetic aspirations with an unexplained hanging corpse and a threat of yet another murder. The detectives' desire for logic, perpetually undercut by the "logic of desire," eventually almost produces the missing crime they attempt to solve.[36]

More consistently than in other Gombrowicz's texts, the decomposition of form in *Cosmos*—its bifurcation into grammar and rhetoric—suggests a disintegration of the common socio-linguistic world. In this context, the title "Cosmos," which implies an ordered universe, unified humanity, and universal language—is from the outset a parody of title, creating a critical distance to the interpretative endeavors of the novel's protagonists. Frequently misread as a sign of the skeptical "crisis" of European culture, this process of decomposition presents instead a radical testimony to the impossibility of inhabiting a common discursive universe:

we no longer share a common universe. There are a dozen different universes competing for our readers. How can we find a language comprehensible to a conservative Catholic, an existentialist atheist, a "realist", a man whose conscious patterns of thought have been formulated by Husserl or Freud and one whose artistic sensibility has been developed in the shadow of surrealism? Different realities, different ways of seeing and feeling. In the four corners of these different horizons the whole diversity of our temperaments appears [*KT*, 134].

The irreconcilable languages and diverse horizons of understanding
no longer reveal a possibility of sharing the same world. What is
"philosophically" disturbing about these "competing" frameworks of
intelligibility, is the erasure of the intersubjective agreements preceding and enabling linguistic exchange among different groups of people. For Cavell, the possibility of such a priori agreements, or attunement, among speakers constitutes the only assurance of
communication, in fact, the only defense against pervasive skepticism
about language. For Gombrowicz, however, intersubjective agreements can no longer be taken for granted. Gombrowicz's question,
then, reflects the central difficulty of both philosophical modernity
and literary modernism: how can we find a language that would be
comprehensible, for instance, to both an existentialist atheist and a
conservative believer, to a realist and a surrealist, to a phenomenolo-
gist and a psychoanalyst? Yet, as we shall see, Gombrowicz is not
merely interested in the "philosophically disturbing consequences" of
the disintegration of the linguistic and social totality, but uncovers in
this process of decomposition also positive implications—the inscription of alterity within the shared forms of life.

In *Cosmos* the impossibility of a shared language is reflected in the
conflict between linguistic norms and unexpected deviations. "An
ordinary introduction to an extraordinary world, to the wings of the
world, if you like" [*KT*, 137], *Cosmos* makes the distinction between
ordinary and extraordinary, norm and perversity, particularly troubling. Even though the text never tires of emphasizing the average
quality of its characters, objects, and setting, its semi-gothic preoccupation with the odd and the eccentric—whether it is a hanging bird or
a distorted mouth—brackets the commonality of the social norms of
signification from the very start. This is not to say that Gombrowicz, as
his critics sometimes suggest, simply situates the task of interpretation
outside the parameters of social norms and hierarchies. Even though
its young characters, Witold and Fuchs, try to escape the world of
social conventions and obligations, and in particular, to evade the
authority of social institutions—family, office, university, and
church—the text does not erase the normative character of signification but rather reveals its eccentric and heterogenous character:

> If a man doesn't see Form as I see it, in its autonomy, its perpet-
> ual malleability, its creative fury, its caprices and its perversions,
> its accumulations and its dissolutions, its intricacies and contin-
> ual confusions, what can *Cosmos* mean to him? [*KT*, 134].

Dramatizing a temporal and dynamic process of composition and decomposition of meaning, Gombrowicz's cosmic construction never reaches a level of generality or unity but repeatedly disintegrates into multiple constellations and unstable combinations of fragments, leaving behind an excess of incomprehensible, eccentric particulars.

One of the crucial questions *Cosmos* confronts is whether this process of disintegration of the common framework of language into an irreducible plurality of forms of life entails a retreat into purely subjective, private in Wittgenstein's terms, attempts to construct meaning. Although frequently read in these terms, *Cosmos* in fact destroys two related illusions underlying the primacy of the subject: first, the illusion of an authentic experience outside social language games, and second, the illusion of a purely subjective interpretation.[37] Part of the difficulty of *Cosmos*, therefore, is that it presents two kinds of failure, two kinds of impossibility: the impossibility of a common discursive universe coupled with the exhaustion of the purely subjective paradigm of interpretation. The text implies that only when the disturbing consequences of both of these impossibilities are confronted, then the encounter with the other—"the creative principle" of art — can be articulated at all. With minute precision, *Cosmos* records how each subjective attempt to construct an intelligible representation of reality fails, how each decoding of the grammar of the world deteriorates into chaos before reaching even a tentative conclusion. Commenting on the failed interpretations of his protagonists, Gombrowicz suggests that:

> The main theme of the novel is the very formation of this story, in other words the formation of a reality . . . in it we see how a certain reality endeavors to arise from our associations, indolently, awkwardly . . . in a jungle of misunderstandings and erroneous interpretations. And at each moment the awkward construction is lost in chaos [*KT*, 137].

For Gombrowicz, the disintegration of the common discursive universe and the erasure of the intersubjective agreements does not posit subjectivity as the alternative center of meaning. On the contrary, as Karpiński suggests, in Cosmos subjectivity is equally "unable to constitute any sphere of meaning."[38] Yet, it is this disintegration of the common discursive universe and the subsequent failure of any subjective efforts to reconstruct meaning that calls for a rethinking of the very opposition between the discursive community and private language, between intersubjectivity and alterity, philosophy and aesthet-

ics. Strategically dramatizing the limits of both subjectivity and intersubjectivity, the rhetoric of failure reveals significations that exceed
both types of rationality. It is this persistent excess—or what the characters refer to as anomalies and eccentricities—that calls for a turn
from the epistemological to the ethical understanding of the irreducible heterogeneity of "forms of life."

In *Cosmos*, such a turn occurs at the moment when we are confronted with the most devastating failure of subjective interpretation.
This exhaustion of subjectivity takes here two forms: characteristic of
the usual composition of Gombrowicz's texts, the narrative and inter-
pretive perspective in *Cosmos* is split into two opposite articulations,
one represented by the young protagonists, Witold and Fuchs, the
other by the retired bank official and seemingly respectable family
man, Leo. This split occurs between a rational hermeneutical attempt
to decipher the grammar of the world and an ecstatic pseudo-
Nietzschean attempt to impose sense on the world and on others
through unconstrained auto-eroticism and sensual enjoyment. If the
first interpretative perspective strives to grasp the unity and totality in
the profusion of details, the second one derives pleasure from the play
with the eroticized particulars. The first orientation attempts to assemble incoherent fragments into meaningful maps and constellations, the
second deliberately intensifies fragmentation of language and particu-
larization of the world. In this conflict between the subject of representation, deciphering meaning inherent in the world, and the subject
of enjoyment, ecstatically projecting the meaning out of its own
desires, Gombrowicz sees two main modalities of subjective interpretation. Yet rather than trying to reconcile their difference—the difference between rationalism and eroticism, logic and desire, objectivity
and subjectivity, totality and fragment—*Cosmos* dramatizes the limits
of both of these interpretative perspectives since both assume the subjective experience as the origin of meaning.

Frustrated and exhausted, the young detectives of sense confront at each step of their investigation an overwhelming impasse of
interpretation:

> The profusion of stars in the moonless sky—incredible!—in these
> swarming imaginings [*w tych wyrojeniach*] some constellations
> stood out, I recognized and identified some of them, the Great
> Bear, the Scales, but others unknown to me were also lurking
> there as if inscribed in the position of the main stars; I tried to
> work out some lines, to tie some figures . . . but this deciphering,
> this imposition [*narzucanie*] of a map suddenly exhausted me, so

I shifted my attention to the garden, though here too I was quickly exhausted by the profusion of things, such as the chimney, a
pipe, the bends in the gutter, or a young tree, as well as more difficult ones because already combinations, such as the bending
and the disappearance of the path or the rhythm of shadows . . .
reluctantly here too I started working out figures, relations, I did-
n't want to, I felt bored, impatient, and irritated, until I realized
that what attracted or perhaps captivated me about these things
was one thing's being behind another; the pipe was behind the
chimney, for instance . . . . I was more surprised by this than it
was necessary, in general I rather tended to exaggeration;
besides, the constellations, this Great Bear, etc., superimposed
something painfully cerebral upon me. . . . The idea of the map
got mixed up into my head [*mapa wmieszała mi się do głowy*], a
map of the night sky, or an ordinary map with the cities . . . [*C*,
19–20, trans, mine; emphasis added *K*, 13–14].

Characteristic of the style of the novel with its endless enumerations,
with its sentences without end or clear semantic relations, this passage—*mise en abyme* of interpretation— dramatizes the limits of interpretation, and, quite literally, the exhaustion of the interpreter. The
project of interpretation presupposes a conventional relation between
the part and the whole, the global and the local, macrocosm (the sky)
and microcosm (the garden). The organizing figure of synecdoche suggests that just as the innumerable stars in the sky have been grouped
together into constellations which enable subjective orientation in a
world without a center (the sky is moonless), so too the profusion of
clues in the provincial garden can be similarly organized in meaningful combinations. What could bring, therefore, these two planes of
interpretation together is the metaphor of a map—a metaphor which
promises to order the confusing multiplicity of details into a rational
or into an aesthetic unity. Evoked as the conventional figure of representation in the text, the map assures both the order of the world and
the triumph of the knowing subject.

And yet, it is the figure of the map that Witold, the narrator of
Cosmos, repeatedly fails "to tie." Throughout the text, the narrator is
uncertain whether the possibility of the map inheres in the world or
whether it is an arbitrary mode of representation imposed by himself.
The task of representation stumbles therefore upon undecidability
where the deciphering of the objective grammar of the world turns
into a subjective projection. It is as if, in a manner anticipating
Levinasian critique of representation, Gombrowicz were suggesting

that the comprehension of the world is implicated from the start in the subjective constitution of being. However, the very idea of projection becomes equally problematic since the young detectives are not sure whether the idea of the map is their own or whether it is forcefully imposed upon them by a certain formal automatism or by conventional expectations of order and symmetry. They are unsure whether they are active or passive interpreters, whether they project their own designs or whether these designs are projected, "superimposed," upon them. That is why they submit to the work of interpretation both compulsively and reluctantly, as if they were proceeding against their own will. Exposing the limits of the will to knowledge, the obsessive desire to decipher the meaning of the anomalous events repeatedly leads to the exhaustion, boredom, and impatience of the interpreters.

What persistently escapes the totality of representation and destroys the grammatical stability of forms of life is an overwhelming excess of details. The young detectives fail to decipher or construct a map because they are fascinated and diverted by the heterogenous combinations between dispersed fragments of sense. In its shift of attention from the general to the particular, *Cosmos* uncovers the negativity of the detail—its power to decompose order, to obstruct a generalizing thought, to fragment the sense of the whole. The excess of random particulars in the text erodes the principles of subordination, hierarchy, and closure: "After so many things that I could no longer enumerate, the nails, the frog, the sparrow, the bit of wood, the pole, the nib, the lemon peel, the cardboard box, etc., the chimney, the cork, the arrow on the ceiling, the gutter, the hand, the hands, etc., etc., the lumps of earth, the bed springs, the ashtray, bits of wire, toothpicks, pebbles, the chicken, warts, gulfs, islands, needles, etc., etc., *ad nauseam*" [*C*, 66–67]. Because of this excess, the task of representation is as if immobilized by two contradictory tendencies—by the clash between the uncontrollable proliferation of possible clues and the grammatical imperative of unity and totality:

> There was an oppressive profusion of possible links and associations . . . . How many sentences can be created with the twenty four letters of the alphabet? How many meanings can be deduced from these hundreds of weeds, clumps of earth, and other small particulars? [*C*, 36, trans. modified; *K*, 29,]

> some tendency toward unification, something as if vaguely connected, could be felt in the series of these events . . . some pressure toward sense, as in a game of charades, when the letters

start arranging themselves into a word [*przebijało się w nich jakieś parcie ku sensowi, jak w szaradach gdy litery zaczynają zmierzać do ułożenia się w słowo*]. But what word? [C, 38, trans. mine; K, 30,]

Witold's gloss on the impasse of representation reflects also a certain crisis of language caused by the unresolvable tension between the multiplicity of linguistic combinations and the pressure toward the unity of meaning, expressed here as the unity of the word.

This "oppressive profusion of possible links" is announced on the level of language as "turbulence" of rhetoric, as a certain figurative disorder. From Aristotle to Derrida, the theorists of rhetoric point out that the function of metaphor is to establish necessary analogies and essential connections, and therefore to perform an implicit generalization and unification of heterogeneity into a unity of being. Yet in *Cosmos* the trope of metaphor perpetually reveals disjunctions underlying analogous relations. Metaphors turn into metonymies, and analogies disintegrate into contiguous associations. *Cosmos* is in fact mostly written in metonymic style, preoccupied with metonymic lists, which fail to provide a synthesis for the profusion of random associations. This tension in *Cosmos* between analogy and contiguity, similarity and heterogeneity, reveals disjunctions underlying both metaphorical and conceptual syntheses:

> Could one speak of a logical thread connecting the sparrow and the bit of wood, linked as they where by a barely visible arrow on our bedroom ceiling, an arrow so indistinct that we had noticed it only by chance? [C, 157].

The most ambiguous sign in the text, the arrow in this passage, functions both as an analogous link and as a mark of disjunction. At the beginning of the story, the characters notice an indistinct trace on the ceiling, which might be an ordinary crack or a purposefully drawn arrow pointing to the next clue. The arrow in question dramatizes the undecidability between necessary links and accidental fissures, between purposiveness and randomness, rational connections and gaps. By becoming the metaphor for the entire construction of the text, this ambiguous figure questions all metaphors and reveals disjunctions underlying all necessary links. As this *mise en abyme* of interpretation suggests, the signification of otherness is announced in language only as a mark of disjunction, a mark that cannot be converted into a meaningful sign.[39]

Another alternative to the impasse of interpretation caused by "the intolerable excess of reality" is proposed in the text by Leo, a retired bank official, for whom the disintegration of the world into a flood of random particulars no longer constitutes a deplorable loss but a possibility of perverse pleasure. In the figure of Leo, Gombrowicz parodies the Nietzschean temptation to seek an alternative to rationality in the repressed other of reason, namely, in the unconstrained experience of pleasure. For Leo, the crisis of interpretation and, consequently, the crisis of subjectivity, can be avoided only when the constraints of reason are surpassed by homoerotic desire.[40] As Leo explains, both erotic and interpretative desires converge on the detail, on the small and the partial; however, if the desire for logic is directed at the unification and subordination of the particulars into a whole, the logic of erotic desire has just the opposite effect: it aims to fragment, to dissimulate, to subdivide. To take the pleasure in the manipulation of the trivial and insignificant is Leo's recipe for enjoying "the pleasures of Paris" at the provincial family table:

> What amuses me, gentle sir and travelling companion, is precisely nothing, the nothing one does the whole of one's life . . . . Years are divided into months, months into days, days into hours, hours into minutes and minutes into seconds, and the seconds go with the wind . . . . They add up to nothing, nothing at all [*C,* 117].

> But if you concentrate on seeking out quite small and insignificant pleasures for yourself, and I do not mean only sexual pleasures, you can enjoy yourself like a pasha making *little bread pellets,* for instance.   . . .   Epicurism, or voluptuousness [*rozkosznisium*], can be of two kinds, it can be like a wild boar, a buffalo or a lion, or it can be like a flea or a mosquito, that is, it can be either a large scale or small-scale and, if the latter, *it must be capable of microscopical treatment, of being divided and sub-divided and appreciated in small doses* [*C,* 127, emphasis added; *K,* 112].

A reaction to the lack of any inherent values, to the slow disintegration of life into "nothing, nothing at all," Leo's microscopic voluptuousness posits pleasure rather than rationality as the source of meaning. Since for Leo the value or meaning of the object depends entirely on subjective desire, this eroticized subjective notion of meaning leads to equally privatized language. Leo in fact constructs for himself his own, entirely incomprehensible for others, hermetic language of pleasure.

Leo's private "berg"-language, is based on endless syntactical and grammatical variations of the empty semantic root ("berg" as a word does not exist in Polish): "That it's berging. Berging with my bamberg with all the bambergity of my bamberg" [*C*, 120]. This attempt to construct a private code of pleasure represents what Cavell calls the aestheticization of language—a desire to divorce language from the intersubjective norms of signification and to turn it into an instrument of entirely private desires.

As Gombrowicz suggests, the aporia of these private language games lies in the unacknowledged connection between pleasure and domination. It is not only the case that Leo's private play with words is empty and nonsensical but also that it cannot, precisely, remain private. Okopień-Sławińska stresses the duplicity of the "berg"-language, its simultaneously private and public, profane and religious character, but it is important to add that this duplicity precisely destroys the very dream of private language.[41] Finding the aestheticization of language insufficient, Leo needs a witness to or an accomplice in his perverse games. Thus at the moment that Leo discloses the secret of his linguistic game to Witold, he inadvertently confesses the impossibility of pure private language. What is at stake in this failure of the private language of pleasure, however, is not merely a delusion of irrational hedonistic self but also a critique of violence. The violence of Leo's erotic games inheres in his simultaneous need and denial of others. Like Fryderyk in *Pornografia*, Leo turns others into duped participants or unwitting witnesses of his private erotic ceremonies and rituals: "and they . . . think I brought them here to admire the view. . . . My wife, my daughter, my son-in-law, the priest, the Lolos and the Tolos, are all here on a pilgrimage in honor to my supreme experience, my superberg . . . . Unknowing pilgrims to the voluptaberg" [*C*, 129]. Private language in this context does not serve just the purpose of expression of subjective pleasure but turns out to be an instrument of deception, domination, and manipulation. This unacknowledged violence exposes the aporia underlying both private pleasure and private language. Born out of the will to power, private language is from the outset caught in the games of power.

This failure of either representation or ecstatic voluptuousness to constitute meaning in the text leads to the unavoidable impasses of subjective interpretation. To overcome these impasses we need to change the perspective of reading, to turn from the "philosophically disturbing" consequences of *Cosmos* to its "creative" possibilities—to return to what Gombrowicz calls "the other as creative principle." As Emmanuel Levinas argues, the signification of alterity cannot be confined to hermeneutics or even to the philosophy of language, but entails a difficult shift to ethics. However, in what way can we talk about the ethical significance of Gombrowicz's "literary testament"? Is it not rather the case that *Cosmos* fails to provide any explicit articulation of ethics, or to suggest any positive moral program?

To insist on the ethical significance of the failure of interpretation is somewhat paradoxical in the context of Gombrowicz's professed antipathy to morality. Gombrowicz's interest in ethics seems to be limited to morality conceived as a constraining cultural force forming and deforming the identity of some of his protagonists, just as, for instance, Catholic morality defines Amalia in *Pornografia*. Gombrowicz distrusts morality for two reasons. First of all, he attacks the way morality has been exploited as a commodity in modern literature, assuring the popularity and success of the "committed" writers. With his usual sardonic humor, Gombrowicz claims that "morality, for the artist, is a sort of sex appeal. He seduces and embellishes himself with it" [*KT*, 80]. That is why he repeatedly writes that "the moralizing tendency of post-war literature—of the Marxists, the Existentialists, the Catholics, Sartre, Camus, Mauriac and so on—never convinced me . . . . This aristocratic morality, this secure morality, this morality in white gloves...bothers me" [*KT*, 79]. Gombrowicz opposes this "secure" morality also for more fundamental, philosophical reasons. Belonging to the order of the subject, morality, for Gombrowicz, expresses the subject's concern with the perfection of his own soul. That is why Gombrowicz often claims that his focus on the intersubjective character of form cannot but destroy morality in the traditional sense: "Our present moral sense is essentially individualistic. It always proceeds from the idea of the immortal soul . . . . So it is hardly ever in harmony with a human world, based on the creation of man by men" [*KT*, 76].

Nonetheless, despite these reservations, Gombrowicz is interested in different possibilities of ethics, even though he admits that his search for the alternative understanding of ethics will be considered destructive by conservative moralists: "Moral constructors will no doubt consider me destructive, but what can I do about that?" [*KT*, 80]. Two of these ethical alternatives to the traditional morality are especially pertinent for our understanding of *Cosmos*. First, Gombrowicz suggests the ethical significance of his decomposition of form: "Perhaps my highest moral aim is to weaken all the structures of premeditated morality and other interhuman dependencies so that our immediate and most moral reflexes can say a word of their own" [*KT*, 80]. Second, Gombrowicz attempts to divorce ethics from the individual experience, even though this move destroys morality in the traditional sense. What his texts explore then is a possibility of ethics apart from both the moral sense of an individual and the intersubjective norms and values: "We might have to acknowledge that what we call 'the moral being' or 'the soul' does not really belong to an individual but is composed of various human beings. I don't know if we can talk of morals in this sense" [*KT*, 77]. As we can see, the question of ethics repeats on a different plane the dilemma Gombrowicz confronts in the context of his philosophy of language: just as it is the case with signification, ethics cannot be reduced either to the intersubjective laws or to the individual moral sense. Although Gombrowicz refuses to formulate a definite answer, we are left with an impression that ethics, like his understanding of signification, is intertwined with the other "as creative principle."

Gombrowicz remarks that the ethical significance of his texts is often written in the margins, as if off the center of the main narrative. Evoked in an equally indirect way, both the linguistic and ethical significance of alterity in *Cosmos* converge on the "shrieking eccentricity of the detail." Gombrowicz plays on the double meaning of the "eccentricity," underscoring both the exteriority of the particular and its deviation from the norm. How is this "eccentricity" to be read if the impasses of subjectivity are to be surpassed? We owe to Emmanuel Levinas's ethics the articulation of alterity as an excess overflowing any subjective attempt to constitute meaning: "the absolutely other is not reflected in consciousness."[42] For Levinas the signification of otherness is announced in the non-coincidence or non-adequation of representation: "The other who provokes this ethical movement in consciousness, and who disorders the good conscience of the coinciding of the same with itself involves a surplus for which intentionality is inadequate."[43] Similarly, in *Cosmos* the eccentricity of details has been consistently presented in terms of a residue or excess, escaping the labor of representation: "There is a sort of excess about reality, and after a certain point it can become intolerable . . . here was this teapot popping up like a jack-in-the box without rhyme or reason, extra, gratis, and for nothing, like a fifth wheel on a coach, an ornament of chaos . . . . This teapot was too much, and I could not swallow it" [*C*, 66–67]. This obstinate residue marks the limit of what is intelligible, and, as the figure of swallowing suggests, the limit of what can be assimilated or incorporated by the subject:

> And worst of it was that it was impossible to place the sparrow on the same plane as the mouth, the sparrow was entirely outside, in a different area altogether, it was accidental, absurd even

[*przypadkowy, niedorzeczny nawet*], so why did it keep haunting me, it had no right to [*C*, 21, *K*, 15, trans. modified].

As Gombrowicz's narrator desperately observes, the impossibility of closure announces alterity that cannot be placed within the totality of things: "it was impossible to place the sparrow on the same plane." In the eccentricity of the particulars, the otherness of the world announces itself as an unsurpassable exteriority, as a residue that "remains entirely outside." Withdrawing into a "different area altogether," otherness signifies as a rupture within the order of representation.

It is precisely this excess that makes the interpretative efforts of Witold and Fuchs not only futile but also "intolerable." In the encounter with the other, the rules of interpretation are unexpectedly reversed because the signification of alterity no longer belongs to the initiative of the narrator. It is at this point that representation conceived as the work or task of the subject reaches its impasse: "a kind of exhausting game of tennis set in, for the sparrow returned me to the mouth and the mouth returned me to the sparrow, I was the ball in the middle, and each was hidden by the other . . . " [*C*, 21, *K*, 15]. Overwhelmed by the excess of the eccentric details, the narrator of *Cosmos* stops being a dominant player or even a participant in the game of interpretation but becomes "a ball in the middle," put into motion beyond his control. "Haunted" or "assaulted" by what he fails to comprehend, Gombrowicz's protagonist is propelled, in ecstatic motion, outside the bounds of his identity.

Hoping to arrest this maddening movement, the work of representation aims to convert the discontinuity and excess into analogical or grammatical relations, but this reconstruction of the meaningful ties can be completed only at the price of violence. Instead of suggesting a positive articulation of ethics, Gombrowicz reveals violence in its absence. In *Cosmos* the increasing threat of violence is intertwined with the subjective attempts to comprehend alterity, to inscribe it into the "same plane" of representation. Unexpected and surprising, the first manifestation of violence in the text seems to be just an act of desperation in response to the "unbearable" excess of things. When, for example, after the night of surreptitious watching, Witold sees a teapot instead of the "true" nakedness of the beautiful Lena, he strangles and hangs her cat: "Yes, strangling the cat had been my furious reaction to the provocation of that senseless teapot . . . . But in that case, priest, you had better look out. For what guarantee is there that I might not . . . do something to you" [*C*, 101]. Grotesque as it is, the hanging cat "fits" into the series of hanging objects, and for the first time reveals the idea of "hanging" as an ordering principle of the detective investigation. As an embodiment of the ordering idea, the hanging cat no longer bespeaks a temporary loss of control but implicates epistemological desire in a violence that might be as systematic as it is logical. On many occasions in his writings, Gombrowicz underscores "the tyranny of syntactic forms," which compromise heterogeneity and otherness by the habits of analogy and symmetry. Yet, unlike Stanley Cavell, for whom "the tyranny" of the inherited conventions and "the intolerance" of grammar remain merely figurative, Gombrowicz explicitly links the tyranny of the forms of life to the obliteration of alterity. In his novels, especially in *Cosmos* and *Pornografia*, Gombrowicz literalizes the metaphor of "tyranny" and presents it as a crime contemplated or committed, beyond any psychological motivations, for the sake of formal symmetry. In *Pornografia* such a project of perfect symmetry is literally executed by the edge of a knife and ends in a seemingly superfluous murder. Similarly, in *Cosmos* the threat of violence as the price of order escalates so persistently that it seems finally inevitable. Its most striking representation is a logical corpse, in fact, the only rational object in the text:

> And by what miracle, though a mere dot in the sky, had it (a bird) imposed itself *like the discharge of a gun, scattering the confusion and chaos?* [*C*, 99, emphasis added]

> The sparrow, the bit of wood, the cat, and now Luis. What consistency, what logic. The absurd corpse was turning into a *logical corpse* [*Trup idiotyczny stawał się trupem logicznym*]—but it was a heavy sort of logic, a rather too personal and private logic of my own [*C*, 155, trans. modified; emphasis added; *K*, 139].

> Besides, a deep satisfaction that at last 'mouth' connected itself with 'hanging.' I connected them! At last. I felt as if I had fulfilled my duty.

> And now *I must go and hang Lena* [*C*, 160, trans. mine; emphasis added; *K*, 143].

"Scattering confusion and chaos," violence underlines both local analogies and main links, becoming in fact the guarantee that the grammatical coherence reflects "the natural order of things." If vio

lence, as in the first passage, is announced in passing merely as a figure of speech, describing the effect of organization (like "a discharge
of a gun"), then by the end of the text, this figurative aspect is literalized, and violence imposes itself as a "natural" necessity, a prerequi-
site of order. In the process of interpretation, violence erases discontinuities and gaps, installing in their place necessary links with a terrible
finality, just as, for instance, when Witold, with "a deep satisfaction
that at last 'mouth' connected itself with 'hanging'," discovers that he
has to hang Lena in order to complete the formal arrangement of the
hanging objects. Even if the logic of these links appear too awkward
and private, it still allows to convert the seeming "absurdity" and
eccentricity of alterity into rationality. Yet, when the other is inscribed
in the rational order, and thus ceases to be "philosophically disturbing," its alterity is utterly obliterated. Expressing the unity of violence
and rationality, "the logical corpse" in Gombrowicz's text points to the
lurid triumph of the formal/rational imperative.[44] The rational corpse
bespeaks the consequences of subordinating the ethical significance of
otherness to the tasks of cognition, representation and knowledge.

By confronting us at the end of his text with rational corpses
crowning the impending achievement of interpretation, Gombrowicz
one more time raises the question about the significance of failure:

> The sparrow was hanging, the bit of wood was hanging, Luis
> was hanging, and I was going to hang her as I had hanged the
> cat. Of course I might not hang her, but what *a let-down, what a
> fiasco*, that would be. Was I to disturb *the natural order of things?*
> (*ale . . . taki zawód sprawiać? Takie pomieszanie szyków*) [C, 161–162,
> emphasis added; K, 144].

As if in a parody of the numerous readings of *Cosmos*, this passage
indeed confirms the critical consensus that Gombrowicz's last novel is
one of the most disturbing texts he ever wrote. Yet, as the ending of the
novel makes clear, it is not the failure of interpretation that is so unsettling but, on the contrary, its impending success. Gombrowicz's protagonist finally knows what it would take to finish the labor of interpretation ("I must go and hang Lena"), and it is only the proverbial
deluge that, in the end, prevents the execution of this final step. The
labor of interpretation stops nothing short of producing the crime it
attempts to solve. What, then, makes *Cosmos* so devastating? What is
so disturbing about Gombrowicz's literary testament is certainly not
the negative philosophical implications of form but the monstrous
ethical consequences associated with the desire for linguistic and aes-

thetic coherence. In that case, we may only wonder why so many Gombrowicz critics respond to the absence of such a fatal resolution with the familiar refrain: "what a letdown, what a fiasco!"

* * *

In a way similar to other literary texts analyzed in this study, *Cosmos* locates the ethical significance of alterity at the interstices between philosophy and aesthetics. Although this peculiar location of ethics implies a conflict or even incommensurability between what Gombrowicz calls the philosophical and the aesthetic implications of language, it is precisely this incommensurability that sustains a double signification of otherness. Irreducible to the coherence of rational discourse, the signification of otherness is, from the philosophical point of view, disturbing and even catastrophic. Yet, if the signification of otherness is not to be limited to a familiar skeptical thesis about the impossibility of truth or knowledge, the philosophical paradigm of language needs to be surpassed. Implicated in this interruption of the bounds of philosophy, modern aesthetics, for Gombrowicz, has the task to uncover and sustain the affirmative signification of the encounter with the other, even though the singularity of this event exceeds the structure of its representation in language. Part of the difficulty of *Cosmos* lies, then, in the necessity of reading this double articulation and double valorization of form. For rather than resolving the disparity between the negative and the affirmative, between the philosophical and the aesthetic, the grammatical and the rhetorical, *Cosmos* articulates this incommensurability as the very possibility of ethics.

NOTES

1. Ludwig Wittgenstein, *Philosophical Investigations,* trans. G. E. M. Anscombe (New York: Macmillan, 1953), #19.

2. *Form* has also been one of the most frequently discussed topics in Gombrowicz's scholarship. For the most comprehensive discussion of the various possibilities of interpreting Form—from sociological and cultural to aesthetic and philosophical—see Jerzy Jarzębski, Pojęcie 'formy' u Gombrowicza," *Gombrowicz i krytycy: Wybór i opracowanie,* ed. Zdzisław Łapiński (Kraków Wydawnictwo Literackie, 1984), 313–346; and "Między chaosem a formą: Witold Gombrowicz," *Prozaicy dwudziestolecia międzywojennego,* ed. B. Faron (Warszawa: Wiedza Powszechna, 1972), 181–218. See also Maria Janion,

Gorączka romantyczna (Warszawa: Państwowy Instytut Wydawniczy, 1975), 167–246; Zdzisław Łapiński, "Ślub w kościele ludzkim" (O kategoriach interakcyjnych u Gombrowicza), *Tworczość* 9 (1966): 93–100; Jan Błoński, "O Gombrowiczu," *Pamiętnik Literacki* 8 (1970): 47; and Artur Sandauer, "Witold Gombrowicz—człowiek i pisarz," *Gombrowicz i krytycy*, 103–127.

3. Peter Bürger, *Theory of the Avant-Garde*, trans. Michael Shaw (Minneapolis: U of Minnesota P, 1984), 48.

4. Witold Gombrowicz, *A Kind of Testament*, ed. Dominique de Roux, trans. Alastair Hamilton (Philadelphia: Temple UP, 1973), 113. Originally published in French, *Entretiens de Dominique de Roux avec Gombrowicz*, Editions Pierre Belfond, 1968. The references to the English edition will be marked parenthetically in the text of this chapter, preceded by TK.

5. For a succinct discussion of Gombrowicz's attitude toward literary traditions, both Polish and European, see Michał Głowiński, *"Ferdydurke" Witolda Gombrowicza* (Warszawa: Wydawnictwa Szkolne i Pedagogiczne, 1991), 29–30, 78–85. Głowiński points to Gombrowicz's combination of his parody of the Baroque traditions and the grotesque. For Gombrowicz's criticism of art, see Małgorzata Szpakowska, "Gombrowicz-teoretyk sztuki," *Gombrowicz i krytycy*, 347–364.

6. For a critical discussion of the major trends in Gombrowicz criticism, see Janusz Sławiński, "The Gombrowicz Case," in *Literary Studies in Poland*, vol. X, *Gombrowicz*, ed. Hanna Dziechcińska (Wrocław: Zakład Narodowy im. Ossolińskich, 1983), 107–113; Zdzisław Łapiński, "Gombrowicz and His Critics," *Literary Studies in Poland*, 115–126; Maria Janion, "Ciemna młodość Gombrowicza," in *Tworczość* 36 (1980): 78-107. See also the special issue of *Pamiętnik Literacki, Wokół recepcji Gombrowicza* 4 (1972) and the special issues of *Tworczość* 37 (1981) and 11–12 (1986). In his *Witold Gombrowicz: studium portretowe* (Kraków: Wydawnictwo Literackie, 1988), 169–338, Tadeusz Kępiński attempts something like a polemical intervention into the canon of Gombrowicz criticism, but what he actually accomplishes is a wholesale (and groundless) rejection of any analysis that considers Gombrowicz to be a major Polish writer. For a discussion of the criticism in English, see Regina Grol-Prokopczyk, "New Gombrowicziana," in *The Polish Review* 26 (1981): 83–86; and Beth Holmgren, "Witold Gombrowicz in the United States," in *The Polish Review* 33 (1988): 409–418.

7. For an excellent account of antinomy in Gombrowicz's aesthetics, see Kazimierz Bartoszyński, "On How Gombrowicz's Antinomies May Cause Problems in Literary Interpretations" *Literary Studies in Poland*, 95–106.

8. Jean-François Lyotard, *The Postmodern Condition: A Report on Knowledge*, trans. Geoff Bennington and Brian Massumi (Minneapolis: U of Minnesota P, 1984), 71–82.

9. For a brief but lucid discussion of the relationship between aesthetics and individuality in bourgeois art, see Peter Bürger, *Theory of the Avant-Garde*, 47–49. In the context of the specificity of the history of Polish literature, what needs to be stressed is that this anti-romantic critique of individuality is inter-

twined in Gombrowicz's work with the opposition to the other romantic tradition, namely, to art's important role in the preservation of the national and cultural independence.

10. Witold Gombrowicz, *Diary* vol. 1, ed. Jan Kott, trans. Lillian Vallee (Evanston: Northwestern UP, 1988), 20. Subsequent references to this edition (vol. 1 and 2) will be marked parenthetically in the text. In contrast to Gombrowicz's novels, this is an excellent translation but in the few instances I felt a need to modify it in order to underscore a competing emphasis. I based my translation on the Polish edition, Witold Gombrowicz, *Dziennik 1953–1966*, *Dzieła*, vol. vii–ix, ed. Jan Błoński (Kraków: Wydawnictwo Literackie, 1988). My modified translations will be marked in the text.

11. For an informing analysis of the philosophical underpinnings of Gombrowicz's aesthetics, see Francesco M. Cataluccio, "Gombrowicz filozof," trans. Katarzyna Bielas, 5–21; Andrzej St. Kowalczyk, "Gombrowicz—Husserl. O fenomenologicznych motywach w *Dzienniku*," 206–226; and Renato Barilli, "Sartre i Camus w *Dzienniku*," trans. Wiktoria Krzemień, 227–239; all three essays are from *Gombrowicz Filozof*, ed. Francesco M. Cataluccio and Jerzy Illg (Kraków Wydawnictwo Znak, 1991).

12. Witold Gombrowicz, "Przewodnik po filozofii w sześć godzin i kwadrans," trans. from French into Polish Bogdan Baran, *Gombrowicz Filozof*, 71–128. Shortly before his death, Gombrowicz, at the request of his friend Dominique de Roux, delivered his lectures in the history of philosophy, from Kant to structuralism. A surprising testimony of Gombrowicz's philosophical interests and passion, these lectures occurred in the unusual, to say the least, circumstances. In the spring of 1969, Gombrowicz, seriously sick and remaining mostly in bed, could no longer write, or even read for more than an hour. When Gombrowicz more and more openly talked about his suicide, and finally asked his friend for help, Dominique de Roux came up with the idea of the series of talks about the history of philosophy as a desperate means to let Gombrowicz forget about his sickness, and above all, to postpone his death. Although Gombrowicz refused several times, finally the grotesque and theatrical character of the event must have appealed to him. Playing philosophical games as a substitute for suicide, reconstructing the philosophical cosmos as a postponement of dying (so much for the disinterestedness of a philosophical reflection)—it sounded after all like a good scene in a novel with a Kafkaesque or a Beckettian touch. Gombrowicz called these lectures, somewhat ironically, "A Guide to Philosophy in Six Hours and Fifteen Minutes". Between April 27 and May 25, Gombrowicz gave thirteen talks starting with Kant and ending with existentialism. The series was supposed to end with a reflection on the dialectical relationship between existentialism and structuralism, but the last planned talk on structuralism never happened. Gombrowicz died on July 24.

13. For an impact of form on Gombrowicz's anthropology, see, for instance, Konstany Jeleński, "Bohaterskie niebohaterstwo Gombrowicza" and Włodzimierz Maciąg, "Antropologia Gombrowicza," both in *Gombrowicz*

Filozof; Michał Głowiński, *Ferdydurke Witolda Gombrowicza,* 8–15; Artur Sandauer, "Witold Gombrowicz—człowiek i pisarz," 103–127; See also works cited in note #3.

14. This linguistic effect of amputation described by Gombrowicz has been frequently compared to Jacques Lacan's linguistic reinterpretation of the castration of the subject. Ewa Thomson, for instance, argues that "Gombrowicz's intuitions about self and Form are similar to what Jacques Lacan, one of the leading structuralists has to say about the problem of distortion of the 'I.'" Ewa M. Thompson, *Witold Gombrowicz* (Boston: Twayne Publishers, 1979), 150. However, the important difference lies in Gombrowicz's conception of language, the conception which is not reducible to the structuralist notion of the symbolic order.

15. However, as Gombrowicz frequently argues, this focus on the linguistic deformation of the subject does not amount to the abandonment of the problematics of subjectivity, as is the case in structuralism, but to its reformulation. For Gombrowicz's critique of structuralism's incapacity to deal with subjectivity, see his interview, "Byłem Pierwszym Structuralistą" ("I Was the First Structuralist"), trans. from French Maciej Broński, in *Gombrowicz Filozof,* 147–151.

16. Witold Gombrowicz, "Preface" to *Pornografia,* trans. Alastair Hamilton, *Cosmos and Pornografia* (New York: Grove, 1985), 8.

17. According to Michał Głowiński, "*subiektywizm Gombrowicza ma character zdecydowanie nie romantyczny. Widoczne jest to także w jego stosunku do literatury czy sztuki w ogólnosci,*" "*Ferdydurke*" *Witolda Gombrowicza,* 10. For a discussion of Gombrowicz's often conflicting relation to Polish literature, see also Konstanty Jeleński, "Tajny ładunek korsarskiego okrętu," in *Kultura* 344 (1976): 21–32 and Czesław Miłosz, *The History of Polish Literature* (London: Macmillan, 1969), 432–437.

18. Gilles Deleuze, *The Fold: Leibniz and the Baroque,* trans. Tom Conley, (Minneapolis: U of Minnesota P, 1993), 81–82. I am grateful to Hanjo Berressem for pointing this reference out to me.

19. Stanley Cavell, *In Quest of the Ordinary: Lines of Skepticism and Romanticism* (Chicago: U of Chicago P, 1988), 148.

20. Cavell, *In Quest of the Ordinary,* 135.

21. For a discussion of the important role played by parody in Gombrowicz's poetics, see Michał Głowiński, "*Ferdydurke*" *Witolda Gombrowicza,* 20–24 and "Parodia konstruktywna (O *Pornografii* Gombrowicza)," in *Gombrowicz i krytycy,* 365–383.

22. Gombrowicz, "Preface" to *Pornografia,* 6.

23. Jan Błoński interprets this conflict between maturity and immaturity as the duality of form and energy. He also points out the philosophical, social, and erotic significance of this linguistic dualism. "O Gombrowiczu," 47.

24. Gombrowicz, "Preface," 5.

25. Kazimierz Bartoszyński, "*Kosmos* i antynomie," in *Gombrowicz i krytycy*, 682.

26. For instance, Andrzej Kijowski writes about "father complex" shaping Gombrowicz's writings in a way similar to Kafka's or Joyce's texts, "Strategia Gombrowicza," in *Gombrowicz i krytycy*, 435.

27. Gilles Deleuze and Félix Guattari, *Kafka: Toward a Minor Literature*, trans. Dana Polan (Minnesota: U of Minnesota P, 1986), 16–28.

28. Bruno Schulz was the first to recognize and theorize that aspect of Gombrowicz's work and it is one of the very few interpretations that Gombrowicz enthusiastically endorsed. For Gombrowicz's commentary on Bruno Schulz's interpretation of *Ferdydurke*, see *A Kind of Testament*, 64–65.

29. Gombrowicz comments in the following way on Buber's concept of the "Thou" in his diaries: "Buber, a Jewish philosopher, described this pretty well when he said that the individualist philosophy we have known up to now has done itself in and the greatest disillusionment that awaits mankind in the nearest future is the bankruptcy of the collectivist philosophy . . . "[*D I*, 20].

30. As Gombrowicz writes in his "Guide to Philosophy," "*Krótko mówiąc, spojrzenie innego zaprzecza prawdzie naszej wolności*," in *Gombrowicz Filozof*, 107-108. For an excellent discussion of the relation between Gombrowicz's works and the philosophy of Sartre, see Bronislawa Karst, *The Problem of the Other and of Intersubjectivity in the Works of Jean Paul Sartre and Witold Gombrowicz*, Dissertation (Ann Arbor: University Microfilms International, 1984).

31. As Miłosz writes, "*Bo wyższe, przygniecione przez swój fałsz, fałsz Formy, tęskni do niższego, tak jak niższe chce stać się wyższym, dojrzałe marzy o tym, żeby odnowić się przez niedojrzałość, tak jak niedojrzałe . . . pragnie dojrzałemu się poddać . . .* " "Kim jest Gombrowicz," in *Gombrowicz i krytycy*, 189.

32. Ewa M. Thompson, *Witold Gombrowicz*, 96.

33. For an alternative interpretation of this obscurity in the context of eroticism, see Antoni Libera, "*Kosmos*: wizja życia—wizja wszechświata," in *Gombrowicz i krytycy*, 387-428.

34. "*Kosmos okazuje się najodważniejszym wysiłkiem przedstawienia kryzysu, który został wywołany przez pojawienie się konsekwentnego sceptycyzmu w europejskiej kulturze.*" Wojciech Karpiński, "Gombrowiczowska przestrzeń," *Gombrowicz i krytycy*, 183; trans. mine.

35. "*Bycie w świecie rozpadło się na dwie części, na niedosiężny świat i zamurowaną świadomość,*" Karpiński, "Gombrowiczowska przestrzeń," trans. mine, 180. Similarly, Kazimierz Bartoszyński argues in his "*Kosmos* i antynomie" that Gombrowicz's last novel reveals the uncertainty of knowledge and quite ostensible distrust of signs. Kazimierz Bartoszyński, "*Kosmos* i antynomie," in *Gombrowicz i Krytycy*, 676.

36. For the Lacanian reading of the relation between the philosophical desire for knowledge and the logic of sexual desire in *Cosmos*, see Hanjo Berressem, "Witold Gombrowicz: Cosmos, the Case of the Hanged Sparrow," in *Polish Review*, 36 (1991): 145–159.

37. Symptomatically, Barbara Górska asserts that Gombrowicz presents in *Cosmos* the failure to construct the meaning of the world by a solitary atheistic individual, deprived of faith in God or in any pre-established order of cosmos. See, "Nota Wydawcy," Witold Gombrowicz, *Kosmos, Dzieła*, tom v, 150.

38. Wojciech Karpiński, "Gombrowiczowska przestrzeń," 180.

39. Emmanuel Levinas describes the relations between the sign and the trace in the following way: "But when a trace is thus taken as a sign, it is exceptional with respect to other signs in that it signifies outside of every intention of signaling and outside of every project of which it would be the aim." "The Trace of the Other," trans. Alfonso Lingis, in *Deconstruction in Context: Literature and Philosophy*, ed. Mark C. Taylor (Chicago, U of Chicago P, 1986), 356–7.

40. For an excellent discussion of the relation between private language and homoerotic desire, see Aleksandra Okopień-Sławińska, "Wielkie bergowanie czyli hipoteza jedności *Kosmosu*," in *Gombrowicz i krytycy*, 698–702.

41. Okopień-Sławińska, "Wielkie bergowanie," 701.

42. Emmanuel Levinas, "The Trace of the Other," 352–3.

43. Levinas, "The Trace of the Other," 353.

44. For a different interpretation of the question of violence and the figure of the corpse as a consequence of the impossible desire for authenticity and the fear of deformation, see Andrzej Kijowski, "Strategia Gombrowicza," 439.

Index